Essays in the
American Catholic Tradition

Essays in the American Catholic Tradition

P. ALBERT DUHAMEL

Boston College

Rinehart & Company, Inc.

NEW YORK

Contents

FOUR   Ideas and Attitudes from Abroad

FIVE   Essays Informal and Critical

SIX   In the Forum of Public Opinion

SEVEN   Reassessments and New Directions

Introduction

In the mid-nineteen fifties the American Catholic tradition came in for a re-examination by Catholic and non-Catholic alike. While historic centers of American Catholicism, such as Philadelphia and Boston, were celebrating the sesquicentennial of their establishment as dioceses of the Roman Church, many Catholics were wondering aloud if their Church, in over a hundred and fifty years of organized apostolic effort, had made its expected contribution to the American intellectual life. Some apologists, recalling that as recently as 1900 Rome still considered the United States as missionary territory, argued that it was premature to evaluate the Church's contribution to American arts and sciences. In 1956 a Catholic, Senator John Kennedy of Massachusetts, came close to winning the Democratic nomination for the office of Vice-President; in 1959 he seemed to be a leading contender for the party's nomination as its Presidential candidate for 1960. Reflective non-Catholics, who remembered the misinformation and prejudice which had marked the elections of 1928 when Al Smith ran for president, felt an obligation to learn more about traditional Catholic attitudes on controversial questions.

The essays in this collection have been brought together to provide Catholic and non-Catholic alike with the means of examining some of the evidence and judging for themselves the Catholic contribution to affairs intellectual and the traditional Catholic attitudes in matters political. For several reasons, the essay was chosen as the literary form most likely to provide this evidence. First, it is the form which can be found in use among the earliest Catholic writers and which, consequently, can provide illustrations of the entire history of the development of the American Catholic tradition. Whether or not America is yet to produce a great Catholic novelist, poet, or dramatist may be subject to discussion, but it is certain that all the writers who have ever been proposed for these distinctions have been relatively latecomers to the scene. Second, the essay is the form most commonly used for apologetic writing, and by far the largest amount of Catholic writing has been apologetic, if not polemic, in intent. It is difficult to name many promising American Catholic poets or novelists who have been able to resist the many pressures calling upon them to undertake an explanation of their artistic or spiritual creeds. Third, the essay is the only form flexible enough to provide for the treatment of the wide range of subjects which had to be represented. It was even hoped that bringing together a number of essays on such a variety of ideas might encourage the general reader as well as the college student to undertake a close study of the nature and potentialities of this versatile literary form.

Consequently every effort has been made to include in this collection only those essays which would, at one and the same time, illustrate the Catholic tradition and the versatility of the literary form. No essay was chosen simply because it was a significant piece of apologetics or because it was a fine piece of writing. Each essay was intended to represent an authoritative consideration of some aspect of American Catholic culture as well as a successful use of the form itself. The collection as a whole is not intended, however, to reflect any particular conception of the nature or evolution of either the tradition or the form. On the contrary, the collection is intended to provide students of literature and history, general readers and conscientious citizens, with material for making up their own minds.

The first, and perhaps most easily defined, stage in the development of American Catholicism is that of the Colonial Period, extending from the first coming of the missionaries in the sixteenth century to the passage of the Stamp Act in 1765. Among the groups of missionaries who have had the greatest influence on the course of early American history the Franciscans and the Jesuits are the most significant. Although they themselves had little time to write much more than letters or reports to their superiors, they have been extensively written about. Parkman's account of Father Marquette's first exploration of the Mississippi captures the spirit of the work of the Jesuits as explorers; Paul Horgan's description of the Franciscans in the Southwest stresses their work as teachers. The Franciscans left an indelible mark on the geography as well as the culture of the regions where they taught. The shifting fortunes of war and political allegiances prevented the Jesuits, however, from establishing themselves permanently as teachers among the Indians and settlers of the Northwest.

In contrast with the work of the Catholic Church in the territories of France and Spain in the New World, Catholicism in the English Colonies was of little importance. In the area of the original thirteen Colonies, Catholicism is practically limited to a single voice and an outstanding example of religious tolerance. Bishop Carroll was the voice, and the Catholic Colony of Maryland was the colony—the only one—which granted full religious freedom. Eloquent as a speaker or writer, Bishop Carroll is an early example of a cultured Catholic turned apologist to allay suspicions and to clarify misunderstandings. Historians frequently forget that the Colonies had limits upon the tolerance they were willing to exhibit towards believers of different persuasions. Maryland alone provided the kind of atmosphere which allowed a man to worry only about his conscience and to trust the state statutes. The problems encountered by Catholicism in the Colonial Period were an accurate foreshadowing of the problems with which it was to be preoccupied for the next one hundred and fifty years. The impressions and conceptions of Catholicism which the English colonists brought with them from the mother country generated what has been called "the most persistent prejudice in the history of the American people."

Shortly after the establishment of the new republic, events occurred abroad which were also to have their influence upon the development of Catholicism for the next hundred years. The French Revolution and the ensuing Napoleonic Wars displaced many people and sent many priests to seek refuge in America. There they established the first parishes and laid the foundations of the earliest dioceses. These were the first real beginnings, roughly one hundred and fifty years ago, of organized Catholic effort within the area of the original United States. From about the time of the Napoleonic Wars to approximately the end of the First World War, American Catholicism was concerned with two major problems: adjusting to a prejudiced environment and providing for the tide of immigrants who brought with them the Old Religion from the Old Countries. Thus almost all of nineteenth-century Catholic writing is concerned with two problems: the significance of a Catholic education for all Catholics, and the Catholic conception of the freedoms which should be guaranteed by the state. Father Hecker's essay on the nature of the relation between church and state in America was selected because it is representative of the many essays on the subject as well as the work of the founder of the Paulist Fathers, whose purpose was to educate and inform the non-Catholic about Catholic belief. Orestes Brownson's essay defining the nature and values of a Catholic education is typical of his creative spirit in contrast to the chauvinistic point of view commonly expressed on that subject at that time. The essay by James Paston, a non-Catholic, was included to show that Catholicism was not without sympathetic understanding on the part of non-Catholics and that Catholics were right in the conception of what were their main problems. Cardinal O'Connell's reminiscences of his early years in the textile city of Lowell illustrate conditions under which Catholic boys grew up and the memories they carried with them when they came into positions of prominence.

At this point the American Catholic tradition was strongly influenced by ideas and attitudes from the writings of English Catholics. The English apologists, Chesterton and Belloc in particular, had a great influence on their American counterparts. No American ever achieved the urbanity of Belloc or rivaled the wit of Chesterton, but many were led to imitate their craftsmanship and taste. From this point on American Catholic writing abandoned a posture of defense along with a concern for parochial issues and adopted a tone which implied that it expected unbiased consideration from rational readers. Instead of limiting themselves to a discussion of local or transitory issues, writers now undertook an examination of the implications of those issues not only for the group which they represented but for all groups. Essays on the rights of all working men replaced the sometimes shrill outcries for justice for some small group.

Several American Catholic writers have commanded a national audience: Sidney Lanier, F. Marion Crawford, Joyce Kilmer, to name but a few. Among these the one who is best remembered for her mastery of the form of the informal essay is Louise Imogen Guiney. Some of the essays from her collection, *Patrins,* are frequently reprinted, and modern readers respond to her art while recognizing the leisurely elements which reflect an earlier taste. It is doubtful if any collection of essays ever succeeds in representing all the uses to which the form can be put. One of the uses, examples of which are common in the daily newspaper but great examples of which are uncommon, is that of dramatic criticism. Among the Catholic writers who won a very large following for dramatic critical reviews was R. Dana Skinner. Throughout most of the Twenties his reviews in *The Commonweal* were respected for their perceptiveness of the significance of experimenters like Eugene O'Neill and for their insight into the regular Broadway openings.

By the end of the First World War, American Catholicism, by now no longer looked upon as a missionary effort by the Vatican, entered upon a distinctive new phase. From this time on it sought a hearing in the forum of public opinion not only as the right of a minority religious group in a secularistic society but as the representative of ideas and attitudes which had much much to contribute to the preservation and development of that society. Weekly Catholic magazines, such as *America,* published by the Jesuits, and *The Commonweal,* published by a group of liberal Catholic laymen, won recognition as spokesmen for opinions shared by large segments of the population as a whole. It is impossible to represent the many writers and opinions which acquired large followings at this time, and any selection is bound to be questioned. Some may object to the inclusion of an essay by Bishop Fulton Sheen as representative of a Catholic attitude towards science, but there is no denying the size of the following he has influenced nor the part this attitude has played in curtailing the contribution American Catholicism could have made to modern science. Others may question the inclusion of a selection by Dorothy Day, for her *Catholic Worker* movement is considered much too radical by many of the more conservative. But certainly anyone familiar with the course of American Catholicism between two World Wars will recognize in Father Gillis, for years the editor of the influential monthly, *The Catholic World,* and Father LaFarge, long-time editor of *America,* two of the most representative writers of the period. The essay by Father Ellard was included to reflect an aspect of Catholic thought with which the non-Catholic is not always familiar, the continuing attempt to increase the participation of the faithful in the liturgy. Several of the movements which developed in the thirties have continued to grow and have had an important effect not only on the way in which Catholics take part in the sacrifice of the Mass but also on the development of Catholic artistic taste.

It is difficult to believe that any question has furnished more material for discussion, in and out of the classrooms of Catholic colleges, than whether or not there is an American Catholic literature. In September, 1959, the *Saturday Review* published an essay by a young Catholic writer which brought the question to the attention of a much wider audience. His conclusion, that there was not, and that any collection of American Catholic writings might easily give the impression that most of Catholic writing had been apologetic, generated a series of replies in Catholic periodicals. Most of the replies seemed willing to admit that there was some truth to his evaluation of the past but that he failed to take into account the promise of the future. Two of the essays in the present collection, rounding out the next to last section, are intended to represent two points of view on the problem of Catholic literature. These two essays are intended to give some idea of the future direction of Catholic writing and thinking. Henry Rago, currently editor of *Poetry,* is experienced as writer and teacher with the problems of the Catholic writer and reader on every level. Thomas Merton, a Trappist monk and author of one of the most popular autobiographies of recent years, illustrates the concern of the Catholic writer with the theoretical explanation of his work.

The first essay in the last section is still the landmark in the self-evaluation entered upon by leading Catholic writers and thinkers in the mid-nineteen fifties. Originally delivered by the author, Monsignor John Tracy Ellis, in a much longer version as an address to the Catholic Commission on Intellectual and Cultural Affairs, it has been widely reprinted and discussed. Essays such as Father Weigel's on Catholic communication with the world are reflections of a continuing attempt to answer the criticism made by Monsignor Ellis and to point out directions for the future.

The last essay in the collection was chosen partly because of its author and partly because of its subject. In 1958 Christopher Dawson, a life-long resident of the British Isles and a scholar with an international reputation for his work in anthropology and European history, became the first professor of Catholic theology in the Harvard Divinity School. The essay, on Christianity and Oriental cultures, published in the same year, reflects a concern with problems which transcend the concerns of one religious group and point to a fulfillment of the directions laid down in other essays in this section. Thus the author's position and his subject mark a break with earlier traditions of prejudice and hostility on the part of the non-Catholic and isolation and parochialism on the part of the Catholic himself.

Whether or not the American Catholic tradition has been as fruitful or significant as it should have been is a matter of opinion. What its future contributions to the American intellectual life may be, is a matter of prophecy. This collection was intended to stimulate a discussion of the past and a recognition of the opportunities of the future.

P. ALBERT DUHAMEL

Boston College
January, 1960

Essays in the
American Catholic Tradition

ONE

Explorers and Educators

Discovery of the Mississippi
FRANCIS PARKMAN

Louis Joliet was the son of a wagon-maker in the service of the Company of the Hundred Associates, then owners of Canada. He was born at Quebec in 1645, was educated by the Jesuits; and, when still very young, he resolved to be a priest. He received the tonsure and the minor orders at the age of seventeen. Four years after, he is mentioned with especial honor for the part he bore in the disputes in philosophy, at which the dignitaries of the colony were present, and in which the Intendant himself took part. Not long after, he renounced his clerical vocation, and turned fur-trader.

.   .   .   .   .

Marquette was born in 1637, of an old and honorable family at Laon, in the north of France, and was now thirty-five years of age. When about seventeen, he had joined the Jesuits, evidently from motives purely religious; and in 1666 he was sent to the missions of Canada. At first he was destined to the station of Tadoussac; and, to prepare himself for it, he studied the Montagnais language under Gabriel Druilletes. But his destination was changed, and he was sent to the Upper Lakes in 1668, where he had since remained. His talents as a linguist must have been great; for, within a few years, he learned to speak with ease six Indian languages. The traits of his character are unmistakable. He was of the brotherhood of the early Canadian missionaries, and the true counterpart of Garnier or Jogues. He was a devout votary of the Virgin Mary; who, imaged to his mind in

"Discovery of the Mississippi," from *France and England in North America,* by Francis Parkman (Boston: Little, Brown & Co., 1869).

1

shapes of the most transcendent loveliness with which the pencil of human genius has ever informed the canvas, was to him the object of an adoration not unmingled with a sentiment of chivalrous devotion. The longings of a sensitive heart, divorced from earth, sought solace in the skies. A subtile element of romance was blended with the fervor of his worship, and hung like an illumined cloud over the harsh and hard realities of his daily lot. Kindled by the smile of his celestial mistress, his gentle and noble nature knew no fear. For her he burned to dare and to suffer, discover new lands and conquer new realms to her sway.

He begins the journal of his voyage thus: "The day of the Immaculate Conception of the Holy Virgin; whom I had continually invoked, since I came to this country of the Ottawas, to obtain from God the favor of being enabled to visit the nations on the river Mississippi—this very day was precisely that on which M. Joliet arrived with orders from Count Frontenac, our Governor, and from M. Talon, our Intendant, to go with me on this discovery. I was all the more delighted at this good news, because I saw my plans about to be accomplished, and found myself in the happy necessity of exposing my life for the salvation of all these tribes; and especially of the Illinois, who, when I was at Point St. Esprit, had begged me very earnestly to bring the word of God among them."

The outfit of the travellers was very simple. They provided themselves with two birch canoes, and a supply of smoked meat and Indian corn; embarked with five men; and began their voyage on the seventeenth of May. They had obtained all possible information from the Indians, and had made, by means of it, a species of map of their intended route. "Above all," writes Marquette, "I placed our voyage under the protection of the Holy Virgin Immaculate, promising that if she granted us the favor of discovering the great river, I would give it the name of the Conception." Their course was westward; and, plying their paddles, they passed the Straits of Michillimackinac, and coasted the northern shores of Lake Michigan; landing at evening to build their camp-fire at the edge of the forest, and draw up their canoes on the strand. They soon reached the river Menomonie, and ascended it to the village of the Menomonies, or Wild-rice Indians. When they told them the object of their voyage, they were filled with astonishment, and used their best ingenuity to dissuade them. The banks of the Mississippi, they said, were inhabited by ferocious tribes, who put every stranger to death, tomahawking all new-comers without cause or provocation. They added that there was a demon in a certain part of the river, whose roar could be heard at a great distance, and who would engulf them in the abyss where he dwelt; that its waters were full of frightful monsters, who would devour them and their canoe; and, finally, that the heat was so great that they would perish inevitably. Marquette set their counsel at naught, gave them a few words of instruction in the mysteries of the Faith, taught them a prayer, and bade them farewell.

The travellers soon reached the mission at the head of Green Bay; entered the Fox River; with difficulty and labor dragged their canoes up the long and tumultuous rapids; crossed Lake Winnebago; and followed the quiet windings of the river beyond, where they glided through an endless growth of wild rice, and scared the innumerable birds that fed upon it. On either hand rolled the prairie, dotted with groves and trees, browsing elk and deer. On the seventh of June, they reached the Mascoutins and Miamis, who, since the visit of Dablon and Allouez, had been joined by the Kickapoos. Marquette, who had an eye for natural beauty, was delighted with the situation of the town, which he describes as standing on the crown of a hill; while, all around, the prairie stretched beyond the sight, interspersed with groves and belts of tall forest. But he was still more delighted when he saw a cross planted in the midst of the place. The Indians had decorated it with a number of dressed deer-skins, red girdles, and bows and arrows, which they had hung upon it as an offering to the Great Manitou of the French—a sight by which, as Marquette says, he was "extremely consoled."

The travellers had no sooner reached the town than they called the chiefs and elders to a council. Joliet told them that the Governor of Canada had sent him to discover new countries, and that God had sent his companion to teach the true faith to the inhabitants; and he prayed for guides to show them the way to the waters of the Wisconsin. The council readily consented; and on the tenth of June the Frenchmen embarked again, with two Indians to conduct them. All the town came down to the shore to see their departure. Here were the Miamis, with long locks of hair dangling over each ear, after a fashion which Marquette thought very becoming; and here, too, the Mascoutins and the Kickapoos, whom he describes as mere boors in comparison with their Miami townsmen. All stared alike at the seven adventurers, marvelling that men could be found to risk an enterprise so hazardous.

The river twisted among lakes and marshes choked with wild rice; and, but for their guides, they could scarcely have followed the perplexed and narrow channel. It brought them at last to the portage; where, after carrying their canoes a mile and a half over the prairie and through the marsh, they launched them on the Wisconsin, bade farewell to the waters that flowed to the St. Lawrence, and committed themselves to the current that was to bear them they knew not whither, —perhaps to the Gulf of Mexico, perhaps to the South Sea or the Gulf of California. They glided calmly down the tranquil stream, by islands choked with trees and matted with entangling grape-vines; by forests, groves, and prairies,—the parks and pleasure-grounds of a prodigal nature; by thickets and marshes and broad bare sandbars; under the shadowing trees, between whose tops looked down from afar the bold brow of some woody bluff. At night, the bivouac,—the canoes inverted on the bank, the flickering fire, the meal of bison-flesh or venison, the evening pipes, and slumber beneath the stars: and when in the morning they embarked again, the mist hung on the river like a bridal veil; then melted before the sun, till the glassy water and the languid woods basked breathless in the sultry glare.

On the 17th of June, they saw on their right the broad meadows, bounded in the distance by rugged hills, where now stand the town and fort of Prairie du Chien. Before them, a wide and rapid current coursed athwart their way, by the foot of lofty heights wrapped thick in forests. They had found what they sought, and "with a joy," writes Marquette, "which I cannot express," they steered forth their canoes on the eddies of the Mississippi.

Turning southward, they paddled down the stream, through a solitude unrelieved by the faintest trace of man. A large fish, apparently one of the huge cat-fish of the Mississippi, blundered against Marquette's canoe with a force which seems to have startled him; and once, as they drew in their net, they caught a "spade-fish," whose eccentric appearance greatly astonished them. At length, the buffalo began to appear, grazing in herds on the great prairie which then bordered the river; and Marquette describes the fierce and stupid look of the old bulls, as they stared at the intruders through the tangled mane which nearly blinded them.

They advanced with extreme caution, landed at night, and made a fire to cook their evening meal; then extinguished it, embarked again, paddled some way farther, and anchored in the stream, keeping a man on the watch till morning. They had journeyed more than a fortnight without meeting a human being; when, on the 25th, they discovered footprints of men in the mud of the western bank, and a well-trodden path that led to the adjacent prairie. Joliet and Marquette resolved to follow it; and, leaving the canoes in charge of their men, they set out on their hazardous adventure. The day was fair, and they walked two leagues in silence, following the path through the forest and across the sunny prairie, till they discovered an Indian village on the banks of a river, and two others on a hill half a league distant. Now, with beating hearts, they invoked the aid of Heaven, and, again advancing, came so near without being seen, that they could hear the voices of the Indians among the wigwams. Then they stood forth in full view, and shouted, to attract attention. There was great commotion in the village. The inmates swarmed out of their huts, and four of their chief men presently came forward to meet the strangers, advancing very deliberately, and holding up toward the sun two calumets, or peace-pipes, decorated with feathers. They stopped abruptly before the two Frenchmen, and stood gazing at them with attention, without speaking a word. Marquette was much relieved on seeing that they wore French cloth, whence he judged that they must be friends and allies. He broke the silence, and asked them who they were; whereupon they answered that they were Illinois, and offered the pipe; which having been duly smoked, they all went together to the village. Here the chief received the travellers after a singular fashion, meant to do them honor. He stood stark naked at the door of a large wigwam, holding up both hands as if to shield his eyes. "Frenchmen, how bright the sun shines when you come to visit us! All our village awaits you; and you shall enter our wigwams in peace." So saying, he led them into his own; which was crowded to suffocation with savages, staring at their guests in silence. Having smoked with the chiefs and old men, they were invited to visit the great chief of all the Illinois, at one of the villages they had seen in the distance; and thither they proceeded, followed by a throng of warriors, squaws, and children. On arriving, they were forced to smoke again, and listen to a speech of welcome from the great chief; who delivered it, standing between two old men, naked like himself. His lodge was crowded with the dignitaries of the tribe; whom Marquette addressed in Algonquin, announcing himself as a messenger sent by the God who had made them, and whom it behooved them to recognize and obey. He added a few words touching the power and glory of Count Frontenac, and concluded by asking information concerning the Mississippi, and the tribes along its banks, whom he was on his way to visit. The chief replied with a speech of compliment,—assuring his guests that their presence added flavor to his tobacco, made the river more calm, the sky more serene, and the earth more beautiful. In conclusion, he gave them a young slave and a calumet, begging them at the same time to abandon their purpose of descending the Mississippi.

A feast of four courses now followed. First, a wooden bowl full of a porridge of Indian meal boiled with grease was set before the guests, and the master of ceremonies fed them in turn, like infants, with a large spoon. Then appeared a platter of fish; and the same functionary, carefully removing the bones with his fingers, and blowing on the morsels to cool them, placed them in the mouths of the two Frenchmen. A large dog, killed and cooked for the occasion, was next placed before them; but, failing to tempt their fastidious appetites, was supplanted by a dish of fat buffalo-meat, which concluded the entertainment. The crowd having dispersed, buffalo-robes were spread on the ground, and Marquette and Joliet spent the night on the scene of the late festivity. In the morning, the chief, with some six hundred of his tribesmen, escorted them to their canoes, and bade them, after their stolid fashion, a friendly farewell.

Again they were on their way, slowly drifting down the great river. They passed the mouth of the Illinois, and glided beneath that line of rocks on the eastern side, cut into fantastic forms by the elements, and marked as "The Ruined Castles" on some of the early French maps. Presently they beheld a sight which reminded them that the Devil was still lord paramount of this wilderness. On the flat face of a high rock, were painted in red, black, and green a pair of monsters,—each "as large as a calf, with horns like a deer, red eyes, a beard like a tiger, and a frightful expression of countenance. The face is something like that of a man, the body covered with scales; and the tail so long that it passes entirely round the body, over the head and between the legs, ending like that of a fish." Such is the account which the worthy Jesuit gives of these *manitous,* or Indian gods. He confesses that at first they frightened him; and his imagination and that of his credulous companions were so wrought upon by these unhallowed efforts of Indian art, that they continued for a long time to talk of them as they plied their paddles. They were thus engaged, when they were suddenly aroused by a real danger. A torrent of yellow mud rushed furiously athwart the calm blue current of the Mississippi; boiling and surging, and sweeping in its course logs, branches, and uprooted trees. They had reached the mouth of the Missouri, where that savage river, descending from its mad career through a vast unknown of barbarism, poured its turbid floods into the bosom of its gentler sister. Their light canoes whirled on the miry vortex like dry leaves on an angry brook. "I never," writes Marquette, "saw any thing more terrific;" but they escaped with their fright, and held their way down the turbulent and swollen current of the now united rivers. They passed the lonely forest that covered the site of the destined city of St. Louis, and, a few days later, saw on their left the mouth of the stream to which the Iroquois had given the well-merited name of Ohio, or, the Beautiful River. Soon they began to see the marshy shores buried in a dense growth of the cane, with its tall straight stems and feathery light-green foliage. The sun glowed through the hazy air with a languid stifling heat, and, by day and night, mosquitoes in myriads left them no peace. They floated slowly down the current, crouched in the shade of the sails which they had spread as awnings, when suddenly they saw Indians on the east bank. The surprise was mutual, and each party was as much frightened as the other. Marquette hastened to display the calumet which the Illinois had given him by way of passport; and the Indians, recognizing the pacific symbol, replied with an invitation to land. Evidently, they were in communication with Europeans, for they were armed with guns, knives, and hatchets, wore garments of cloth, and carried their gunpowder in small bottles of thick glass. They feasted the Frenchmen with buffalo-meat, bear's oil, and white plums; and gave them a variety of doubtful information, including the agreeable but delusive assurance that they would reach the mouth of the river in ten days. It was, in fact, more than a thousand miles distant.

They resumed their course, and again floated down the interminable monotony of river, marsh and forest. Day after day passed on in solitude, and they had paddled some three hundred miles since their meeting with the Indians; when, as they neared the mouth of the Arkansas, they saw a cluster of wigwams on the west bank. Their inmates were all astir, yelling the war-whoop, snatching their weapons, and running to the shore to meet the strangers, who, on their part, called for succor to the Virgin. In truth they had need of her aid; for several large wooden canoes, filled with savages, were putting out from the shore, above and below them, to cut off their retreat, while a swarm of headlong young warriors waded into the water to attack them. The current proved too strong; and, failing to reach the canoes of the Frenchmen, one of them threw his war-club, which flew over the heads of the startled travellers. Meanwhile, Marquette had not ceased to hold up his calumet, to which the excited crowd gave no heed, but strung their bows and notched their arrows for immediate action; when at length the elders of the village arrived, saw the peace-pipe, restrained the ardor of the youth, and urged the Frenchmen to come ashore. Marquette and his companions complied, trembling, and found a better reception than they had reason to expect. One of the Indians spoke a little Illinois, and served as interpreter; a friendly conference was followed by a feast of sagamite and fish; and the travellers, not without sore misgivings, spent the night in the lodges of their entertainers.

Early in the morning, they embarked again, and proceeded to a village of the Arkansas tribe, about eight leagues below. Notice of their coming was sent before them by their late hosts; and, as they drew near, they were met by a canoe, in the prow of which stood a naked personage, holding a calumet, singing, and making gestures of friendship. On reaching the village, which was on the east side, opposite the mouth of the river Arkansas, they were conducted to a sort of scaffold before the lodge of the war-chief. The space beneath had been prepared for their reception, the ground being neatly covered with rush mats. On these they were seated; the warriors sat around them in a semicircle; then the elders of the tribe; and then the promiscuous crowd of villagers, standing, and staring over the heads of the more dignified members of the assembly. All the men were naked; but, to compensate for the lack of clothing, they wore strings of beads in their noses and ears. The women were clothed in shabby skins, and wore their hair clumped in a mass behind each ear. By good luck, there was a young Indian in the village, who had an excellent knowledge of Illinois; and through him Marquette endeavored to explain the mysteries of Christianity, and to gain information concerning the river below. To this end he gave his auditors the presents indispensable on such occasions, but received very little in return. They told him that the Mississippi was infested by hostile Indians, armed with guns procured from white men; and that they, the Arkansas, stood in such fear of them that they dared not hunt the buffalo, but were forced to live on Indian corn, of which they raised three crops a year.

During the speeches on either side, food was brought in without ceasing; sometimes a platter of sagamite or mush; sometimes of corn boiled whole; sometimes a roasted dog. The villagers had large earthen pots and platters, made by themselves with tolerable skill,—as well as hatchets, knives, and beads, gained by traffic with the Illinois and other tribes in contact with the French or Spaniards. All day there was feasting without respite, after the merciless practice of Indian hospitality; but at night some of their entertainers proposed to kill and plunder them,—a scheme which was defeated by the vigilance of the chief, who visited their quarters, and danced the calumet dance to reassure his guests.

The travellers now held counsel as to what course they should take. They had gone far enough, as they thought, to establish one important point,—that the Mississippi discharged its waters, not into the Atlantic or sea of Virginia, nor into the Gulf of California or Vermilion Sea, but into the Gulf of Mexico. They thought themselves nearer to its mouth than they actually were,—the distance being still about seven hundred miles; and they feared that, if they went farther, they might be killed by Indians or captured by Spaniards, whereby the results of their discovery would be lost. Therefore they resolved to return to Canada, and report what they had seen.

They left the Arkansas village, and began their homeward voyage on the seventeenth of July. It was no easy task to urge their way upward, in the heat of midsummer, against the current of the dark and gloomy stream, toiling all day under the parching sun, and sleeping at night in the exhalations of the unwholesome shore, or in the narrow confines of their birchen vessels, anchored on the river. Marquette was attacked with dysentery. Languid and well-nigh spent, he invoked his celestial mistress, as day after day, and week after week, they won their slow way northward. At length they reached the Illinois, and, entering its mouth, followed its course, charmed, as they went, with its placid waters, its shady forests, and its rich plains, grazed by the bison and the deer. They stopped at a spot soon to be made famous in the annals of western discovery. This was a village of the Illinois, then called Kaskaskia,—a name afterwards transferred to another locality. A chief, with a band of young warriors, offered to guide them to the Lake of the Illinois; that is to say, Lake Michigan. Thither they repaired; and, coasting its shores, reached Green Bay at the end of September, after an absence of about four months, during which they had paddled their canoes somewhat more than two thousand five hundred miles.

Marquette remained, to recruit his exhausted strength; but Joliet descended to Quebec, to bear the report of his discovery to Count Frontenac. Fortune had wonderfully favored him on his long and perilous journey; but now she abandoned him on the very threshold of home. At the foot of the rapids of La Chine, and immediately above Montreal, his canoe was overset, two of his men and an Indian boy were drowned, all his papers were lost, and he himself narrowly escaped. In a letter to Frontenac, he speaks of the accident as follows: "I had escaped every peril from the Indians; I had passed forty-two rapids; and was on the point of disembarking, full of joy at the success of so long and difficult an enterprise,—when my canoe capsized, after all the danger seemed over. I lost two men, and my box of papers, within sight of the first French settlements, which I had left almost two years before. Nothing remains to me but my life, and the ardent desire to employ it on any service which you may please to direct."

Marquette spent the winter and the following summer at the mission of Green Bay, still suffering from his malady. In the autumn, however, it abated, and he was permitted by his superior to attempt the execution of a plan to which he was devotedly attached,—the founding, at the principal town of the Illinois, of a mission to be called the Immaculate Conception, a name which he had already given to the river Mississippi. He set out on his errand on the twenty-fifth of October, accompanied by two men, named Pierre and Jacques, one of whom had been with him on his great journey of discovery. A band of Pottawattamies and another band of Illinois also joined him. The united parties—ten canoes in all—followed the east shore of Green Bay as far as the inlet then called Sturgeon Cove, from the head of which they crossed by a difficult portage through the forest to the shore of Lake Michigan. November had come. The bright hues of the autumn foliage were changed to rusty brown. The shore was desolate, and the lake was stormy. They were more than a month in coasting its western border, when at length they reached the river Chicago, entered it, and ascended about two leagues. Marquette's disease had lately returned, and hemorrhage now ensued. He told his two companions that this journey would be his last. In the condition in which he was, it was impossible to go farther. The two men built a log-hut by the river, and here they prepared to spend the winter, while Marquette, feeble as he was, began the spiritual exercises of Saint Ignatius, and confessed his two companions twice a week.

Meadow, marsh and forest were sheeted with snow, but game was abundant. Pierre and Jacques killed buffalo and deer and shot wild turkeys close to their hut. There was an encampment of Illinois within two days' journey; and other Indians, passing by this well known thoroughfare, occasionally visited them, treating the exiles kindly, and sometimes bringing them game and Indian corn. Eighteen leagues distant was the camp of two adventurous French traders,— one of them a noted *coureur de bois,* nicknamed La Taupine, and the other a self-styled surgeon. They also visited Marquette, and befriended him to the best of their power.

Urged by a burning desire to lay, before he died, the foundation of his new mission of the Immaculate Conception, Marquette begged his two followers to join him in a *novena,* or nine days' devotion to the Virgin. In consequence of this, as he believed, his disease relented; he began to regain strength, and, in March, was able to resume the journey. On the thirtieth of the month, they left their hut, which had been inundated by a sudden rise of the river, and carried their canoe through mud and water over the portage which led to the head of the Des Plaines. Marquette knew the way, for he had passed by this route on his return from the Mississippi. Amid the rains of opening spring, they floated down the swollen current of the Des Plaines, by naked woods, and spongy, saturated prairies, till they reached its junction with the main stream of the Illinois, which they descended to their destination,—the Indian town which Marquette calls Kaskaskia. Here, as we are told, he was received "like an angel from Heaven." He passed from wigwam to wigwam, telling the listening crowds of God and the Virgin, Paradise and Hell, angels and demons; and, when he thought their minds prepared, he summoned them all to a grand council.

It took place near the town, on the great meadow which lies

between the river and the modern village of Utica. Here five hundred chiefs and old men were seated in a ring; behind stood fifteen hundred youths and warriors, and behind these again all the women and children of the village. Marquette, standing in the midst, displayed four large pictures of the Virgin; harangued the assembly on the mysteries of the Faith, and exhorted them to adopt it. The temper of his auditory met his utmost wishes. They begged him to stay among them and continue his instructions; but his life was fast ebbing away, and it behooved him to depart.

A few days after Easter he left the village, escorted by a crowd of Indians, who followed him as far as Lake Michigan. Here he embarked with his two companions. Their destination was Michillimackinac, and their course lay along the eastern borders of the lake. As, in the freshness of advancing spring, Pierre and Jacques urged their canoe along that lonely and savage shore, the priest lay with dimmed sight and prostrated strength, communing with the Virgin and the angels. On the nineteenth of May he felt that his hour was near; and, as they passed the mouth of a small river, he requested his companions to land. They complied, built a shed of bark on a rising ground near the bank, and carried thither the dying Jesuit. With perfect cheerfulness and composure he gave directions for his burial, asked their forgiveness for the trouble he had caused them, administered to them the sacrament of penitence, and thanked God that he was permitted to die in the wilderness, a missionary of the faith and a member of the Jesuit brotherhood. At night, seeing that they were fatigued, he told them to take rest,—saying that he would call them when he felt his time approaching. Two or three hours after, they heard a feeble voice, and, hastening to his side, found him at the point of death. He expired calmly, murmuring the names of Jesus and Mary, with his eyes fixed on the crucifix which one of his followers held before him. They dug a grave beside the hut, and here they buried him according to the directions which he had given them; then re-embarking, they made their way to Michillimackinac, to bear the tidings to the priests at the mission of St. Ignace.

The Desert Fathers

PAUL HORGAN

An early Franciscan on the river said that its human life seemed to show on a map the shape of a cross. The upright stem, north and south, was the river itself along which clustered the great house-towns, and the arms reached east and west to settlements of other Indian people. It was an approximate image, but it expressed the dedication of the friars to their inner and immaterial motive. Their spirit and their flesh were one in purpose. They came to take nothing and they brought with them nothing that could be measured. Like the founder of their order, Saint Francis of Assisi, they could have said that they "had been called to the way of simplicity," and that they always "wished to follow the 'foolishness of the cross,'" by which they meant the innocence that made worldly men smile. Certainly it was the act of a fool, in terms of shrewd mankind, to go into barbarian wilderness at times alone and unprotected to preach the love of Christ. The Castilian Saint John of the Cross said, "Where there is no love, bring love and you will find love." The martyrs of Puaray, and Fray Juan de Padilla in Quivira, had made their ultimate demonstration. "They killed him," said another Franciscan of Fray Agustín Ruíz, "and threw his body into the Rio del Norte, which flows along the edge of this pueblo." And at Taos, when Fray Pedro de Ortega came to offer his faith to the Indians, he was refused a place to live, and to eat was given tortillas made of corn meal and the ground-up flesh of field mice, mixed with urine. These he ate with words of relish, remarking that for "a good appetite there is no bad bread." The Indians marvelled. "They go about poor and bare-foot as we do," said Indians elsewhere, "they eat what we eat, sit down among us, and speak to us gently."

In one respect the Indians and the friars were close together from the beginning. Both had profoundly religious character, and saw life's essentials best explained through the supernatural. But as the friars believed that their faith enclosed all faiths and purified

them in the fire of divine love, until God's relation to man shone
forth in the image of Christ Who was the Son of Man, so did they
think to bring love to replace the fear that animated all objects,
creatures and forces in the Indian's pagan world. The gift they sought
to give the Indian was the sense of his individual human soul, and the
need, and the means, of its salvation.

But if the friar in himself was poor and managed with very little,
his work in the aggregate required extensive organization. The friar's
immaterial mission was enclosed in a system that rested on a rigid
hierarchy and showed itself in massive monuments. At the pueblo of
El Agua de Santo Domingo, that stood on the banks of Galisteo
Creek a short way east of the river, the Franciscan order established
the religious headquarters of the whole kingdom of New Mexico.
There resided the Father President, and there he held his yearly
chapters when all his friars would come in from their lonely posts in
the outlying missions. Santo Domingo was a little Rome, the seat
of an authority that bowed to no secular power in matters of the
spiritual welfare of men and women. In the mountains to the north-
east was the new political capital of the colony at Santa Fe, founded
in 1610, after Oñate's recall. Between the river pueblo and the mountain capital much was in dispute throughout the seventeenth century
and would be composed only in slowly gathering tragedy.

Meanwhile the work of the religious reached into the river towns
to the north and south; into the pueblos of the west, and to the saline
towns over the eastern mountains. Nominally, even the Apache
nations who roamed the plains and alternately traded with and attacked the settled pueblo people were part of a missionary parish.
The Apaches, wrote a Father President in his report, "are very spirited
and belligerent . . . a people of a clearer and more subtle understanding, and as such laugh at other nations that worship idols of wood
and stone. The Apaches worship only the sun and the moon. . . .
They pride themselves on never lying but always speaking the truth."
It was an optimistic vision of mass murderers of whole towns. To
such peoples went "missions of penetration," consisting of a travelling
friar who preached, converted where he could, and if he lived, returned to Santo Domingo, or to the settled "mission of occupation"
to which he was assigned; for many of the outlying missions in Indian
towns were organized as field headquarters from which faith and

civilization were carried to other towns that had no permanent pastor. Such other towns were designated *visitas*.

Fifty churches were built in New Mexico by twenty-six friars in the first quarter of the seventeenth century. First came the word of God and the conversion of the Indians; and then, with no other power but example and patience, the solitary Franciscan father led his parishioners in building a church. In choosing the site for his church he considered many things. He looked into the hearts of the Indians and seeing all that mankind was capable of in good and evil, he felt that a church surrounded by the town was subject to being overwhelmed from within. He looked at the country beyond the town and he saw that the strongest fortress should stand first in the way of invaders. Considering ceremony, he saw how a church must have approaches for processions, and remembering functions, he knew it must be close to community life. Accordingly, at the edge of the pueblo he marked out a site for the church where it could stand by itself, yet be tied to the walls of the town.

He had large papers scratched with drawings. The people looked from these to his face and then to the straggled marks on the baked ground. He was all things: architect, engineer, carpenter, mason, foreman, building master to apprentices who themselves were masters of a building style. He did not scorn their methods or their designs. He saw their perfect economy of material and purpose in what they built. Remembering vast vaults of stone, the flutings of arches and echoing heights, sombre color in glass and every intricacy of grille and recess and carved screen, he saw that reduced to essentials, even the great churches of Europe and Mexico had a plain strong purpose, which was to enclose the attention of men and women in safety and direct it toward the altar. Here were wanted walls and roof as soon as possible. They must be made of materials already used and understood by the people, and to them must be added new methods understood by the friar. He had with him, assigned by the Father President at Domingo, and paid for by the King of Spain, ten axes, three adzes, three spades, ten hoes, one medium-sized saw, one chisel, two augers, and one plane; six thousand nails of various sizes, a dozen metal hinges, two small locks, several small latches, and one large latch for the main church door. With him, too, he brought the principle of the lever, the windlass and the block and fall. Out of his belief and his technique, combined with native materials and the

Indian's reproduction of earth forms in building, a new style was ready to come, massive, stark, angular, and powerfully expressive of its function.

Until they worked under Spaniards, the Indians built their walls of puddled clay and rock. Now the first lesson of the friar was to teach the making of adobes—earthen bricks. Clay was disintegrated rock. The adobe was a restoration of clay to coherent form—a sort of return to rock. With their new hoes, people went to work mixing water and earth in an excavated tray. Only Indian women did this work, for as theirs was the ancient task of enclosing life so they had always made the dwelling rooms of the family. Men, as craftsmen of arms and tools, learned carpentry, and made wooden molds after the friar's instructions. Into the wet clay, straw was mixed as a binder, and the clay was then pressed into the molds to take the shape of large bricks. A brick weighed sixty pounds, and measured ten by eighteen by five inches. It was about all the load a man or woman could carry over and over, as the rows of drying bricks grew longer.

Sometimes foundations were dug and filled with loose stone footings, sometimes the walls rose directly from unopened ground. The walls were deep—six to nine feet thick, and one side wall was several feet thicker than the other. The people wondered why this was as the width was marked out on the ground, and as the walls rose they discovered why, but meanwhile the dried bricks were brought by a long line of workers, and laid in place. The entire pueblo worked on the church. While women mixed earth, and men molded bricks, other men and boys went to the mountains to bring back timbers. With rock and chisel they shaped these. The friar drew patterns for them to follow and out of the wood came beams, corbels, door panels, doorframes, window embrasures. If someone knew where deposits of selenite or mica were to be found, men were sent to bring in a supply so that thin layers of the translucent mineral could be worked into windowpanes. The days were full and the walls rose slowly but all could see progress, and it made them one in spirit. The church was from twenty to forty feet wide, and sixty to a hundred feet long. Its ceiling was to occur at about thirty feet. On one of its long flanks, against the thicker of the two walls, were laid out living quarters for the friar and his Indian staff in a row of little square rooms with low roofs. These formed one side of a patio, the other sides of which held more rooms or a covered cloister. In certain towns the walls of the convent quadrangle took in a round sunken kiva previously used by the Indians. Rooms in the patio were planned for teaching classes, for cooking, dining, and storage of grain and other supplies.

Nowhere in the church or its convent was there a curved wall line, or arch, or dome. As the walls rose to their limit, the purpose of the wider wall became plain. Down on the ground the great tree beams were about to be hoisted up to span the church. Their weight needed a heavy support, and the dozens of men on top of the wall working to bring them up needed room to stand. The wide wall made a fulcrum for the great levers of the beams, and served as a broad platform on which men could work. Scaffolding was little used. Indians had ladders by which to enter their houses and kivas from the roof, and these were put to work too in acts of building. As the church walls achieved their height, carved wooden corbels were laid into the bricks to support crossbeams. Oxen dragged one timber at a time to the base of the walls and men hauled it upright, tipping it against the massive fulcrum at the top, and laying it across the nave. Such beams, or vigas, were of unequal length. Their ends projected beyond the walls and were often left so. Now between the beams were placed branches of uniform size to close the ceiling, and above these rose the parapet of the walls high enough to hide a man. Crenellations were let into the parapet for sighting with musketry or arrows. Over the whole roof went load after load of loose earth, which was packed down by feet, and hardened by water and sun.

The river churches followed two designs. One was that of a long narrow straight box; the other that of a cross, with shallow transepts. Where transepts occurred, the builders lifted a higher roof over them and the sanctuary in a gesture of grace; for where this higher portion rose above the long nave, they placed a clerestory window reaching the width of the nave that took in the light of the sky and let it fall upon the altar, while the rest of the interior remained in shadow. The only other occasional windows were two or three small, high openings in the thinner of the long walls.

Entering by the main door anyone had his attention taken to the altar by many cunningly planned devices of which the first was the pour of wide and lovely light from the clerestory whose source was hidden by the ceiling of the shadowy nave. The builders used the science of optical illusion in false perspectives to make the nave seem longer, the approach to heaven and altar more august and protracted. The apse, tall and narrow, tapered toward the rear wall like the head of a coffin. Where there were transepts, the body of man was prefigured all-evidently—the head lying in the sanctuary, the arms laid into the transepts, and all the length of the nave the narrow-ribbed barrel and the thin hips and the long legs inert in mortal sacrifice. Many churches added one further symbol and illusion: the rear wall of the sanctuary was built upon another axis than that of the nave. It suggested two things—the fall of Christ's head to one side as he hung on the cross; the other, a farther dimension to the house that honored Him. All such variation of symmetry, and modulation of perspective, combined with inexact workmanship and humble materials, resulted in an effect of spontaneity and directness, like that in a drawing made by a child to fulfill a great wish. The wish, the emotion, transcended the means, and stood embodied forth in grave impersonal intimacy.

Over the adobe texture was placed by the women a plaster of mud. They applied it with the palms of their hands and sometimes smoothed it with a patch of sheepskin bearing fleece. The outer walls in time bore the same marks of the weather as the ancient natural forms of earth all about—little watercourses that ran making wrinkles which when dry came to resemble the marks of life in an old sunbrowned face. And yet with even such sensitive response to the elements, an unattended adobe building weathered down only one inch in twenty years. In any proper town the walls were replastered after every rainy season. The walls were renewed so long as human life used them. Some stood for centuries after being abandoned, and still stand in part, above talus of their own yielding as they go ever so slowly back to the earth.

The interior walls received a coat of whitewash and on this in pure colors the people painted designs, as though they were decorating great unrolled surfaces of clay pots. Scrolls, parrots, columns; flowers and cornstalks; symbols of sun, rain, lightning, thunder and the oblique slantings of terraced forms that took an impression of the landscape receding from the river. Many of the frescoes had not only an Indian but also a strangely Byzantine air, as though a new hybrid culture must turn back to relive all the stages of its various influences.

Finally, before the front of the church a walled enclosure was completed where the blessed dead could lie, and where, against the façade an outdoor altar could be set in a sort of atrium to accommodate large crowds on feast days and Sundays.

From a little distance then the finished building gave its purpose with hard grandeur in its loom and weight, its grace of plain angular shadow, and the wide sunlight on its unbroken faces, where the shadows of the vigas bladed down the walls making a sundial that told not hours but centuries. The whole mission with church, convento, cloister and walled burial field seemed like a shoulder of earth emerging out of the blind ground as a work of living sculpture. To see the true beauty of those structures it was necessary first of all to love and to believe in their purpose.

.   .   .   .   .

And when the mission was built and furnished it was both fortress and sanctuary. When outside its blind heavy walls a wind rose, there within were peace and security, where the many candle flames never wavered as they shone on flowers of colored paper. "It all looked very holy," remarked a friar of such a church in 1634. And yet, if he knew Spain, and its sacred treasures, he perhaps looked upon his mud walls and his rough-chiselled timbers and bitterly told himself that here he had contrived no beauty or splendor, remembering such an altar vessel as the monstrance of Toledo that took nine years to fashion out of three hundred and thirty pounds of silver, until it was eight and a half feet high, with two hundred and sixty small statues amongst jewelled pillars, so that in its exposition the Blessed Sacrament appeared to hover in midair surrounded by a shining cloud. He could only say to himself that there was work to be done as well as possible with the materials at hand. Ending his day only to dedicate the morrow, he recited the prayer written by his founder Saint Francis that said ". . . grant that I may not so much seek to be consoled as to console; to be understood as to understand; to be loved as to love; for it is in giving that we receive; it is in pardoning that we are pardoned; and it is in dying that we are born to eternal life."

And when the morrow came, there were many tasks to guide. The convento and the church were staffed by Indians—a bell ringer, a cook, two or three sacristans, a porter, two boys who kept order in the friars' cells, some women to grind corn, an old man who scratched at the beginnings of a garden within the clay walls of the patio. With-

out seeing themselves so, the Franciscan priests of the early river
were great artists of community life. If they desired to bestow and
maintain the standards of civilization in their wilderness, they had
first to show the Indians the whole image of the cultivated life that
came from Europe. Many of the friars were extraordinarily versatile,
and most of them were wholly without that pride of learning which
in the universities and coteries of the day often allowed both the
scholar and his knowledge to die unused by life. The friars put their
learning to work.

Lessons were organized and conducted with discipline. At dawn
every day but Sunday the bellman went to ring the church bell for
Prime. The pupils, young and old, came to the classrooms which they
at once swept out. They then took their places and the pastor came
to teach.

He was quick at languages, and for immediate understanding of
the Indians, learned the native tongues rapidly, and taught the Christian story in the people's own words. The earliest book to be printed
in the New World appeared in Mexico in 1539 under the imprimatur
of Zumárraga, the first Bishop of Mexico. It was a catechism in
Spanish and Nahuatl. Some of the friars came to the river after
preaching for years in Mexico in the native dialects. Once having
reached the understanding of the Indian, they developed it with
classes in many subjects. They first taught Latin, so that the responses
at Mass and vespers could properly be made. Eventually they taught
Spanish so that daily life might link the wilderness people to the all-
powerful source of national life in Madrid. The Indians learned to
speak and to write in those new ways, through which such amazing
information came to them. The past found a way to exist in the
Indian mind.

Along with words, the Indians learned music. Boys were formed
into choirs and trained in the sacred chants of the Church. In one
pueblo, out of a thousand people who went to school the pastor chose
and trained a "marvelous choir of wonderful boy musicians." In
another, the singing boys "with their organ chants . . . enhanced the
divine service with great solemnity." Winter and summer, in the river
dawns and twilights the heavenly traceries of the polyphonic style rose
to the blunt clay ceilings of the coffinlike churches; and the majestic
plainness of antiphonal chants echoed from sanctuary to nave as the
people together stolidly voiced the devotions composed by Fray

Geronimo Ciruelo and shipped north to the river in 1626. A little organ with gilt pipes went to Santa Fe in 1610, and a few decades later eighteen of the kingdom's churches had organs. The friars taught how to play them, and how to make and play stringed musical instruments, and flutes, and bassoons, and trumpets, after the models shipped from abroad. On great feast days, the level Indian voices were enriched by ardent stridencies from pierced cane, hollowed gourd, and shaped copper. A tradition lasting centuries had an imitation of nature at work in the worship of the Mass. From the choir loft over the main door of the church came first softly then mounting in sweet wildness the sounds of a multitude of little birds calling and trilling in controlled high spirits. On the gallery floor a dozen little boys lay before pottery bowls half-filled with water. Each boy had a short reed pierced at intervals which he fingered. He blew through one end while the other rested in the water, from which rose the liquid notes of songbirds adoring God. At the elevation of the Host or other moments of high solemnity it was proper on great feast days to fire a salute of musketry amid the rolling of the bells.

The Franciscan school taught painting. Indians learned not so much how to hold a brush or use color—they knew that—as how to see, look, formalize a representation. A whole new notion of what the world looked like came to the Indians; yet without greatly affecting their decorative styles, for they continued to draw more the spirit, the idea of a subject, than its common likeness.

Joy and laughter were praised by Saint Francis, and there was no reason why the river fathers should not by these means as well as any other reach into the minds and hearts of their taciturn children. The Spanish delight in theatre, scarcely a hundred years old, was already a deeply rooted taste; and the friars, like the lay colonists, gave plays on suitable occasions. In the pueblos, the comedies were meant to instruct as well as entertain. Ancient Nativity stories were acted out by well-rehearsed Indians, who took the parts not only of the Holy Family and their ecstatic attendants but also represented a little party of Indians in their own character. When in the play it was asked who were these strangers come to attend the birth of the Infant Savior, the answer said that they too were men for whom the Son of God was born on earth that He might save them. A dignifying love reached out to the Indians in the audience. Sometimes the plays were hilarious, and all could laugh at the embarrassments and defeats

cleverly visited upon Satan, whose exasperation would know no
bounds. Any play telling the story of people brought a sense of community and self-discovery.

The Franciscan teaching turned everywhere, lifted up the soil,
planted new seeds, and put the soil back. Among the first new crops
was one directly related to the Mass. Cuttings of fine grapevines were
brought across the sea from Spain and sent up the long trail from
Mexico—a light red grape and a purple one, from which the fathers
made sacramental white and red wines. New fruits were set out in
orchards—peaches, apples, pears, plums, cherries, quinces, figs, dates,
pomegranates, olives, apricots, almonds, pecans, walnuts. Later when
the missions rose by the river at the gateway to Mexico, lemons and
nectarines were planted to thrive in the mild winters, and oranges,
which had first been planted in the New World by Bernal Diaz del
Castillo landing with Cortés. Together with the fields of newly introduced vegetables, the orchards were irrigated from the river with improved methods long known to the friars from their Mediterranean
culture. With the foundation of horses, cows and sheep brought by
the colony, the friars taught the Indians how to herd and how to breed
the animals for improvement of the stock. There were workable
resources in the kingdom observed by the well-educated priests, who
said that with patience and labor much could be done with the ores
in the mountains. The treasure hunters had come and gone, unwilling
to work for what they wanted. New Mexico was officially reported as
a poor country. But a Father President of the Franciscan province in
1629 disagreed: "As for saying that it is poor, I answer that there
nowhere in the world has been discovered a country richer in mineral
deposits." He listed the very localities of the river kingdom where he
had seen deposits, and went on scornfully to say that all such news
meant nothing to the Spaniards in Mexico, who if they had merely
a good crop of tobacco to smoke were content. It seemed odd to him
that they should be so indifferent, when Spaniards "out of greed for
silver and gold would enter Hell itself to get them."

.   .   .   .   .

Knowledge, a full mind, made a companion in the empty wilds
when the friars went forth from their clay citadels to preach among
the Indians far east or west of the river. They might be accompanied
by a dozen soldiers "more," as a Father President said, "for the pious

sentiment of not abandoning such a sacred enterprise than for protection or defense, which would have been very limited considering the large number of people they were to meet, all as skilful at arms as they were tenacious in their wars." The friars, he said, "know much hardship in crossing the river each time their ministering demands it, since the river is very swift and subject to bad floods." But all was endurable in the natural world for the sake of that which came to pass in the spirits of those whom they sought in simplicity and love. An Indian cacique came to a father missioner bringing him a marvelously tanned buffalo hide. Unfolding it, the friar saw a painting that showed a green sun and a gray moon, and above them each a cross.

"What does this painting mean?" he asked, and the cacique replied,

"Father, until now we have not known other benefactors greater than the sun and the moon. They light us and warm us, and make our plants produce and the flowers germinate. Thus because of so many benefits we have worshipped them as the arbiters of our lives. But since we heard you tell us who God is who created the sun and the moon, in order that you may know that we now worship only God, I had these crosses, which are the emblem of God, painted above the sun and the moon."

. . . . .

TWO

Catholicism in the Colonies

Religious Liberty in Catholic Maryland

J. MOSS IVES

When it is said that there was religious liberty, separation of state and church, independence of king and parliament and an exercise of self-government in early Catholic Maryland, this is not stating the entire case. There was something of greater importance than any of these things. There was equality of civil rights. When the early settlers and lawmakers once acknowledged that no preference should be given in the exercise of religious worship, they were bound to acknowledge that there should be no discrimination in the exercise of the right to participate in governmental affairs. It has been said that religious liberty is the parent of civil liberty, but there can be no real civil liberty unless there is equality in the privileges and duties of citizens.

In no other colony was the voting franchise so freely given and so free from restriction. Here it was dependent neither on church membership nor ownership of property. Furthermore no one was taxed to support a church or clergy not of his own faith. With the exception of the simple Act for Church Liberties there was no reference made to the subject of religion in any of the early laws of the colony. No fines were imposed for non-attendance at church, and no one was punished for exercising any particular form of church worship. No provision was made for the subsidy of any church nor for the support of the clergy of any church. Like the Royal Charter of Maryland, the early codes were as remarkable for what they omitted as for what they contained.

The contrast between Puritan Massachusetts and early Catholic Maryland is the contrast between a theocracy and a democracy. What has been called the Puritan Commonwealth and the Puritan Republic was in reality a theocracy, a government of the clergy, by the clergy, and for the clergy. There, the power of the government was in the control of a small minority and this ruling minority was the Puritan clergy. In Maryland, the Catholic missionaries who were the only clergy in the colony, abstained from all legislative activity and excused themselves from attendance at the assemblies.

The power of the clergy was early made manifest in the proceedings of the Massachusetts General Court. It was seldom that a measure was carried over their objection and no man sat in the assembly who was obnoxious to them. At the head of the Puritan theocracy was the Reverend John Cotton who has been described as "the unmitered pope of a pope-hating commonwealth." It was this same John Cotton who said he did not concede that God ever ordained democracy "as a fit government either for church or commonwealth; as for monarchy and autocracy, they are both of them clearly approved and dictated ,by scripture."

The power of the clergy in Massachusetts was supreme over the legislature, the courts and the people. The clergy made the laws. The magistrates were little more than sheriffs to execute the laws. The people were made to conform to the rule of the clergy by all manner of penal statutes which invaded the privacy of their homes, regulated their dress, and attempted to control their thoughts. The magistrate decided cases "according to rule of scripture," but if no rule of scripture could be found to fit a particular case, then he had recourse to the advice of the clergy. Frequently men were banished for no other reason than that "they were not fit to live with us." It was the clergy who decided the question of fitness. The clergy was sustained by the magistrates, and the magistrates in turn supported the clergy.

The law-makers were the clergy, and their guide was not the English common law, but the Mosaic code interpreted to conform to their own ideas. The Puritan clergy had a fondness for legislation that became an obsession. They believed the law to be a panacea for all ills. Laws were passed demanding church attendance, enforcing respect for churches and ministers, prohibiting the building of any but the orthodox meeting houses, and prohibiting the preaching and practice of any kind of religion except what was strictly orthodox. No man was given the voting franchise unless he was a member of the orthodox church in good and regular standing.

On Sunday nothing was lawful except to go to church. Absence from church service was punishable by a fine and in order to prevent back-sliding the constables were enjoined to "duly make search throughout the limites of their towns" for absentees during the time when services were being held, and if any were found, to hale them within the church portals. Attendance at church service was not enough. A man must not fall asleep during the sermon and the sermons were long, never less than an hour, sometimes two hours. In 1643, a man was fined for falling asleep in church and striking the man who woke him up. Later the same culprit was severely whipped for falling asleep again. After that he evidently kept awake during the sermon, for there is no record of any further conviction.

A man could not kiss his wife in public on Sunday. A sea captain who had returned from a voyage of three years, on a Sunday morning did not wait until he entered his house before kissing his wife, but indiscreetly kissed her on the door step in full sight of passersby. He sat in the stocks for two hours for his "lewd and unseemly behavior on the Sabbath Day."

Against other sects, the Puritans directed their legislative shafts, Baptists, Quakers and Catholics receiving particular attention. Baptist ministers were fined, imprisoned and flogged for attempting to hold services. Laws were passed for the banishment of all Quakers, Catholic priests and Jesuits, and for the hanging of those who might return after banishment. Four Quakers, including a woman, returned from banishment and were hung on Boston Common. The law against Catholic priests was never invoked, for the missionaries in America had the good sense not to intrude where they were not wanted and where apparently their services were not needed. They never entertained any hope of converting the Puritans. Ministering to those of their own faith and attempting to convert the Indians were their chief concern.

The only record of a member of the Catholic clergy invading the sacred precincts of the Bay Colony during the early days of the theocracy was in the case of Father Gabriel Druilletes, a Jesuit missionary, who was sent to Boston with credentials from the Governor-General of Canada to negotiate with the Massachusetts authorities a proposed alliance against the warring tribes of the Iroquois. Armed

with credentials from his government, he was exempt from the law
providing for banishment of a priest. He was received kindly and
graciously, invited to dine with Governor Dudley at Roxbury and
with Governor Bradford of the Plymouth colony. When he dined
with Bradford it was on a Friday and the governor "considerately
gave him a dinner of fish." He was also the guest of the Reverend
John Eliot, Puritan missionary to the Indians, who invited him to
spend the winter. Father Druilletes' mission apparently failed but the
incident showed that the Puritan could tolerate a Catholic priest even
if he were a Jesuit, when the law allowed him to do so.

A study of the early Maryland codes will show that they were
more constructive and remedial than penal. There were far more laws
for the encouragement of husbandry, the security of property rights
and the protection of the liberties of the people than there were for
the restriction of liberties and the punishment of offenders. While
the laws of Massachusetts fairly bristled with definitions of criminal
offences, only a few of the early laws of Maryland related to crimes
and penalties. Of the eighteen pages of the code of 1642 only two relate to crime. The list of capital offenses was practically the same as
recognized in England, and both the civil and criminal codes were
but restatements of English law, reduced and modified to meet the
simple needs of the young colony.

While Massachusetts was building jails in every county to harbor
those who violated her many penal laws, there were no jails in Maryland. In 1642, eight years after the landing of the *Ark* and the *Dove,*
when Captain Ingle was arrested for piracy and treason he escaped
from the sheriff at St. Mary's. The sheriff excused his apparent
neglect of duty by reporting that there was no public jail "but his
owne hands." He was expected to entertain prisoners in his home.

The Puritans were a long time finding out that men could not
be re-created by legislation. The theocracy lasted for over a half
century and it is amazing how this rule by a minority could have
survived as long as it did. A large number of the people of the colony
were deprived of the vote, not being members of the established
church in good and regular standing. This number kept increasing
until in the last days of the theocracy fully five-sixths of the people
were disfranchised.

Coming down to Virginia, there will be found the same laws of
compulsory church attendance as in Massachusetts, except that the

Church of England was substituted for the church of the Puritans. Wilstach says:

> Church attendance on the Maryland side of the river was enforced by the Catholics in their own way. It was a matter of moral discipline. To miss Mass was a sin. The offender punished himself. On the Virginia side failure to attend church was made a wilful misdemeanor and the State punished the offender.

Anyone who absented himself from church in early Virginia forfeited a pound of tobacco, and if his absence continued for a month, he forfeited fifty pounds of the same commodity. All churches and ministers must conform to the Church of England and all churches were built at the public expense. Penalties were imposed on parents for not sending their children to church, and upon children for refusing to learn the catechism.

The first legislative assembly in America was introduced in Virginia, but it cannot be said that because of this the germs of real American democracy first took root in the soil of this colony. From the very beginning the Church of England was established in Virginia. The oath of supremacy was required of all inhabitants and the freeman's vote was given only to conformists.

The preliminary meeting of the assembly was held in the English church at Jamestown in 1619. The assemblymen first sat in the choir of the church. The Governor was in the seat he was accustomed to occupy when attending church service. The sergeant was at the choir rail ready for any emergency. The meeting was opened with prayer by the minister of the Church of England. The members of the assembly withdrew into the body of the church, each taking the oath of supremacy before being admitted to his seat.

The idea of a legislative assembly in Virginia was probably original with Sir Edwin Sandys. George Calvert was a member of the Second Virginia Company and a member of the provisional council for the management of the affairs of the colony after the revocation of the charter. Although in the discharge of his duties as Secretary of State in the Court of James it may appear that he was opposed to some of the policies of Sandys, yet he was in entire agreement with the latter on the question of religious liberty. As Dr. Andrews says: "What Sandys may have seen as a vision Calvert prepared to carry into practical effect."

Calvert in the preparation of his charters adopted the Virginia plan of a popular assembly but his plan went further in that it granted equal rights of citizenship and allowed for separation of state and church.

The first assembly, the records of which have been preserved, was that of 1623. This assembly provided for religious conformity and uniformity. All persons must yield "readie obedience" to the canons of the Church of England "under pain of censure."

In 1642 "Popish recusants" were disabled from holding office and Catholic priests arriving in the colony were to be expelled within five days. At different times both Puritans and Quakers were ordered to be banished with severe penalties in the event of return. Baptists were also discriminated against. Any one who disparaged a minister of the Church of England without bringing sufficient proof "to justify his reports" incurred a fine of five hundred pounds of tobacco and must publicly ask the minister for forgiveness.

In both Massachusetts and Virginia discriminatory laws and compulsory attendance upon an established church afforded barren soil for the growth of the principle of equality before the law. Without some recognition of this principle we may look in vain for the real foundation of the American form of government.

In some of the other colonies there were later established more liberal forms of government than are to be found in early Massachusetts and Virginia, but in all respects not as liberal as the early government of Maryland. Thomas Hooker and his band of followers who came to the meadowlands of Hartford and Wethersfield, Connecticut, to get away from the Puritan theocracy, adopted in the exercise of self-government a set of principles and laws which formed the first written constitution in America. The one great drawback in Connecticut, however, was the fact that although church membership was not made a prerequisite for voting, the Congregational Church was the established church of the colony. The church was a public charge and all inhabitants, regardless of creed, were taxed to pay for its support; its buildings were erected at public expense and its ministers were called by the town meeting.

It was near the time when the control of the government of Maryland was taken from the third Lord Baltimore that William Penn received the charter for his princely domain. His charter followed some of the features of the Maryland charter, but Penn failed to obtain two concessions which were granted to the first Lord Baltimore

—the guarantee of the rights of English freemen to the colonists and freedom from taxation imposed by parliament. Despite these handicaps he did all within his power to follow where Calvert had led the way, and made a substantial contribution to the cause of liberal government.

In the same year that Penn came to America, James, the Duke of York, appointed Colonel Thomas Dongan, an Irish Catholic,. governor of the colony of New York. Dongan established a democratic form of government and religious freedom. John Austin Stevens in his contribution to Winsor's *Narrative and Critical History of America,* declares that "no more democratic form of government existed in America or was possible under kingly authority"; than that established in New York by Governor Dongan. The first act of the assembly in 1683 was that which bore the title of "The Charter of Liberties and Privileges granted by His Royal Highness to the Inhabitants of New York and its dependencies." The supreme legislative authority under the King and the Duke, was vested in a governor, council and the "people met in general assembly." The franchise was free to every freeholder, there was no church establishment and there was freedom of conscience and religion. It is a noteworthy fact that in the only two colonies which had Catholic governors, both civil and religious liberty were established which continued as long as these colonies were under Catholic rule. It is equally significant that both these Catholic governors (Leonard Calvert and Colonel Dongan) had Jesuits for their spiritual advisers. One of Dongan's advisers during the short time he was governor of New York was Father Thomas Harvey who afterwards came to Maryland.

Professor Andrews cites as an early measure of religious liberty an act passed by the General Court of the Province of Maine in 1649, "oddly enough," he says, "but six months after the passage of the more famous and misunderstood act concerning religion by the Maryland assembly." This act declared that:

All good people of this province who are of a church way and be orthodox in judgment and not scandalous in life shall have liberty to gather themselves into a church estate, providing they do it in a Christian way, with due observance of the rules of Christ revealed in his word and every church hath full liberty of election and ordination of all her officers from time to time, provided they be able, pious and orthodox.

Assuming that the real purpose of this act was to grant religious liberty it can be seen that any of its several provisos, especially the proviso as to orthodoxy, might easily stand in the way of allowing full liberty to all sects and all creeds. Then too, this act is to be interpreted in the light of the royal charter granted by Charles I to Sir Ferdinando Gorges for the Province of Maine. In the charter there was an express provision that "the religion now professed in the Church of England and ecclesiastical government now used in the same, shall forever professed and with as much convenient speed as may be, settled and established in and throughout said province and premises and every of them."

Gorges was granted proprietary rights much the same as was Baltimore, together with the "liberties and immunities as the Bishop of Durham within the bishopric or County Palatine of Durham in our Kingdom of England now hath." The charter to Gorges was not granted until 1639, some sixteen years after Baltimore received the Charter of Avalon. Evidently some of the King's advisers cautioned against any vagueness and uncertainty such as had crept into the Avalon and Maryland charters, and to take no chance with the Maine charter so far as the establishment of the Church of England was concerned, so church establishment was made mandatory. There may be toleration under church establishment but not real religious liberty.

Maryland, Pennsylvania, Maine and New York were all proprietary colonies, as were also the Carolinas and New Jersey. Professor John M. Mecklin in his recent work, *The Story of American Dissent*, says:

The proprietary colonies were inclined to be tolerant. Founded primarily for the purpose of trade, they welcomed any group of immigrant irrespective of religious affiliations who were economic assets. Often the tolerant ways of life built up in proprietary colonies persisted after the colonies were transferred to the crown and offered the stubborn and effective resistance to all efforts to enforce a religious establishment. This was especially true of the Carolinas, New Jersey and New York where Anglican establishment was never more than a mere shell. The same was also true of Maryland where, however, it was not so much the exigences of trade as the effect of liberal ideas inculcated under Lord Baltimore that later proved a hindrance to the effective functioning of the Anglican establishment.

The claim to priority in the field of civil and religious liberty must after all be yielded to Maryland, for here in the early days of the colony can be found the first full recognition of the basic American principle of equality before the law.

The Address of the Roman Catholics To George Washington, Esq. President of The United States

Sir,

We have been long impatient to testify our joy, and unbounded confidence on your being called, by an Unanimous Vote, to the first station of a country, in which that unanimity could not have been obtained, without the previous merit of unexampled services, of eminent wisdom, and unblemished virtue. Our congratulations have not reached you sooner, because our scattered situation prevented our communication, and the collecting of those sentiments, which warmed every breast. But the delay has furnished us with the opportunity, not merely of presaging the happiness to be expected under your Administration, but of bearing testimony to that which we experience already. It is your talent, in war and in peace, to afford security to those who commit their protection into your hands. In war you shield them from the ravages of armed hostility; in peace, you establish public tranquility, by the justice and moderation, not less than by the vigour, of your government. By example, as well as by vigilance, you extend the influence of laws on the manners of our fellow-citizens. You encourage respect for religion; and inculcate, by words and actions, that principle, on which the welfare of nations so much depends, that a superintending providence governs the events of the world, and watches over the conduct of men. Your exalted maxims, and unwearied attention to the moral and physical improvement of our country, have produced already the happiest effects. Under your administration, America is animated with zeal for the attainment and encouragement of useful literature. She improves

An Address From The Roman Catholics of America, To George Washington, Esq., President of the United States (London: Printed by J. P. Coghlan, Duke-Street, Grosvenor-Square; and Sold by Messrs. Robinsons, Pater-Noster-Row, M, DDC, XC).

her agriculture; extends her commerce; and acquires with foreign nations a dignity unknown to her before. From these happy events, in which none can feel a warmer interest than ourselves, we derive additional pleasure, by recollecting that you, Sir, have been the principal instrument to effect so rapid a change in our political situation. This prospect of national prosperity is peculiarly pleasing to us, on another account; because, whilst our country preserves her freedom and independence, we shall have a well founded title to claim from her justice, the equal rights of citizenship, as the price of our blood spilt under your eyes, and of our common exertions for her defence, under your auspicious conduct—rights rendered more dear to us by the remembrance of former hardships. When we pray for the preservation of them, where they have been granted—and expect the full extension of them from the justice of those States, which still restrict them:—when we solicit the protection of Heaven over our common country, we neither omit, nor can omit recommending your preservation to the singular care of Divine Providence; because we conceive that no human means are so available to promote the welfare of the United States, as the prolongation of your health and life, in which are included the energy of your example, the wisdom of your counsels, and the persuasive eloquence of your virtues.

John Carroll,   In behalf of the Roman Catholic Clergy.
Charles Carroll, of Carrollton, ⎫
Daniel Carroll,   ⎪   In behalf of the Roman
Dominick Lynch,   ⎬   Catholic Laity.
Thomas Fitzsimmons.   ⎭

Answer To The Roman Catholics
In The United States Of America

Gentlemen,

While I now receive, with much satisfaction, your congratulations on my being called, by an unanimous Vote, to the first station in my Country—I cannot but duly notice your politeness in offering an apology for the unavoidable delay. As that delay has given you an opportunity of realizing, instead of anticipating, the benefits of the general Government,—you will do me the justice to believe, that your testimony of the increase of the public prosperity, enhances the pleasure, which I should otherwise have experienced from your affectionate Address.

I feel that my conduct, in war and in peace, has met with more general approbation, than could have reasonably been expected: and I find myself disposed to consider, that fortunate circumstance, in a great degree resulting from the able support, and extraordinary candour, of my fellow-citizens of all denominations.

The prospect of National prosperity now before us, is truly animating; and ought to excite the exertions of all good men, to establish and secure the happiness of their Country, in the permanent duration of its freedom and independence. America, under the smiles of Divine Providence—the protection of a good Government—and the cultivation of Manners, Morals, and Piety—cannot fail of attaining, an uncommon degree of Eminence, in Literature, Commerce, Agriculture, Improvements at home, and Respectability abroad.

As Mankind become more liberal, they will be more apt to allow, that all those who conduct themselves worthy members of the Community, are equally entitled to the protection of Civil Government. I hope ever to see America among the foremost Nations in examples of Justice and Liberality. And I presume that your fellow-citizens will not forget the patriotic part, which you took in the accomplishment of their Revolution, and the establishment of their Government—or the important assistance, which they received from a Nation, in which the Roman Catholic Faith is professed.

I thank you, Gentlemen, for your kind concern for me. While my Life and Health shall continue, in whatever situation I may be, it shall be my constant endeavour to justify the favourable sentiments which you are pleased to express of my conduct. And may the Members of your Society in America, animated alone by the pure spirit of Christianity, and still conducting themselves, as the faithful subjects of our free Government, enjoy every temporal, and spiritual felicity.

March 12, 1790

George Washington

⌘ THREE ⌘

A Century of Adjustment
and Apologetics

Letter to the Candid and Unprejudiced
People of America

BISHOP JOHN ENGLAND

Charleston, S.C., Oct. 3, 1831.

To the Candid and Unprejudiced People of America.

My Friends:—I am desirous of closing this series of letters. I have trespassed upon your patience and been tedious in exhibiting evidence to prove that of which most of you have been long since convinced, viz., that the evangelicals complained that under the pretext of placing men of good principles in civil office, they were not permitted to exclude from all places of public honour, public trust, and public emolument, all men who did not belong to their party. Thus they sought to monopolize the stations of government to the exclusion of infidels, of Papists, and of the ungodly and the heterodox. That is they aim at a practical violation of the constitution of the United States. The rabid fury with which they assail Roman Catholics is abundant evidence of their disposition. The moment any member of that church is chosen to any office worth naming, that instant he and his church are villainously outraged: laboured and polished essays, and vile and vulgar contumely are flung abroad amongst the public, and you are called upon to protect your endangered liberties. These productions are seen in Europe, they are noticed in Catholic nations, and our country is viewed by men of literature and of acquirements in no very flattering way. Yet, what care the evangelicals for this? Their object is to perpetuate ancient prejudices for their private emolument: and if they succeed, the public may indeed hiss them, but they will applaud themselves. Hence they are reckless of the character of the nation, provided they possess the influence of power, or are able to count a large share of dollars in their stock.

Hitherto they have been defeated in their efforts, and they on that account complain of the men in power. The Congress refused to declare that this was a country of any religious denomination, or to assume any power of religious legislation, upon the express plea that they received no such commission. Hence they are to be considered infidels. They declined the honour of being "nursing fathers of the church," upon the principle that they were only appointed to be political representatives of the states and of the people. For this they are denominated anti-Christians. By means of petitions, of suggestions, of disquisitions, and various modes of influence, efforts were made to procure the enactment of a law upon the basis, that the public business should be regulated upon the principle of observing one divine law, as interpreted by one portion of the people,—and that portion the evangelical. Should that basis be laid, it would be sufficiently ample to sustain any edifice they might think proper to erect; for if the divine law as interpreted by this division were to be made the rule of legislation in one case, why not in another? Let one precedent be given, and the question would not be, what enactments it would sanction, but to what it would not extend. The Congress refused to be influenced, and therefore we find it charged with "Sabbath-breaking," and its members with licentiousness. Thus, because the constitution is not violated, it is said that religion is destroyed. The principle for which Protestantism affected to contend is, that no man should have dominion over the conscience of another, but that every man should be the interpreter of God's law in his own behalf, and that no man should presume to force his interpretation upon another. Yet the practice of those self-styled Protestants is, to endeavour to compel others to submit to their interpretation. If the Congress desires to transport the mail, it compels no one to be the carrier. The conditions are known to all, and he who feels them interfere with his notions of religion is not forced to carry it. In like manner no one is compelled to drink whiskey; the distiller may make it if he will; and the grocer may sell it; but no one is compelled to buy or to drink it. What would our evangelicals say, if Congress were to enact that no butcher should sell meat to a Catholic on Friday or Saturday, and that if any tavern-keeper furnished it to him he should forfeit his license and be fined? Yet the principle is the same. Congress has no power to compel the evangelical member to observe one law according to the interpretation of his sect, nor to compel a Catholic to observe another according to the discipline and interpretation of his spiritual authority. Our government therefore very properly declined to interfere:—and it has thus called forth the vituperation of the saints. But though baffled, they will not desist.

What is now their plan? You see it is in operation. In our country everything is carried by the ballot-box. The holy ones saw that although they are at present a minority: yet by perseverance they might become a majority. Dr. Ely in the exultation of his heart proclaimed the mode by which it was to be effected. His brethren denied in a variety of ways that their object was what the Doctor developed: yet no one was deceived. The editor of the *Telegraph* now avows that the public understood the Doctor correctly, and that no one except an infidel need be ashamed to avow as the Doctor did, that by means of Sabbath schools, the rising generation might be so trained up as that in a few years, by concerted action at the ballot-boxes, none but men of good principles, that is men of the evangelical school, should hold public offices. And is there any question of this being not only a feasible plan, but one in which, if the saints can train up the children to their purposes, they must necessarily succeed?

From the remarks which I have previously made, it is clear that the framers of the constitution neither intended nor felt themselves authorized to make ours a sectarian government: and yet, if the saints succeed in their plan, will it not become, to all intents and purposes, sectarian? No; we are told this is impossible, for though there is a concert between those who hold evangelical principles, yet these persons are so divided into sects, that no one of the five or six which compose their aggregate could acquire an ascendency over the others, and in their minor differences we have the guarantee of our liberty; should any one of them arrogate to itself any predominance, the others would unite against the ambitious division, and defeat its unholy purposes. Suppose, my friends, that such would be the case; I ask, why should the aggregate of those sects be permitted

to exclude the great body of their fellow-citizens, whom those elect
designate as Papists, intemperate, anti-Christian, dissolute, infidel,
gamblers, and Sabbath-breakers? Are not these men American citizens? And why are they to be disfranchised? Is it a crime for them
to avail themselves of the Protestant principle, that each individual
is to regulate his own religious conduct and belief without being
accountable to his fellow-citizens, or liable to any civil or political
disability, for his exercise of this right? But we are told that these
systems lead, necessarily, to demoralization and to the ruin of our
liberties: and that the lovers of liberty and good order should, therefore, discountenance them. The assumption is only an opinion which
might be erroneous; and which I believe and know to be so in fact.
I am of opinion that the principle of justification by faith, which I
take to be characteristic of Evangelical Protestantism, is, if carried
into practice, more demoralizing and destructive to our freedom,
public and personal, than even infidelity. The evangelical Protestant
will proclaim this to be a grievous mistake, and would deprecate as
tyranny my being permitted to exclude him from office because of
my opinion. He would in this be sustained by the spirit of our institutions, by the principles of our constitution, and by the patriotism of
the republic. Shall I not, then, be equally sustained by the same
powers in my objection to his being permitted to exclude me, a Roman
Catholic, and my fellow-citizens, who, though Christians, are neither
Evangelicals, nor Papists. Shall he be permitted to exclude the Jew,
the anti-Christian, the Deist? Would he not have excluded Charles
Caroll and Thomas Jefferson?

     But he tells us, that he leaves us all in possession of our eligi-
bility, and even of our right of voting, and he asks whether we are
warranted to tell him and his associates that they shall be debarred
from their right of voting for those men, whose religious principles
and moral conduct they approve. I must, indeed, upon the general
principle, concede all that he claims. But what would you say to the
Catholics of those sections where they predominate, were they to
treat Protestants in this way? What would the holy men themselves
say, if that to which their conduct and efforts would naturally urge
the public were reduced to practice, and that whilst they are a
minority, all those against whom they have conspired were to enter
into a league of co-operation, and to exclude from office every member of an evangelical church or society? The saints have conspired to

act upon this principle against the body of the people; upon what ground could they then complain, if their own principle were turned against themselves? The consequence would indeed be unpleasant. We should have religious rancour superadded to our political differences. But will not this consequence arise whether the principle be acted upon by the saints or by the sinners? There is no way of avoiding it but by abandoning the principle itself; it is one at open variance with all our republican institutions.

Thus, even though the variety of their sect should appear to give you security against the usurpation and predominance of any one of the subdivisions of which this Christian party in politics is composed; yet their combination promises to elevate the party upon the ruins of your rights; and to produce consequences of the most disastrous character to the country itself.

When it is said that the variety of sects precludes the possibility of usurpation, I am led to consult my experience rather than my imagination. I know many villages, especially in our Southern States, in which, at their origin, the inhabitants were of various Protestant sects, and I may, indeed, say, generally evangelical. Neither the numbers nor the means of the sects warranted the erection of separate churches, and the maintenance of different settled pastors; they united their efforts to build a common church, in which the pastors of all would have equal rights. They went on harmoniously for a time, and each pastor, as he visited, was welcomed to the church; but year after year began to give a greater singleness of character to the trustees; though the church was open to divers preachers, yet he was taught in accord with the great body of the trustees, always had a preference, and occasionally a stipend. His services were more frequent; he then became a resident; and he appeared statedly in the pulpit; the others, upon their arrival, generally found it thus preoccupied. They could now seldom find an opportunity of holding forth, save on some week-day, and not always then. Disgusted, disappointed, and uniformly out-voted, the few dissident trustees resigned. There was on the side of their co-trustees an affectation of regret. Why could not brethren live together in harmony, as from the beginning? The board of trustees was now filled up, and they were, for the first time, all members in accord with the preacher. They who had departed were consoled; they were encouraged to do something for themselves; perhaps fifty or a hundred dollars, together with the promise of a subscription to aid them, was taken as a full compensation for the church which originally belonged to a community of five or six sects, but which now had become the property of one, and that one not always the most numerous, of the first owners. I could reckon up several churches whose history is here described, and almost in every instance they have fallen into the hands of one sect, and that the one which has most frequently put forward the fact of the diversity of sects in the evangelical combination as the guarantee for the safety of equal rights, and equal powers. . . . I need not make the application. You, my friends and fellow-citizens, have intellect equally strong as he who addresses you, and your conclusion is his. Thus, even if the monopolizing aggregate of five or six sects was to continue with a balance of power between the parties, still would their act be palpable and vile aggression upon the rights of their fellow-citizens; and their present variety of sects is no guarantee against the future predominance of the most industrious, the most insinuating, the most ambitious, and the most hypocritical.

Let us now see the manner in which the principle of Dr. Ely is to be reduced to practice. The principle is, that by training up the children in Sabbath-schools, such an influence can be created upon their minds as will necessarily operate at the ballot-boxes. They are not to be trained up to any special modification of federalism or democracy, but they are to be a Christian party in politics. Their teachers are to be Christians; the lessons, the expositions, the whole system of instruction is to be under the guidance of a board of saints. The only principle upon which the voters, as they grow up, are to be united is uniformly to support Christians, and to oppose profane and ungodly candidates. The Christian is not a Papist, is not an infidel, is not an anti-Christian—any man against whom there exists the suspicion of being suspected of anything condemned by the saints, is one of the ungodly. The board of local directors, and that of general directors, can easily testify for or against the Christianity of candidates. But who are to sustain their nominations? The candidate has necessarily some private and some political friends; then add to these the whole host of the children trained up at Sabbath-schools, now become men capable of voting, you see the Christian party in politics. But observe how industriously the agents are engaged. Thirty-eight thousand dollars have been expended last year, in exploring the valley of the Mississippi, merely preparatory to the introduction of their system. One of their collectors told a respectable gentleman in Georgia, who hesitated to subscribe, that the true object was to destroy the power of Popery in the great regions of the West, so as to deprive it of any political influence. Already in successful operation in various other quarters, the grand directors of the scheme saw that the West was not sufficiently organized; taking advantage of the religious feeling of the community, when they found themselves foiled in their premature efforts to seize upon the capital, they are so far from abandoning their plans that they have only retired to render them more effectual, and now, under the pretext of religion, they organize an extensive politico-religious association. And they are likely to succeed to the extent of their wishes; at least they have every reasonable prospect of success.

One word more before we part. The political press has not as yet been fully enlisted in their cause, and of this they piteously complain. Yet already they have in the various sections of the Union, a vast number of their own presses. And the great bulk of the political press is favourable to their Sunday-school schemes, their Bible schemes, their missionary schemes, their colonization schemes, their temperance schemes, and their emancipation and education schemes —which are all the various branches of the great Christian party in politics, and yet that press is accused, as "it is well known that too many of the conductors of the political press, instead of informing the people as watchmen ought, of the dangers which threaten the republic, are wholly engaged in promoting the supposed interests of their favourite candidate;" and they add, "It would not be difficult to show by facts, that the evils of this course are incalculable." The object of this party is to procure the election of "men of good principles"—and yet the political press is accused of deserting its post by advocating the election of favourite candidates. How shall we understand this? There is but one explanation. The political press has not yet taken its lessons respecting candidates from the Christian party in politics.—When it shall have done this, it will have performed its duty.

My friends, I have done with this writer. I am an enemy to intemperance, but I am also an enemy to pharisaical restraint. I am a friend to the bringing children together for religious instruction on the Sunday; but I am an enemy to organizing them into political factions to promote ambition under the guise of piety. I am a friend to the liberal and pious education of a respectable ministry, and to their being sent to cultivate the desert places of our land; but I am an enemy to training up youth in ferocious hatred to a portion of their fellow-citizens, whose tenets they are taught to misrepresent; and thus unfitted for the work of peace, are sent to brandish swords of devastation, and to apply the torches of incendiaries. I am a friend to the diffusion of the Gospel; but an enemy to vilifying of those who preserved it through the vicissitudes of ages, of revolutions, of barbarism, of philosophy, of infidelity, of crime, and of corruption. I am an ardent admirer, a devoted enthusiast, and a sworn friend to the liberties and the constitutions of our American confederation; and therefore I am irreconcilably inimical to every effort whether of fraud or of folly to violate their principles by disfranchising any portion of our citizens under the pretext of their religious mistakes.

I have exhibited to you the malignity and rancour which pervade the article that called me forth. I have shown you how it exhibits the settled design of degrading and disfranchising, not only the Roman Catholics of these United States, but also a vast multitude of their fellow-citizens. I have shown you that the Christian party in politics, not only has not ceased to exist, but is strong, active, compact, powerful, extensive, industrious, prudent, wealthy, and ambitious. The means which it has selected, have been judiciously chosen, and are likely to insure its predominance. It calls upon the people not only to tax themselves for its support, but also to pray for its success; and like its precursor in England, it is careful whilst they pray, to take such steps as will conduce to the efficacy of the appeal. Whilst Aaron and Hur sustain the hands of Moses upon the mountain, the sword of Josue smites powerfully upon the plain. It is for you to say whether our civil and religious rights are to share the fate of Amelec.

Yours, respectfully,
John England
Bishop of Charleston

Catholic Schools and Education
ORESTES BROWNSON

The importance of education in general needs in no sense to be dwelt on in our country, for no people are or can be more alive to its utility and even necessity than are the American people, especially in the non-slaveholding states; and no people have, upon the whole, made more liberal provisions for its general diffusion. There would seem to be just as little need of dwelling on the importance and necessity of Catholic schools and Catholic education for our Catholic population. All Catholics feel, or should feel, that education, either under the point of view of religion or of civilization, is useful and desirable no further than it is Catholic. Catholic truth is universal truth, is all truth, and no education not in accordance with it is or can be a true or a useful education, for error is never useful, but always more or less hurtful. Every Catholic, then, indeed every man who loves truth and wishes to conform to it, must be in favor of Catholic schools and Catholic education, if they are Catholic in reality as well as in name.

So believing, our bishops and clergy, supported by various religious communities, have lost no time in making the imposing effort to provide under their own direction schools, academies, colleges, and universities for all our Catholic children and youth. They have felt the necessity of giving our children a Catholic education, as the best and surest way of securing their temporal and spiritual welfare, of promoting Catholic interests, and of converting this whole country to the Catholic faith. Yet, strangely enough, they are very far from receiving the hearty and undivided support of our whole Catholic community. Great dissatisfaction has been expressed, and in quarters entitled to respect, with our colleges and female academies, and not a few whose love of Catholicity and devotion to the church cannot be questioned, refuses to join in the movements for parochial schools, or the establishment of separate schools for our children under the care of our clergy. . . .

"Catholic Schools and Education," by Orestes A. Brownson, from *The Works of Orestes A. Brownson,* ed. by Henry F. Brownson (Detroit: Thorndike & Nourse, 1884). (Originally printed in *Brownson's Quarterly Review,* January, 1862.)

There are a great many people, honest people, but not over and above stocked with practical wisdom, who imagine that whatever is done or approved by Catholics in any age or country, in any particular time or locality, must needs be Catholic, and that opposition to it is necessarily opposition to Catholicity itself. These people never doubt that schools and colleges, under the patronage and direction of the bishops, religious orders and congregations, and the regular and secular clergy, must necessarily be truly Catholic in character and tendency, and hence they conclude that dissatisfaction with them or opposition to them must indicate a heterodox tendency, or the absence of a thoroughly Catholic disposition. They transfer to the bishops and clergy as individuals the veneration and respect due only to the priest-hood and the prelacy, and to the individual members of the church the infallibility that can be predicated only of the church as the living body of Christ. But we are permitted neither by Catholic faith nor by Catholic duty to make this transfer, and all experience proves that there is neither wisdom nor justice in making it. It does not necessarily follow that schools and colleges are Catholic because founded and directed by religious orders and congregations approved by the church, or by bishops and parish priests; and therefore it does not follow that dissatisfaction with the schools and colleges, or even op-position to them, is any indication of a heterodox tendency, or of any want of true Catholic faith and devotion. Such schools may them-selves fail to educate in a truly Catholic spirit, or to give a truly Catholic character to their pupils, and thus leave it possible that the dissatisfaction or the opposition should arise not from the fact that they are Catholic, but from the fact that they are not Catholic, or that, in spite of their name and profession, they are really sectarian and heterodox. The dissatisfaction, in such case, instead of being a reproach to those who feel and express it, would be no mean proof of their Catholic discernment, their strong desire for really Catholic education, and earnest devotion to Catholic interests.

There need be no question as to the purity of motive and honesty of intention on the part of those who are engaged in founding or supporting schools and colleges for imparting a Catholic education, or even of those who tolerate the expression of no opinion adverse to the system of schools adopted, or to the quality of the education imparted. The bishops and secular clergy, the religious orders and congregations of both sexes engaged in the work of education, are animated, we doubt not, by the most sincere desire to do good, and are doing what they in their best judgment believe the most likely of any thing in their power to promote the interests of our holy religion, and to provide a truly Catholic education for our children. Any hostile criticism which should in any sense impeach their motives or intentions would be manifestly unjust, and should not be tolerated. But the subject of Catholic education itself cannot be prudently withdrawn from discussion, either private or public; nor can its discussion be confined to the prelates and clergy alone. The laity have, to say the least, as deep an interest in it as have ecclesiastics or the religious, and they have in regard to it the common right of all men to judge for themselves. Parents have certain duties growing out of their relation as parents which they cannot throw upon others, and they must themselves discharge them according to the best of their ability. They are bound by the law of God to give their children, as far as in their power, a truly Catholic education, and they are free to criticise and to refuse to support schools, though professing to be Catholic, in which such education is not and cannot be expected to be given. They are not obliged to patronize schools, because founded or directed by Catholics, any more than they are to support a tailoring or a hatting establishment, because owned by a Catholic who employs Catholic workmen, or because recommended by bishops and parish priests. We protest against the assumption that so-called Catholic schools, collegiate or conventual, parochial or private, because under the control of Catholics, participate in the immunities of the church, of the priesthood, or of the prelacy, and are sacred from public investigation and public criticism; or that we are necessarily bound by our Catholic faith and Catholic piety to patronize or defend them any further than we find them Catholic institutions in fact as well as in name.

The first question, then, for us Catholics to settle relates to the catholicity of the education imparted in our so-called Catholic schools. Catholicity, as we have elsewhere shown, is the idea in its plenitude, and therefore the catechism tells us that the church is catholic, because "she subsists in all ages, teaches all nations, and maintains all truth." She, then, is catholic (potentially) in space and time, and (actually) in idea—as she must be, since her life is the life of the Word made flesh, of him who was at once "perfect God and perfect man"—and therefore the whole truth living and individuated in both the divine and human orders in their dialectic union. It is for this reason that the catechism says she "maintains all truth"; and it is because she maintains all truth, and all truth in its unity and integrity, that she is called the *Catholic* Church; and it is because she is catholic in idea, that is, embracing in her ideal all truth, human and divine, that is she is actually or potentially catholic in space and time.

Catholic would say *universal,* and when predicated of truth means universal truth, all truth, and all truth in and for all ages and nations. They whose views are not universally true, are not applicable to all times and places, and to all subjects, may have truth under some of its aspects, but they are not Catholics. They are heterodox, sectarian, or national. Men cease to be Catholics, in the full sense of the term, by denying the universality of the idea or life the church is living, the principle she is evolving and actualizing in the life of humanity, and alike whether they deny this universality in relation to space or in relation to time, in relation to the natural, or in relation to the supernatural. They deny Catholicity who deny that it embraces the whole truth in the human order, as they do who deny that it embraces the whole truth in the divine order. To deny it in relation to the natural order is as much to deny Catholicity, as it is to deny it in relation to the supernatural; and we depart as widely from it in denying its catholicity in time, as we do in denying its catholicity in space. . . .

Catholic education must recognize the catholicity of truth under all its aspects, and tend to actualize it in all the relations of life, in religion and civilization. Its tendency is to aid the church in the fulfilment of her mission, which is the continuous evolution and actualization of the idea, or the life of the Word made flesh, in the life of humanity, or completion in mankind of the incarnation completed in the individual man assumed by the Word. The completion of this work is the complete union of men, through Christ, with God, the finite with the infinite—the true term of human progress, or final cause of the divine creative act. . . .

It is with this ideal standard of Catholic education that we have the right to compare our Catholic schools, and we must judge them as they, by the instruction they give, and the influence they exert, tend or do not tend to its realization. We hazard little in saying that our so-called Catholic schools, in their actual effect, tend rather to depart from this standard than to approach it. They practically fail to recognize human progress, and thus fail to recognize the continuous and successive evolution of the idea in the life of humanity. They practically question the universality of the idea by failing to recognize as Catholic the great principles or ideas natural society is evolving and actualizing in its career through the ages. They do not educate their pupils to be at home and at their ease in their own age and country, or train them to be living, thinking, and energetic men, prepared for the work which actually awaits them in either church or state. As far as we are able to trace the effect of the most approved Catholic education of our days, whether at home or abroad, it tends to repress rather than to quicken the life of the pupil, to unfit rather than to prepare him for the active and zealous discharge either of his religious or his social duties. They who are educated in our schools seem misplaced and mistimed in the world, as if born and educated for a world that has ceased to exist. They come out ignorant of contemporary ideas, contemporary habits of mind, contemporary intelligence and tendencies, and large numbers of them sink into obscurity, and do nothing for their religion or their country; or, what is worse, abandon their religion, turn their backs on the church, and waste all their energies in seeking pleasure or in accumulating worldly wealth. Of the young men educated in our colleges, a certain number have become priests and religious, and fill the ranks of the clergy and continue the religious orders. Of these we have nothing to say. But, of the others, we would ask: Do we find them up to the level of contemporary civilization, and foremost in all those movements fitted to advance intelligence, morality, and the general well-being of society? Do we find them showing by their superior intelligence, their superior morals, and their loftier aspirations the superiority of their religion and the salutary influence it is fitted to exert on civilization? With very few exceptions, we fear we must answer: This is not the case. Comparatively few of them take their stand as scholars or as men on a level with the graduates of non-Catholic colleges, and those who do take that stand, in most cases, do it by throwing aside nearly all they learned from their alma mater, and adopting the ideas and principles, the modes of thought and action they find in the general civilization of the country in which they live.

Whence comes it that such, in general terms, has been thus far in our country the effect of what we proudly call Catholic education?

We cannot ascribe it to any innate incompatibility between Catholic truth and the civilization of the country, for that would be to deny the catholicity of the idea; nor to any repugnance between it and modern society, because that would be to deny its catholicity in time. The cause cannot be in Catholicity itself, nor can it be in our American order of civilization, for Catholicity, if catholic, is adapted to all times and to all nations. . . . The cause of the failure of what we term Catholic education is, in our judgment, in the fact that we educate not for the present or the future, but for a past which can never be restored, and therefore in our education are guilty of a gross anachronism.

We do not mean, and must not be understood to say that the dogmas, that is, the mysteries, as defined in the infallible speech of the church, are not scrupulously taught in all our schools and colleges or that the words of the catechism are not faithfully preserved and duly insisted upon. We concede this, and that this gives to our so-called Catholic schools a merit which no others have or can have. Without the external word, the life of the internal expires, and when it is lost or corrupted, there are no means, except by a new supernatural intervention of Almighty God, of renewing the interior Christian life. This fact is of the first importance, and must never be lost sight of or underrated. The man who has not lost his faith, although his faith is inoperative, or, as theologians say, a "dead faith," is always to be preferred to him who has no faith at all; because he has in him a recuperative principle, and it is more easy to quicken it into activity, than it is to beget faith in one who has it not. The education given in our schools, however defective it may be, must always be preferred to that given in schools in which the dogma is rejected or mutilated, and can never be justly censured, save when compared with its own ideal, or with what it should be and would be, were it truly and thoroughly Catholic.

The fault we find with modern Catholic education is not that it does not faithfully preserve the symbol, that it does not retain all the dogmas or mysteries, so far as sound words go, but that it treats them as isolated or dead facts, not as living principles, and overlooks the fact that the life of the church consists in their continuous evolution and progressive development and actualization in the life of society and of individuals. They themselves, since they are principles and pertain to the ideal the church is evolving and actualizing, must be immutable, and the same for all times, places, and men. They are the principles of progress, but not themselves progressive, for the truth was completely expressed and individuated in the Incarnation. The progress is not in them, but in their explication and actualization in the life of humanity. The truth contained in them is always the same, can neither be enlarged nor diminished; but our understanding of them may be more or less adequate, and their explication and application to our own life and to the life of society may be more or less complete. Their evolution is successive, progressive, and continuous. This fact, which lies at the bottom of Dr. Newman's theory of development, though not always presented by him in an orthodox sense, is what our Catholic education seems to us to overlook, and practically to deny. It seems to us to proceed as if the work of evolution were finished, and there remained nothing for the Christian to do, but to repeat the past. It aims not at the continuous evolution and realization of the Catholic ideal; but to restore a past age, an order of things which the world has left behind, and which it is neither possible nor desirable to restore, for it could be restored, if at all, only as a second childhood. It is now "behind the times," and unfits rather than prepares the student for taking an active part in the work of his own day and generation. It either gives its subjects no work to do, or a work in which humanity takes no interest and will not work with them, a work which all the living and onward tendencies of the age obstinately resist, and which, if there is any truth in what we have said, is adverse alike to the present interests of both religion and civilization.

    .   .   .   .   .

It is very widely and, we fear, very generally believed, that true Catholic duty requires us to take our stand for a past civilization, a past order of ideas, and to resist with all our might the undeniable tendencies and instincts of the human race in our day. We are required by the present dominant sentiment of Catholics, to resist progress in every sense and direction, except in the purely ascetic life of individuals, and to content ourselves with the explication and application of the dogmas of the church, the great and immutable principles of Catholic life, given in past times, and embalmed in the opinions of the theologians of other ages, and the dry, technical, and well-nigh unintelligible formulas of the schools. Hence Catholic education, or rather the education adopted and generally approved by Catholics in our age, especially in our country, fails to produce living men, active, thinking men, great men, men of commanding genius, or generous aims, and high and noble aspirations; and hence it also fails to enable the church to take possession of humanity, and to inspire and direct its movements.

But the objection we urge has a peculiar force and application to Catholic education in our country. Our Catholic population, to a great extent, is practically a foreign body and brings with it a civilization foreign from the American, and in some respects inferior to it. The great majority of our congregations are of foreign birth, or the children of foreign-born parents, and the greater part of our bishops and clergy, and of our professors and teachers, have been born, or at least educated, abroad, and they all naturally seek to perpetuate the civilization in which they have been brought up. Those even of our clergy and of our professors and teachers who have been born and educated in the country, have been educated in schools founded on a foreign model, and conducted by foreigners, and are, in regard to civilization, more foreign than native. We state the fact as it is. We are not condemning it; we may regret it, but we could hardly expect it to be otherwise. The original settlers of the country were, for the most part, non-Catholic, and but comparatively few of their descendants have been or are Catholics. The very large Catholic population now in the country has not been the growth of the country, but has been chiefly supplied by a foreign and a very recent migration. This is the fact,—a fact which is no fault of the Catholic population, but a fact that must be taken into the account in forming a judgment of the Catholic education in our own country. Catholics from the Old World necessarily bring with them their own civilization which, whether we speak of France or Italy, Ireland or Germany, is, to say the least, different from ours, and, in some respects, even hostile to it.

But this is not all. The civilization they actually bring with them, and which without intending it they seek to continue, is, we being judges, of a lower order than ours. It may be our national prejudice and our ignorance of other nations, but it is nevertheless our firm conviction, from which we cannot easily be driven, that, regarded in relation to its type, the American civilization is the most advanced civilization the world has yet seen, and comes nearer to the realization of the Catholic ideal than any which has been heretofore developed and actualized. We speak not of civilization in the sense of simply *civility,* polish of manners, and personal accomplishments, in which we may not compare always favorably with the upper classes of other nations; but of the type or idea we are realizing, our social and political constitution, our arrangements to secure freedom and scope for the development and progress of true manhood. In these respects American civilization is, we say not the term of human progress, but, in our judgment, the furthest point in advance as yet reached by any age or nation. Those who come here from abroad necessarily bring with them, therefore, a civilization more or less inferior to it, and which, in relation to it, is a civilization of the past. If they educate, then, according to their own civilization, as they must do, they necessarily educate for a civilization behind the times and below that of the country.

. . . . .

The great body of our Catholics, no doubt, wish to americanize, and conform to the civilization of the country, but they have hitherto americanized, so far as they have americanized at all, in a southern rather than in a northern sense. The type of the Americanism they aim to adopt is in Maryland, not in Massachusetts; Baltimore, not Boston; and nothing can exceed the hostility of the Maryland type, which, properly speaking, is the Virginia type, to the Boston, or New England type. Indeed, it is these two orders of civilization that meet in mortal combat in the civil war which now threatens the integrity of the American nation. The war is a struggle for life and death, a struggle between a civilization based on slavery, represented by the South, and a civilization based on constitutional liberty and the rights of men, represented by the free states. And, in this struggle, if, as is the fact, the interest and loyalty of Catholics lead them in large numbers to take sides with the North, their sympathies are very generally with the South; and we cannot doubt that, if the South were the loyal party, they would much more readily fight with the South than they now fight with the North. Even, then, where our Catholics aim to be American, it is not American in the sense of the highest, truest, and most advanced Americanism; but in the sense of the lowest, the least advanced, that which is least remote from barbarism, and the furthest removed from that which the church as well as humanity demands, and never ceases to struggle to obtain.

We are also borne out in our views by the political history of the country. Politically, the southern leaders have for a long time formed their association with the least intelligent, the least advanced classes in the free states, and these southern leaders are those our Catholic population have followed with the most alacrity. This fact proves, on the one hand, that the South represents the lowest order of civilization in the country, and that Catholics are more easily engaged in supporting it than in supporting the superior civilization represented by the northern states. It is not too much to say that the great influx of the Catholic peasantry of different European states into the country, and the conferring on them, almost on their arrival, of political franchises, have done not a little to corrupt our politics, and to lower the standard of our civilization. Their orthodoxy, as yet, has done less to advance, than their inferior civilization has done to corrupt and lower, our civilization and morals. However humiliating this fact may be to us as Catholics, there is no use in attempting to deny it, or to disguise it. It is a fact which all intelligent Americans see and know, and it is one which we ourselves should dare look in the face. The opposition to us represented by "Native-American," or "Know-Nothing" parties or movements, is not opposition to us as orthodox Catholics, nor, in itself considered, to us as foreigners, but simply as representatives of a civilization different from the American, and, in many respects, inferior and opposed to it. We have practically, if not theoretically, insisted that our orthodoxy and our foreign and inferior civilization are inseparable; and the heterodox American people have in this agreed with us, and hence their opposition to us, and ours to them. Heterodoxy, with the heterodox of our country, is no longer a living principle, and is retained only because associated, accidentally associated, with a superior and more advanced civilization. Orthodoxy is opposed not because there is any opposition to it on its own account, but because it is believed to be inseparably wedded to that inferior and less advanced civilization that has come hither with it from the Old World, and which many honest Catholics think, if they ever think at all on the subject, is identical with it.

Now, the objection to Catholic schools, especially those for the people at large, is that they tend, and for a time at least must tend, to perpetuate the association of orthodoxy with this inferior civilization, and thus injure alike the country and the church. These schools must be taught chiefly by foreigners, or, if not by foreigners, at least by those whose sympathies and connections, tastes and habits are un-American; because what is wanted by their founders and supporters is not simply the preservation of orthodoxy, but the perpetuation of the foreignism hitherto associated with it. Schools which should associate real Americanism with orthodoxy would be hardly less offensive or more acceptable to them than the public schools themselves. They must, therefore, be conducted and taught by men who will keep up the old association, and prevent the association of real Americanism with orthodoxy. Yet it is precisely this latter association which is desirable both for civilization and for religion, and it is only by breaking the old associations, and forming the new in good faith, as we are in fact required to do by orthodoxy itself, that Catholics can cease to be in this country an isolated foreign colony, or a band of emigrants encamped for the night, and ready to strike their tents, and take up their line of march on the morrow for some other place.

These are some of the reasons which have led many of our most intelligent, most earnest, and devout Catholics to form their unfavorable judgment of Catholic schools and Catholic education, as they now are, and for some time are likely to be, in the United States. They are solid reasons as far as they go, and fully justify the dissatisfaction with them we began by recognizing. They prove that here and elsewhere, but especially here, Catholic education, or the education given by Catholics, is below the wants of the age and country, and prove that, from the seminary down to the primary school, it stands in need, whether we consult the interest of orthodoxy or that of civilization, of a wide, deep, and thorough reform. Yet, after long reflection and much hesitation, some would say opposition, we must say that we do not regard them as sufficient reasons for abandoning the movement for Catholic schools and education supported by our bishops and clergy. It may be that the movement was premature, and that it would have been better to have used for a longer time the schools of the country, as the early Christians did those of the empire, before attempting to establish schools of our own, save for the education of the clergy. But it is too late to discuss that question now. The movement has, wisely or unwisely, been set on foot, and gone too far to be arrested, even if it were desirable to arrest it. Our bishops and clergy have decided that the movement shall go on, and the Catholic cause can never be promoted by any anti-hierarchical action. Much good may be done that is not done by or under the direction of the hierarchy; but no good end can ever be obtained in opposition to it. This consideration is of itself sufficient to deter us from opposing the movement, and of inducing us to accept it at least as *un fait accompli,* and to make the best we can of it.

That we are to have schools and colleges of our own, under the control of Catholics, we take it is a "fixed fact." Whether the movement for them is premature or not, it is idle, if nothing worse, to war against it. Let us say, then, to those who regard the education actually given by Catholics as we do, and who have not seen their way clear to the support of primary schools under the control of Catholics as a substitute, in the case of Catholic children, for the common schools of the country, that we regard it as our duty now to accept the movement, and labor not to arrest it, or to embarrass it, but to reform and render truly Catholic the whole system of Catholic education, from the highest grade to the lowest. Let it be our work not to destroy Catholic education, but to reform and advance it. The first care of all Catholics should be the preservation of orthodoxy, and, in the actual state of our Catholic population, it may be that orthodoxy will be better preserved by schools under Catholic direction than it can be by sending our children to the public schools. The objections we have set forth are, after all, only temporary and accidental. They grow out of the present and past state of our Catholic population, and must disappear under the slow but effectual operation of time and causes already in operation amongst us. We might gain something under the point of view of civilization by adopting the schools of the country; but, as our prelates and clergy are strongly opposed to them, and have done much to bring them into disrepute with Catholics, we should probably lose, under the point of view of orthodoxy, more than would thus be gained. Schools under the control of Catholics will, at least, teach the catechism, and though they may in fact teach it as a dead letter, rather than as a quickening spirit, it is better that it should be taught as a dead letter than not be taught at all. It is only by preserving the dogma intact that we do or can preserve the Christian ideal, or have the slightest chance of securing our final destiny. The hopes of the world for time and eternity are dependent on the preservation of the orthodox faith.

·   ·   ·   ·   ·

Relation of Church and State in America

I. T. HECKER, C. S. P.

What relation does Catholicity hold to the discovery of America and the settlement of this country? The discovery of the Western continent was eminently a religious enterprise. Columbus had in vain sought aid for his great undertaking from his native city, Genoa; from Portugal, England, Venice, and the court of Spain; and it was after these fruitless applications that Juan Perez, the prior of La Rabida, took up his cause and pleaded it with so much earnestness and ability in a letter to Queen Isabella that she at once sent for Columbus and offered to pledge her jewels to obtain funds for the expedition. The motive which animated Columbus, in common with the Franciscan prior and Isabella the Catholic, was the burning desire to carry the blessings of the Christian faith to the inhabitants of a new continent, and it was the inspiration of this idea which brought a new world to light.

This inspiration has never died out; if the Spanish and French missionaries did not accompany the first discoverers, they followed speedily in their tracks, and the work of the conversion of the aborigines was earnestly begun. In a short time they traversed the whole northern continent from the mouth of the St. Lawrence to California, and from the Gulf of Mexico to Hudson's Bay. Sometimes missionaries were slain, but the fearless soldiers of the cross continued unceasingly their work of converting the natives and bringing them into the fold of Christ. The pages of history which narrate the self-sacrificing labors of the missionaries to the Indians are among the brightest in the annals of the Church.

The raising of the red men to the height of the Christian faith was but one of the fruits of the discovery of the new continent; another was to offer an asylum to all who in other lands were persecuted and oppressed on account of their religious convictions. Among the first to seek this relief from oppression on the virgin soil of the New

"Relation of Church and State in America," taken from a chapter of *The Church and the Age,* by I. T. Hecker, published by the Paulist Press, New York, N.Y. Reprinted by permission of the publisher. [n.d.]

World were the English Catholic colonists under Lord Baltimore. To their honor it is to be said that, both by the original design of the proprietary, Lord Baltimore, and by the legislative enactments of the freemen of the province, there reigned, while their rule lasted in Maryland, a perfect equality among all Christian denominations, and to all were secured the same rights and privileges, civil and religious. This act on the part of the colonists of Maryland was in harmony with the dictates of right reason and the authentic teachings of faith; for all attempts to bring by coercion men who differ in their religious convictions to uniformity in the profession of religious belief, if successful, would logically put an end to all rational religion. Compulsion never gave birth to faith, which is "not by any means a blind assent of the mind," [Vatican Council, De Fide, ch. iii] but essentially an intelligent and voluntary act. Convinced of this, as Catholics, the idea of religious tolerance flowed naturally and consistently in the minds of the first settlers on the shores of the Potomac. It was a noble act on their part to proclaim that within the province and jurisdiction of Maryland no Christian man should be molested in worshipping God according to the dictates of his conscience, and whoever supposes that the Syllabus teaches anything to the contrary seriously mistakes its meaning. Honor, then, to the pilgrim fathers of St. Mary! who, when the other settlements had a state-supported church and were intolerant of all others, asked for themselves no favor, but offered equal rights to all; thus excluding the secular authority of the state from interfering in matters of religion—a principle for which the popes, in their struggles with the secular powers for the rights of the Church, have always contended, and for which they still have to contend. Let, then, those Catholic Anglo-Americans have their due share of praise for the religious toleration of which they were the first to give an example—an example, furthermore, which had a formative influence in shaping the republic and its free institutions. For the principle of the incompetency of the state to enact laws controlling matters purely religious is the keystone of the arch of American liberties, and Catholics of all climes can point to it with special delight.

The connection between the republic and the Catholic Church, if satisfactorily treated, requires that the fundamental principles of the republic should be clearly stated, and their relation with Protestantism first be disposed of. This is what we now attempt.

The republic of the United States is the result of the gathered political wisdom and experience of past ages, shaped by a recognition of man's natural rights and a trust in his innate capacity for self-government beyond what had found expression in the prevailing political systems of Europe. The fundamental articles of the American political creed and the formative principles of the republic are embodied in the Declaration of Independence, whence they passed gradually into the constitutions of the several States and into the Constitution of the United States, and have step by step worked their way more or less perfectly into the general and special laws of the country. These articles consist principally in the declaration "that all men are created equal; that they are endowed by their Creator with certain inalienable rights; that among these are life, liberty, and the pursuit of happiness; that to secure these rights governments are instituted among men, deriving their just powers from the consent of the governed."

These declarations can be looked upon only by superficial thinkers as "glittering generalities," for some of them are divine and fundamental truths, and all are practical verities, having a ground both in reason and revelation. They are divine, inasmuch as they declare the rights of the Creator in His creature; they are fundamental, for without the enjoyment of the natural rights which they proclaim man is not a man, but a slave or a chattel; they are practical, for man is, or ought to be, under his Creator, the master of his own destiny and free from any dominion not founded in divine right. The Creator invested man with these rights in order that he might fulfil the duties inseparably attached to them. For these rights put man in the possession of himself, and leave him free to reach the end for which his Creator called him into existence. He, therefore, who denies or violates these rights offends God, acts the tyrant, and is an enemy of mankind. And if there be any superior merit in the republican polity of the United States, it consists chiefly in this: that while it adds nothing and can add nothing to man's natural rights, it expresses them more clearly, guards them more securely, and protects them more effectually; so that man, under its popular institutions, enjoys greater liberty in working out his true destiny.

Since Christianity claims to be God's revelation of the great end for which He created man, it follows that those rights without which he cannot reach that end must find their sanction, expressed or implied, in all true interpretations of its doctrines.

.   .   .   .   .

There exists a necessary bond and correlation between the truths contained in the Declaration of Independence and the revealed truths of Christianity, since the truths of the natural order serve as indispensable supports to the body of revealed truths of faith. Deny to man reason, and religion can have to him no more meaning than to a brute or a machine. Deny the certitude of reason, and there is no foundation for certitude in supernatural faith. Deny the innate freedom of the will, and the basis for all morality is undermined, and the fountain-head of personal, political, and religious liberty dried up. Deny to man the gifts of reason and free-will, and the natural rights of man which flow from these gifts are the wild fancies of a dreamer, and a republic founded upon them becomes the baseless fabric of a vision.

The following principles will throw more light on the value of human nature, and of the bearing of the truths of reason upon the supernatural truths of faith, and make our road still easier. Reason is the organ of truth, and acts upon the truth which lies within its domain with infallible certitude. The action of reason implicitly or explicitly precedes faith; reason can admit the claims of no authority which does not appeal with entire trust to its jurisdiction for verification; it can accept none that does not accord and blend with its dictates. Man is by nature in possession of his free-will; therefore freedom is a birthright, and he holds it in trust from his Creator and is responsible for its right use. Human nature, as it now exists, is essentially good, and man naturally seeks and desires his Creator as the source of his happiness. Man has lost none of his original faculties and has forfeited none of his natural rights by Adam's fall, and therefore is by nature in possession of his natural rights, and it is rightly said: "Among these are life, liberty, and the pursuit of happiness." "God has created all men equal" in regard to these rights, and therefore no one man has the natural right to govern another man; and all political authority in individuals is justly said to be derived, under God, from the consent of the collective people who are governed. The people, under God, associated in a body politic, are the source of the sovereign political power in the civil state. The light of reason is the light of God in the soul, and the natural rights of man are conferred by God directly upon man; and therefore a religion which does not affirm the value of human reason and defend the natural rights of man is baseless, and by no manner of means revealed by his Creator, but is a delusion or an imposition and worthy of no respect. With the light of these statements, which are in conformity with her authoritative teaching, the connection of the Catholic Church with the American republic can easily be understood; the light which they shed lays bare to the view of all men the real motives which actuate Catholics in their devotion to popular rights, and places above all suspicion the sincerity of their love for popular institutions.

The American people in the Declaration of Independence avowed unequivocally their belief in the value of human nature, made a solemn act of loyalty to human reason, grounded their popular government on a solid foundation, and opened the door which leads directly to the truth. The truths asserted were not the fruits of philosophical speculations, but evident truths of human reasons; and the rights affirmed were not the declamations of political dreamers, but rights inseparable from man's rational nature. Nor were these truths and these rights proclaimed to the world for the first time on the 4th of July, 1776, by the Continental Congress of the colonies; for they are as old as human nature, and will be found among the traditions of all races of civilized men. They are not lifeless abstractions but living truths, concreted more or less in all political governments, in their institutions and laws. Freedom is no tender sapling, but a hardy tree and of slow growth, whose roots are grounded in and entwined around the very elements of human nature, and under the shelter of its stout branches man has reached, through many struggles, his existing state of manhood.

The War of Independence was a struggle for man's sacred rights and liberties, and in support of these rights and liberties the colonists, as British subjects, cited the Magna Charta outlined by Cardinal Langton and his compeers, and won by them from King John in the meadow of Runnymede. Upon these inherent and acknowledged rights of man, and upon the conclusion derived from them that no taxation without representation ought to be permitted, the founders of the American state based their claims. To maintain these rights, which they had received as a legacy from our common Catholic ancestors, the war for independence began, was fought, was won;

upon them the republic was erected, and stands unchanged and immovable. Had the farseeing Count de Maistre been as well acquainted with the history of the American colonies as he was with the history of his own country or that of England, he would not have hazarded the statement, advanced in his *Considerations on France,* that "he did not believe that the United States would last" or that "the city of Washington would accomplish the object for which it was projected." All the conditions which he considered as essential to form a nation, and the vital principles necessary to produce a constitution, were existing and gave birth to the republic. The republic came forth from these into existence as naturally as the flower expands from the bud. The illustrious count's distrust of our political principles was in contradiction to his own political doctrines no less than to the truths of his Catholic faith. He whose intellectual vision is open to the light of first principles and their main bearings, and is not altogether a stranger to true history, knows full well that the Catholic Church has battled her whole life-time for those rights of man and that liberty which confer the greatest glory on the American republic.

That the pages of history testify to the close relationship existing between popular governments and the Catholic faith is shown by the fact that all republics since the Christian era have sprung into existence under the influence of the Catholic Church, were founded in the ages of faith and by a Catholic people. The republic of San Marino has existed in an entirely Catholic population in the heart of Italy one thousand years or more; and that of Andorra, on the borders of Spain and France, has stood the same number of years. But these republics are small in numbers and in extent of territory? Grant it; yet they are large enough and have existed long enough to illustrate the principle that republicanism is congenial with the Catholic religion and at home in a Catholic population. Then, again, we have the Italian republics in Catholic ages—those of Venice, Pisa, Genoa, Milan, Florence, Padua, Bologna. In fact, there were no less than two hundred republics spread over the fair land of Italy. The principal Italian cities may be regarded as model republics. Some were founded in the ninth, others in the tenth or eleventh, century, and lasted several hundred years. Venice stood one thousand years and more. The Swiss republic was founded in mediaeval times, and counts among its heroes and martyrs of political liberty William Tell and Arnold von Winkelried, both of whom were faithful sons of the Catho-

lic Church. The republics in South America, though rather quarrel-
some, are at least the growth of a population altogether Catholic.
How can we explain that the love of liberty and popular institutions
should thus spring up spontaneously and exclusively on Catholic soil,
unless it be that republicanism and Catholicity have one common
root?

From this point of view it is a matter of no surprise that Catholics
were the first to proclaim religious freedom among the original
colonists, and were also among the first and stanchest patriots in the
war for independence. None will be found among the signers of the
Declaration of Independence whose position in society and wealth
were equal to those of Charles Carroll, the intelligent, sincere, and
fervent Catholic layman. The priest who became the first bishop and
first archbishop in the hierarchy of the Catholic Church in the United
States was the intimate friend of Benjamin Franklin, and, an associate
with him, invited by Congress to engage the Canadians to be neutral
if they were not ready to join their efforts for independence. Washington, with his characteristic impartiality, publicly acknowledged at
the close of the war the patriotic part which Catholics as a class had
taken in the great struggle for liberty. No one can appreciate the
depth of conviction and the strength of affection of Catholics for
republican institutions unless he sees, as they do, the same order of
truths which serve as the foundation of his religious belief underlying
the free institutions of his country. The doctrines of the Catholic
Church alone give to popular rights, and governments founded
thereupon, an intellectual basis, and furnish their vital principle.
What a Catholic believes as a member of the Catholic Church he
believes as a citizen of the republic. His religion consecrates his
political convictions, and this consecration imparts a twofold strength
to his patriotism.

What a Catholic believes as a citizen of the republic he believes
as a member of the Catholic Church; and as the natural supports and
strengthens the supernatural, this accounts for the universally acknowledged fact that no Catholics are more sincere in their religious
belief, more loyal to the authority of the Church, more generous in
her support, than the Catholic republican citizens of the United
States. Catholicity in religion sanctions republicanism in politics, and
republicanism in politics favors Catholicity in religion.

·   ·   ·   ·   ·

On the other hand, the affirmation of any one truth, logically followed out, leads to the knowledge and affirmation of all truth. The American republic began afresh in the last century by the declaration of certain evident truths of reason. The law of its progression consists in tracing these truths out to their logical connection with all other truths, and finally coming to the knowledge of all truth, both in the natural and supernatural order, ending in the affirmation of universal truth and the union with the source of all truth—God. The dominant tendency of the American people is towards the law of the positive sequence of truth. The course of Europe was that of negation; the course of the United States was that of affirmation. The first was destructive, the second was constructive. The one was degrading, the other was elevating. That bred dissension, this created union. Europe, under the lead of the religious revolution of the sixteenth century, turned its back on Catholicity and entered upon the downward road that ends in death; the republic of the United States, in affirming man's natural rights, started in the eighteenth century with its face to Catholicity, and is in the ascending way of life to God.

From this point of view the Declaration of American Independence has a higher than political meaning, and it may be said to be the turning-point in history from a negation to an affirmation of truth: interpreting democracy not as a downward but as an upward movement, and placing political society anew on the road to assist man in the fulfilment of his divine destiny.

Christianity, like republicanism, has in the last analysis to rely for its reception and success on reason and conscience and the innate powers of human nature, graciously aided from above as they always are. Let it once be shown that the Catholic interpretation of Christianity is consonant with the dictates of human reason, in accordance with man's normal feelings, favorable to the highest conceptions of man's dignity, and that it presents to his intelligence a destiny which awakens the uttermost action and devotion of all his powers, and you have opened the door to the American people for the reception of the complete evidence of the claims of the Catholic Church, and prepared the way for the universal acceptance of her divine character.

There is a general conviction abroad that the people's share in the government of a nation ought to be enlarged. It must be admitted that the American republic has contributed not a little to form and support this conviction. But the principles of the republic are not, like those of an Utopia, in the air; they are fixedly rooted in the ground of reason and revealed truth. If the framers of the republic set aside certain privileges and institutions inherited from pagan, barbaric, or feudal times, it was not to break with the past, but because these things were unserviceable to a people with the spirit and in the circumstances of the colonists. They were, besides, no less inharmonious with the more rational ideas of equity due to Christian influences; and by their omission the founders of the republic providentially advanced political government, at least for all peoples similarly situated.

When the nature of the American republic is better understood, and the exposition of Christianity is shaped in the light of its own universal principles so as to suit the peculiarities of the American mind, the Catholic Church will not only keep her baptized American children in her fold, but will at the same time remove the prejudices existing in the minds of a large class of non-Catholics, and the dangers apprehended from the influence of republicanism will be turned into fresh evidence of the Church's divine character.

To sum up: He who does not see the hand of Divine Providence leading to the discovery of the western continent, and directing its settlement and subsequent events towards a more complete application to political society of the universal truths affirmed alike by human reason and Christianity, will fail to interpret rightly and adequately the history of the United States. It is also true that he who sees Heaven's hand in these events, and fails to see that Christ organized a body of men to guard and teach these universal truths to mankind, with the promise of His presence to the end of the world, will fail to interpret rightly and adequately the history of Christianity. He is like a man who sees the light but has his back turned to the sun which gives it. But the discerning mind will not fail to see that the republic and the Catholic Church are working together under the same divine guidance, forming the various races of men and nationalities into a homogeneous people, and by their united action giving a bright promise of a broader and higher development of man than has been heretofore accomplished.

Our Roman Catholic Brethren

JAMES PASTON

One thing can be said of our Roman Catholic brethren, and especially of our Roman Catholic sisters, without exciting controversy,—they begin early in the morning. St. Stephen's, the largest Catholic Church in New York, which will hold five thousand persons and seat four thousand, was filled to overflowing every morning of last November at five o'clock. That, however, was an extraordinary occasion. The first mass, as housekeepers are well aware, usually takes place at six o'clock, summer and winter; and it was this that I attended on Sunday morning, December 8, 1867, one of the coldest mornings of that remarkably cold month.

It is not so easy a matter to wake at a certain hour before the dawn of day. One half, perhaps, of all the inhabitants of the earth, and two thirds of the grown people of the United States, get up in the winter months before day-light; and yet a person unaccustomed to the feat will be utterly at a loss how to set about it. . . . People who get up at five every morning can do without an alarm-clock; and those who get up at five once in five years, even if by any chance they should possess an alarm-clock, forget in the five years of disuse how the little fury is set so as to hold in all night and burst forth in frenzy at the moment required. . . . Our Roman Catholic brethren, in some way or ways unknown, habitually overcome this difficulty; for fifty thousand of them, in New York alone, are frequently at church and on their knees before there are any audible or visible indications of the coming day. . . .

There was scarcely any one astir to keep an adventurer in countenance, when I set off to attend Sunday mass, and I began to think it was all a delusion about the six-o'clock mass. At ten minutes to six, when I stood in front of the spacious St. Stephen's Church in Twenty-Eighth Street, there seemed to be no one going in; and, the vestibule being unlighted, I was confirmed in the impression that early mass did not take place on such cold mornings. To be quite sure of the fact,

"Our Roman Catholic Brethren," by James Paston. Reprinted from *The Atlantic Monthly,* April, 1868.

however, I did just go up the steps and push at the door. It yielded to pressure, and its opening disclosed a vast interior, dimly lighted at the altar end, where knelt or sat, scattered about one or two in a pew, about a hundred women and ten men, all well muffled up in hoods, shawls, and overcoats, and breathing visibly. There was just light enough to see the new blue ceiling and its silver stars; but the sexton was busy lighting the gas, and got on with his work about as fast as the church filled. That church extends through the block, and has two fronts. As six o'clock approached, female figures in increasing numbers crept silently in by several doors, all making the usual courtesy, and all kneeling as soon as they reached a pew. At last the lower part of the church was pretty well filled, and there were some people in the galleries; in all, about one thousand women and about one hundred men. Nearly all the women were servant-girls, and all of them were dressed properly and abundantly for such a morning. There was not a squalid or miserable-looking person present. Most of the men appeared to be grooms and coachmen. . . .

There is a difference between Catholics and Protestants in this matter of praying. When a Protestant prays in public, he is apt to hide his face, and bend low in an awkward, uncomfortable attitude; and, when he would pray in private, he retires into some secret place, where, if any one should catch him at it, he would blush like a guilty thing. It is not so with our Roman Catholic brethren. They kneel, it is true, but the body above the knees is bolt upright, and the face is never hidden; and, as if this were not enough, they make certain movements of the hand which distinctly announce their purpose to every beholder. The same freedom and boldness are observable in Catholic children when they say their nightly prayers. Your little Protestant buries its face in the bed, and whispers its prayer to the counterpane; but our small Catholic brethren and sisters kneel upright, make the sign of the cross, and are not in the least ashamed or disturbed if any one sees them. Another thing strikes a Protestant spectator of Catholic worship,—the whole congregation, without exception, observe the etiquette of the occasion. When kneeling is in order, all kneel; when it is the etiquette to stand, all stand; when the prayer-book says bow, every head is low. These two peculiarities are cause and effect. A Protestant child often has some reason to doubt whether saying its prayers is, after all, "the thing," since it is aware that some of its most valued friends and relations do not say theirs.

But among Catholics there is not the distinction (so familiar to us) between those who "belong to the church" and those who do not; still less the distinction (nearly as familiar in some communities) between believers and unbelievers. From the hour of baptism, every Catholic is a member of the church, and he is expected to behave as such. This is evidently one reason for that open, matter-of-course manner in which all the requirements of their religion are fulfilled. No one is ashamed of doing what is done by every one in the world whom he respects, and what he has himself been in the habit of doing from the time of his earliest recollection. A Catholic appears to be no more ashamed of saying his prayers than he is of eating his dinner, and he appears to think one quite as natural an action as the other.

On this cold morning the priest was not as punctual as the people. The congregation continued to increase till ten minutes past six; after which no sound was heard but the coughing of the chilled worshippers. It was not till seventeen minutes past six that the priest entered, accompanied by two slender, graceful boys, clad in long red robes, and walked to his place, and knelt before the altar. . . .

At ten minutes to seven the priest put on his black cap, and withdrew; and soon the congregation was in full retreat. But by this time another congregation was assembling for the seven-o'clock mass; the people were pouring in at every door, and hurrying along all the adjacent streets towards the church. Seven o'clock being a much more convenient time than six, the church is usually filled at that hour; as it is, also, at the nine-o'clock mass. At half past ten the grand mass of the day occurs, and no one who is in the habit of passing a Catholic church on Sunday mornings at that hour needs to be informed that the kneeling suppliants who cannot get in would make a tolerable congregation of themselves.

What an economy is this! The parish of St. Stephen's contains a Catholic population of twenty-five thousand, of whom twenty thousand, perhaps, are old enough and well enough to go to church. As the church will seat four thousand persons, all this multitude can hear mass every Sunday morning. As many as usually desire it can attend the vespers in the afternoon. The church, too, in the intervals of service, and during the week, stands hospitably open, and is usually fulfilling in some way the end of its erection. How different with our churches! There is St. George's, for example, the twin steeples of which are visible to the home-returning son of Gotham as soon as the

Sound steamer has brought him past Blackwell's Island. In that stately edifice half a million dollars have been invested, and it is in use only four hours a week. No more; for the smaller occasional meetings are held in another building,—a chapel in the rear. Half a million dollars is a large sum of money, even in Wall Street, where it figures merely as part of the working capital of the country; but think what a sum it is when viewed as a portion of the small, sacred treasure set apart for the higher purposes of human nature! And yet the building which has cost so much money stands there a dead and empty thing, except for four hours on Sunday! Our Roman Catholic brethern manage these things better. When *they* have invested half a million in a building, they put that building to a use which justifies and returns the expenditure. . . .

While these successive multitudes have been gathering and dispersing something has been going on in the basement of St. Stephen's, —a long, low room, extending from street to street, and fitted up for a children's chapel and Sunday-school room. The Protestant reader, it is safe to say, has never attended a Catholic Sunday school, but he shall now have the pleasure of doing so. It ought to be a pleasure only to see two or three thousand children gathered together; but there is a particular reason why a Protestant should be pleased at a Catholic Sunday school. Imitation is the sincerest homage. The notion of the Sunday school is one of several which our Roman Catholic brethren have borrowed from us. This church, hoary and wrinkled with age, does not disdain to learn from the young and bustling churches to which it has given all they have. The Catholic Church, however, claims a share in the invention, since for many ages it has employed boys in the celebration of its worship, and has given those boys a certain training to enable them to fulfil their vocation. Still, the Sunday school, as now constituted, is essentially of Protestant origin. Indeed, the energetic and truly catholic superintendent of St. Stephen's School, Mr. Thomas E. S. Dwyer, informed me, that, before beginning this school, he visited all the noted Sunday schools in New York, Protestant, Catholic, and Jewish, and endeavored to get from each whatever he found in it suitable to his purpose.

· · · · ·

The reader, perhaps, may be curious to know what kind of hymns our Roman Catholic brethren teach their children to sing

[at Sunday school]. Well, cut out of their hymn-books one tenth of
their contents, in which the saints are invoked and a few Catholic
peculiarities are referred to, and they would be found suitable to any
Protestant Sunday-school. There is, for example, a "Song of the
Union," which might very properly be sung in Faneuil Hall on the
Fourth of July:—

> "Ere Peace and Freedom, hand in hand,
> Went forth to bless this happy land,
>   And make it their abode,
> It was the footstool of a throne;
> But now no sceptre here is known,
>   No King is feared but God.
>
> Americans uprose in might,
> And triumphed in th' unequal fight,
>   For Union made them strong:—
> Union! the magic battle-cry,
> That hurled the tyrant from on high,
>   And crushed his hireling throng!

. . . It is a beautiful thought, to gather the children of a community, for a short time—an hour and a half, no more—on Sunday
morning, in some very inviting and perfectly salubrious place, where
they shall enjoy themselves in singing songs and hymns, and hear
something cheering and beneficial, and to join in any other exercises
which the affectionate ingenuity of their elders may be able to devise.
It is a lovely idea, and one which civilization, having once possessed
can never again let go. So far, the idea has been carried out imperfectly; and it will perhaps never be made the most of until the
churches all give up the attempt to expound the universe, and settle
down to the final grand vocation,—that of inculcating virtue, instructing ignorance, and cheering human life. . . .

Protestants who visit Catholic institutions for the first time, and
converse with those who have charge of them, are surprised to find
how little good Catholics differ from other good people. These
teachers of the St. Stephen's Sunday school, for example, their *tone,*
manner, feeling, cast of countenance, remind you continually of
Protestant persons engaged in the same calling. They are as candid
and open as the day. They are as truly and entirely convinced of the
truth of their religion as any Protestant ever was of his, and their
habitual feeling towards Protestants is—compassion. They think
their religion is altogether sweet and engaging, full of comfort and

hope; and they yearn to see all the world partaking of its joys and consolations. Just as we in our ignorance pity them, so do they in their ignorance pity us. The habitual feeling of good Catholics, with regard to their Church and the rest of the world, was well and truly expressed by the late pastor of St. Stephen's, Dr. Cummings:—

> "World of Grace! mysterious Temple!
>   Holy, Apostolic, One!
> Never changing, ever blessing
> Every Age and every zone;
> Church, sweet Mother! may all nations
>   Know thee, love thee as of yore:
> May thy children learn to prize thee,
> Daily, Hourly, more and more."

Ignorant Catholics, of course, like ignorant Protestants, sometimes despise or hate those who differ from them on subjects which are far beyond all human comprehension. But the general feeling of our Roman Catholic brethren towards us is a tender and warm desire that we should immediately abandon our gloomy and abortive religion, and come back to the true fold, where all is cheerfulness, certainty, and love,—especially, *certainty!* There is nothing they pity us so much for as the doubt and uncertainty in which they suppose many of us are living concerning fundamental articles of faith. A Catholic cannot doubt; for the instant he doubts he ceases to be a Catholic. His church is "infallible"; hence his doctrine must be right. His priest is the director of his soul; he has but to obey his direction. Thus a good Catholic has intellectual satisfaction and peace of conscience both within his reach; and he truly pities those who grope in mental darkness, and carry the burden of their sins, without the possibility of ever being *quite* sure they are forgiven. The priest says: "I absolve thee"; but it is on certain conditions named, with which a person can comply, and with which he can *know* he has complied.

There is an impression among Protestants that the Catholic priests are not believers in their own creed; but that, being convinced of the necessity which exists in unformed minds of believing something absurd and fictitious, they recognize that necessity, and have organized superstition without sharing it. We sometimes hear Protestants parodying the ancient remark concerning the Roman augurs, and wondering whether two priests can ever look one another in the face without laughing. That there are Catholic statesmen and mon-

archs who take this view of the religion they profess is probable
enough. Voltaire himself admitted, when his house had been robbed,
that hell was an excellent thing to frighten thieves with, and he con-
signed to it the particular thieves in question most heartily. His friend,
Frederick of Prussia, who was as thoroughgoing an unbeliever as
himself, was in the habit of laughing at Voltaire's zeal against the
faith of Christendom; and used to tell him, that, even if he could
succeed in destroying that faith, which he could not, every ignorant
mind would immediately attach itself to falsehoods still more extravagant and pernicious. At that day, too, there were not wanting in
France abbés and bishops who passed their lives in deriding the
church from which they derived their subsistence. But even then and
there the vast majority of the working clergy were perfectly sincere
and very laborious pastors, and gave the hungry peasant the greater
part of the little comfort he enjoyed.

No candid person can associate much with the Catholic priests
of the United States without becoming aware of the entireness and
strength of their faith in the doctrines they teach,—without being
convinced of their fidelity to the vows they have taken. Why remain
priests if they have ceased to believe? It is not the life a false man
would choose in *this* country. What with the early masses, the great
number of services, the daily and nightly calls to the bedside of the
dying, the labor and anxiety of hearing confessions, the deprivation
of domestic enjoyments, the poverty (the Archbishop of New York
has but four thousand dollars a year and his house), and what with the
social stigma which in some communities the very name of Catholic
carries with it,—there are few vocations in which a fervent believer
would find more joy, and in which a hypocrite would suffer so much
weariness and disgust. In one sickly time, two years ago, an assistant
priest of a populous New York parish was summoned sixty-five times
in eight days to administer the communion to dying persons, and
forty-five of those times were between sunset and sunrise. The salary
of an assistant priest, in these dear times, is four hundred dollars a
year, a room, and a portion of the fees he receives for marriages,
baptisms, and masses for the dead,—the whole being a bare subsistence, averaging about eight hundred dollars a year. The pastor of a
church receives six hundred dollars a year, a house, and a portion of
the fees just mentioned. In a few very extensive city parishes the
priest may get a little more money than he really needs; but the great

majority receive just enough for the three necessities,—food, clothes, and charity.

The manner in which our Roman Catholic brethren select and train their priests insures at least sincerity. It is a training which, in favorable cases, develops every noble trait of human nature except one,—the sceptical, question-asking faculty, to which all improvement, all progress, is due. Some of the sweetest, purest, and loveliest human beings in this earth are Roman Catholic priests. I have had the pleasure, once in my life, of conversing with an absolute gentleman: one in whom all the little vanities, all the little greedinesses, all the paltry fuss, worry, affectation, haste, and anxiety springing from imperfectly disciplined self-love,—*all* had been consumed; and the whole man was kind, serene, urbane, and utterly sincere. . . .

Sincere! The sincerest believers in the world are our Roman Catholic brethren. Faith, like every other faculty or habit, grows strong by exercise. Every time a Catholic attends mass, he is required to perform the most tremendous act of faith ever attempted by the human mind since its creation. Whatever may be weak or wanting in Catholics, they abound in faith.

Our Roman Catholic brethren are acquiring so great an estate in the United States, and acquiring it so rapidly, that it becomes a matter of public concern how they get it, what they do with it, and, especially, what they *will* do with it by and by, when it shall have become the largest property held in the country by or for an organization. Other organizations usually live from hand to mouth; but, somehow, the Catholics always contrive to have a little money ahead, to invest for the future. The Catholic Church, seven tenths of whose members are exempt from the income tax because their income is under a thousand dollars a year, is a capitalist, and has the advantage over other organizations which a man has over his fellows who, besides earning his livelihood, has a thousand dollars to operate with. There are spots in the Western country, over which the prairie winds now sweep without obstruction, that will one day be the sites of great cities. Our Roman Catholic brethren mark those spots, and construct maps upon which, not existing towns alone are indicated, but probable towns also. . . .

Look at our island of Manhattan! Sixty-seven years ago there were but one or two small Catholic churches upon it. It was not until 1808 that there was such a personage as a Roman Catholic bishop of New York. Run over the diocese now, and what do we find? Churches, 88; chapels attached to institutions, 29; colleges and theological seminaries, 4; academies and select schools, 23; parochial schools, one to nearly every church; charitable asylums and hospitals, 11; religious communities of men, 6; of women, 10. But this enumeration, as every New Yorker knows, conveys no ideas of the facts. Everything which our Roman Catholic brethren buy or build is bought or built with two objects in view,—duration and growth. Hence massive structures, and plenty of land! Wherever on this island, or on the lovely waters near it, you observe a spot upon which nature and circumstance have assembled every charm and every advantage, there the foresight and enterprise of this wonderful organization have placed, or are placing, something enormous and solid with a cross over it. The marble cathedral which is to contain ten thousand persons is going up on the precise spot on the Fifth Avenue which will be the very best for the purpose as long as the city stands. Yet, when that site was selected, several years ago, in the rocky wilds beyond the cattle-market, no one would have felt its value except a John Jacob Astor or a Roman Catholic Archbishop. This marvellous church so possesses itself of its members, that Catholic priests are as wise and acute and pushing for the church as the consummate man of business is for his own estate. Our excellent and zealous friends, the Paulist Fathers, when they planted themselves on the Ninth Avenue opposite Weehawken, bought a whole block; and thus, for less money than one house-lot will be worth in five years, secured room enough for the expansion of their community and its operations for ten centuries! And there is the Convent of the Sacred Heart, in the upper part of the island,—the old Lorillard country-seat; and the great establishments of the Sisters of Charity on the Hudson, where Edwin Forrest built his toy-castle,—were ever sites better chosen? Mark, too, the extent of the grounds, the solidity of the buildings, and the forethought and good sense which have presided over all the arrangements.

All these things cost money, though bought and built with most admirable economy. Fifty million dollars' worth of land and buildings the church probably owns in the diocese of New York; one half of which, perhaps, it acquired by buying land when land was cheap, and keeping it till it has become dear. Protestants will not fail to note the wisdom of this, and to reflect upon the weakness and distracted inefficiency of *our* mode of doing business. But the question remains: How was the other half of this great estate accumulated in half a century by an organization drawing its revenues chiefly from mechanics, small store-keepers, laborers, and servant-girls? Why, in the simplest way possible, and without laying a heavy burden on any one. The glory of the Catholic Church, as we all know, is, that it is the church of the poor; and in this fact consists its strength, as well as its glory.

. . . By the unstimulated, generosity [of the poor] and the efficiency of its clergy, all our cities will be covered with costly Catholic structures, which will constantly increase in splendor and number. In some New England villages, and in several New England towns, the Catholic church is already much the most solid, spacious, and ornate ecclesiastical edifice in the place. It must be so; for the poor, besides being more generous than the rich, are hundreds of times more numerous, and their pennies flow in a continuous stream. Nor do they confine their gifts to copper coin. "An Irish housemaid," says a paragraph just afloat, "has given a stained-glass window to the Catholic Church at Concord, New Hampshire." Nothing more credible. Two servant-girls, in this very house where I am now writing, educated their brother for the priesthood,—keeping on, year after year, spending nothing for their personal gratification, literally nothing, but sustaining him respectably, until one ecstatic day they went off in their Sunday clothes, their two faces radiant with joy, to see him ordained. Having accomplished this work, they next saved the sum requisite ($250 each) for their honorable admission into a laborious religious order, in which they now are. And yet the self-indulgent Parlor has the insolence to think itself morally superior to the self-denying Kitchen. The Recording Angel, if there is such a book-keeper, has something to enter to the credit of the Kitchen much oftener, probably, than he has to that of the apartments above it.

. . . . .

Among our Roman Catholic brethren the instinct of organizing and co-operating is wonderfully developed. I have before me a list, not complete, of the Catholic orders, which contains the names of two hundred and fifty-one varieties, each of which is an expression and a permanent gratification of the desire of some benevolent soul.

One example: Two hundred and fifty years ago, a French priest, named Vincent de Paul, was requested by a lady of his flock to call the attention of the congregation to the case of a destitute family lying sick a mile from the town. He did so, and with such effect that the poor people were supplied with food in profusion, so that much of it was spoiled before they could consume it. This priest, being one of those men whom every event instructs, was led to reflect upon the need there was in every large town of having the benign impulses regulated, and the gifts of the benevolent husbanded, so that none of them should be wasted, and the supply should never be exhausted. The result of his meditations we behold in the order of the Sisters of Charity, which all the world approves, and will ever approve. But this was not all the good arising from Father Vincent's reflections. To-day nearly every Catholic parish in large towns, in Europe, Asia, Africa, America, and Australia, has within it a society called a "Conference of St. Vincent de Paul," the object of which is the systematic and judicious relief of the poor of the parish. . . .

There is no end to the charities of our Roman Catholic brethren and sisters, and all that they do in this way is done with the efficiency and power of a disciplined organization. An admirable case in point is that of a community in Paris, which consists of an equal number of blind and seeing sisters. In each cell there is one of each; and it is part of the occupation of the sister who can see to aid, wait upon, and read to the sister who is blind. It does the heart good merely to know that such a sweet device as this has ever been conceived. There is a little book published in Paris (and we ought to have such in our cities) which contains a catalogue and brief account of all the charitable organizations there. . . . It contains a description of one hundred and ninety-two benevolent societies and systems. Any one would be puzzled to think of a malady, misfortune, deprivation, or peril for which there does not exist in Catholic Paris some organized remedy, mitigation, or prevention. . . .

In the diocese of New York there are sixty-one parochial schools, in which about twenty-five thousand pupils are taught, greatly to the relief of the cruelly crowded public schools. The religious instruction given in these schools consists of a lesson in the catechism, the saying of a few short Catholic prayers, the reading of the Gospel for the day, and an occasional exhortation; the whole occupying, on the average, twenty minutes a day. But it is not for the sake of the direct religious instruction that the pastors are so desirous of having parochial schools. There are several orders in the church which are devoted to the work of instruction,—the Christian Brothers, some of the Sisters of Charity, the Ladies of the Sacred Heart, and many more. It is from these orders that the teachers of the parochial schools are drawn; and it is the *Catholicizing* effect, upon the minds of the children, of these still, self-contained, cheerful persons, that the pastors chiefly value. There is a marvellous economy, too, in the system; for these pious sisters and devoted brothers only require the necessaries of life. Dr. Morrogh pays into the treasury of the Sisters of Charity two hundred dollars per annum for each sister employed in his school! The sisters live at the house of their order in Fifteenth Street, and go forth every morning to the schools to spend a laborious day in instructing ignorance, returning at noon and at night to their religious home. It will cost Dr. Morrogh about eight thousand dollars to sustain his school, possibly ten thousand. It would cost the city of New York eighteen thousand dollars.

.   .   .   .   .

Of course there is shadow to be put into the picture. This amazing organization, or system of organizations, is the accumulated practical wisdom of many thousand years; but it is the work of imperfect human beings, and partakes of their imperfection. "There is a provision in nature," says Goethe, "to prevent trees from growing up into the sky." Else, Commodore Vanderbilt would own all the railroads, and we should all turn Catholics immediately. Every Protestant knows, or thinks he knows, precisely what the defect is which prevents this interesting tree from growing up into the sky, and spreading its branches over the whole earth. I think I know. I think it is because there is not a sufficient provision in it for adapting its doctrine to the advancing mind of the race. Perhaps, however, it is the modernized mind that is at fault.

Our Roman Catholic brethren, for example, firmly believe that miracles are daily wrought among them . . . . A good Catholic, no matter what his rank or culture, believes in such things without an effort. . . . For my part, if the President and Vice-President, if the whole Cabinet, both houses of Congress, and the judges of the Supreme Court, had all sworn that they had seen [a miracle] done, and I myself had seen one, still I would think it more probable that all those witnesses, including myself, were mistaken, than that a miracle had been performed. Such is the incredulity of a modernized mind, especially if that modernized mind has occasionally served on a jury, and so learned the value of human testimony.

How different with Catholics! "Why!" says Father Hecker, "we do not worship a dead God! Where is the improbability? No one doubts God's ability to heal his faithful servants; why should we find it so hard to believe that he does so? Protestants usually admit that miracles were once performed, and they still use language in their prayers which implies an expectation of miraculous aid. We Catholics have a living practical *faith* in Providence, which you Protestants think you have, and have not. And where is your authority for saying that, during a certain period of the world's history, miracles were wrought, but that there came a moment when they ceased to be wrought? Why is it rational to believe in a miracle which occurred Anno Domini 32, but wholly irrational to believe in one wrought Anno Domini 1868?"

These are not the precise words of the able and devoted Superior of the Paulists, but such are some of his ideas. I did not, do not, cannot answer his questions. My office is merely that of reporter, and, with the permission of the gentle reader, I will continue my report in a future number of this magazine. I have yet to relate the special measures now on foot for the conversion of us all, and the grounds upon which our Roman Catholic brethren rest their confident expectation of being in another generation or two the dominant church of the United States.

Early Years in Lowell

WILLIAM CARDINAL O'CONNELL

Originally Lowell was a little country village and the inhabitants were Puritans by religion and farmers by occupation. When some of

"Early Years in Lowell," from *Recollections of Seventy Years,* by William O'Connell (Boston: Houghton Mifflin Co., 1934). Reprinted by permission of The Pilot Publishing Company.

the well-to-do New-Englanders began to turn their attention from farming to manufacturing, they at once grasped the very exceptional position of the little town at the junction of the Concord and Merrimac Rivers. Water power was then practically the only power used for industrial purposes, as gas and electricity were virtually unknown. So they immediately saw the exceptional opportunity for setting up industries in the valley of the Merrimac and established a few mills for making cotton cloth, the raw cotton being transported by ships to Boston, and then by canal and over the road to the district in question. In a very few years nearly the whole course of the Merrimac saw the growth of industrial villages, and of these Lowell was the largest and most important. The little village began to grow by leaps and bounds. At first the farmers, their sons and daughters came into Lowell from the surrounding villages, and even from New Hampshire and Vermont. They worked in the new mills in the winter and went back to their farms in summer. The owners of the mills soon found themselves growing rich. Most of them were residents of Boston, and besides being interested in the cotton industry they became merchants, selling their own products, shipping their goods to India, China, and all parts of our own country. Both the mill-owners and operatives were all of the same stock, English Puritan, and the town, like all the other towns of New England, was under Puritan theocratic rule.

Just about this time, between 1846 and 1850, on account of the famine in Ireland, there was an enormous influx of Irish immigrants into the country. They possessed the usual vigor and courage of the Irish everywhere, and with their faith undimmed they faced, in the new world, a situation that otherwise would have become intolerable. They were given only the hardest work and the lowest pay. They were herded in a quarter of the town and told to stay there, like the Jews in the Ghetto;—and these outer portions of the villages were designated Dublin or Cork in derision. All this was doubly true in New England, with its strict Puritan population and inherited hatred of everything Irish. Hundreds of these valiant sons and daughters of Saint Patrick, undaunted by the inimical atmosphere surrounding them, made their way to the town of Lowell and settled down to work in the industries then beginning to thrive enormously.

Among this incoming and unwelcome group of sturdy Irish stock and sterling Catholic faith were my own parents. They went their lonely way amid these inhospitable surroundings, labored in-

dustriously and lived uprightly. The conditions facing them would
have been almost unendurable to a weaker stock and less faithful
people. As a matter of fact, hundreds died under the cruel and gruel-
ling conditions of life. As if things were not hard enough for them,
the mill-owners imported bosses or superintendents from Manchester
and Birmingham and the mining districts of England, and a more
brutal, ignorant, and cruel set of men can scarcely be imagined. Their
chief work and task was to act as slave-drivers of the immigrant
Irish population, for which they were handsomely recompensed. The
day's labor began at six in the morning and ended at seven at night,
with a half-hour free at noon, just time enough hurriedly to eat a
frugal lunch. Those newcomers, first almost entirely Irish, later
French-Canadian Catholics from the Provinces, were treated precisely
as if they were part of the machinery which ground out the millions
being produced for the rich managers and mill-owners, who spent
the money, not in Lowell, but in New York, Boston, Paris, and
London.

Lowell and its new population, which began to increase year by
year by the thousands, got all the hard work and almost nothing else—
certainly not compassion, pity or understanding of the almost in-
supportable condition of labor of that time. Nevertheless, though
many succumbed and were buried in early graves, the strong and the
resolute settled into conditions as they were and made the best of
their lot. And to their eternal credit let it be said of them, with their
meagre wages, the fruit of endless toil, they brought up good families,
faithful to their religion, and by dint of indomitable perseverance
succeeded in giving many of their children the very best kind of
education. I remember so well, as a child, hearing the sonorous bell
of the near-by mill ringing out the reveille at five in the morning. I
can hear now the bustle in the household, the raking of the fires and
the preparation of the morning meal for those who had to be at their
looms or spinning-wheels at six, and I can hear the scuffling feet passing under my window, hurrying on in the darkness of the early morn
to the grinding work they would be obliged to perform until night
fell again.

The mills were surrounded by high brick walls, with gates at
various intervals. At five minutes past six these gates were closed, and
woe betide the worker who was a few minutes late. His pay was
docked and if tardy more than twice he was fired. I remember often

standing outside those same gates at twelve o'clock at noon, when the gates were opened for the half-hour allowed for luncheon, and the workers stormed out in enormous crowds to get whatever food they could in that brief interval. There were, of course, many gay and happy faces and much laughter, but one saw in the midst of this the wan and weary faces of those too weak to stand such drudgery. Again, many a time I stood outside those gates at seven in the evening and saw the laborers at the end of a long, weary day, their bodies drooping with fatigue and all the joy and laughter gone out of them. These are sights and thoughts that burned into my soul as a young boy, for among these workers were those of my own flesh and blood, the nearest and dearest on earth to me; and even then my soul was tortured by the thought that out of this sacrifice had to come the means that would make my education possible and my whole life different. Were it not that the whole Catholic population, living under such grueling conditions, with hard labor their daily lot and the antipathy of brutal bosses the atmosphere of their toil, found their great strength and consolation in the exercise of their faith, they inevitably would have succumbed to the conditions imposed on them. But at that very time every exercise of devotion in the churches, every mission beginning early in the morning and resumed again at eight at night, brought them in thousands to their various parish churches, and there, lifted up by faith above the toil and turmoil of the life of the mills, the whirring of the spindles and the noise of the looms, they snatched a glimpse of heaven. Their hearts were softened and touched, and again and again into their weary eyes came the dew of bitter tears, as they thought of the old home far away with its pleasant hills and valleys, the cheerful cottage and the old church on the hillside. They knew that God was with them amid all the difficulties of their hard lives. They brushed away the tears and looked with unfailing hope to the day when, by the fruits of their labor and faith, they would enter into better conditions of life, with a little house of their own and a happy family about them, and in this hope was their salvation, physically and spiritually. God blessed and fructified that hope in the case of thousands of these faithful children of old Erin amid the strange and unwelcome atmosphere of New England.

Of course, the conditions of the workers as they were then could not last, though the capitalists and mill-owners did their best to prolong them. I remember well when the workers began agitation for a ten-hour law for workers. I was still a child, but the memory of that agitation and its achievement is very vivid in my mind. At first the operators of the mills used threats of dismissal toward anyone who dared to show sympathy with this movement for more human conditions of labor. They even threatened to burn down the houses of the chief agitators. Violence, as always, was met by violence, and the threat came back, "You burn our houses and we will burn your mills." The situation grew more and more perilous for those whose money was invested in the industries of Lowell, and this called a halt on threats and intimidation. After several years of public agitation of this measure, the ten-hour bill finally became a law in Massachusetts. There was rejoicing in all the mills among the operatives, because at last they were allowed some measure of home life and a little less inhuman slavery. Even then there was a threat to cut the wages in view of the fewer hours, although at that time the owners were receiving unheard-of incomes from the labor of these poor people, whom they still seemed to regard as bits of machinery whose only work was to turn out money for them.

The wonder is that the people, goaded to desperation by an unfeeling capitalistic class, did not become out-and-out anarchists. It was well for the mill-owners and capitalists that the operatives, whom they treated so shabbily and unfeelingly, had the strongest possible faith in God and were strengthened by their religion, which was by all odds the most beautiful part of their drab lives. It was nothing short of a miracle wrought by faith that those thousands of virtuous, capable and hard-working people, condemned for their race and despised for their faith—but who, nevertheless, were the producers of the big fortunes of their employers—did not take events into their own hands and read a salutary lesson to the merciless mill-owners, fattening upon the product of their labor, and to the bigots who made their daily lives miserable.

This might easily have happened, for at that very time came the rise of the "Know-Nothing" Movement, whose effect was to torment still more these inoffensive and industrious Catholic workers. This movement was, as usual, led by fanatical ministers, who preached hatred from their pulpits, and very shortly the whole ignorant Puritan population was in a fury. In the streets Catholics were met by taunts and gibes. The bitterness of their feeling was summed up in their two epithets—Paddy and Papist. Protestant mobs surrounded Catholic churches and threatened violence to priests and worshippers. At last, their leader, called by them the "Angel Gabriel," worked the Protestant mob into such a fury that they threatened to burn the churches. This, of course, was more than these defenseless people could stand, and though the priests, with a courage that was heroic, counseled patience to their flocks, the latter could stand it no longer. A score of strong, vigorous Irish Catholics, with whatever instruments of defense they could get, sticks and shovels and spades, stood guard around their little churches, and, as defenders of the faith, dared their enemies to go further.

There were riots and mobs here and there all over New England, and a contemptible crew of fanatics in Maine had gone so far as to tar and feather a holy priest, Father Bapst, as others had burned the convent in Charlestown. But the limit had been reached at last, and when those persecuted people finally turned and showed their pluck, the fanatics fled like the cowards they were and always are. It is hard for any of us now to realize such conditions as I have described in the time of my own youth.

I lived and grew up under those conditions, so I knew them well, and this information is, therefore, first hand. To repeat, therefore, the religion of the people of Lowell was strict Puritanism, with a strong mixture of anti-Popery, and a very open dislike for everything Irish and Catholic. A certain very small minority of the Protestants were either Episcopalians or Unitarians, and, be it said to their credit, they, and only they, showed some largeness of mind and spirit, which helped to make tolerable the lives of the early Catholic settlers of Lowell. As for myself, both in school and out of school, in fact, everywhere except in Church and home, I was clearly conscious of this sentiment of petty animosity. It certainly did not tend to make life joyous or childhood happy. Nevertheless, the influence of Church and home produced in my own childhood a happiness which nothing seemed capable of spoiling.

I was born and brought up, fortunately, in one of the pleasant outlying districts of the city, called "Chapel Hill," so called because the Episcopalians had a small chapel in the district, a mission of the larger parish of Saint Ann in the heart of the city. The pastor of this parish was Dr. Edson, a saintly and kindly soul, whose influence did much to soften the petty antipathy of those who were fortunate enough to belong to his parish. Nearly all our neighbors belonged to the chapel, which accounts for the kindliness of spirit exhibited toward our family and the few other Catholic families living in that locality. My mother was in excellent relations with all the women of that district, and whenever there was any sickness in the neighborhood, she was called even before the doctor, and this, naturally, helped to make the kindlier relations which responded to her goodness and charity. My father, too, was most highly respected. He was a quiet gentle soul, who oftentimes overlooked offense with a smile, and both he and my mother, by the exercise of heroic restraint, succeeded in making a highly honorable place for themselves and their family amid circumstances which, in the beginning, were anything but friendly. They understood perfectly well that the cause of this animosity was the fact that they were devout Catholics. Whenever we children brought home complaints of the petty spites and injustice of our teachers or playmates, my mother would lift her finger commanding silence, and then, in a manner that I can never forget, explain to us that as our ancestors had suffered for the faith we, too, must be prepared to do the same, always adding, "You will see the day, yet, when all these people and their children will regret the attitude they now take against us. Poor things," she would say, "you know they are dreadfully ignorant of the truth of our religion. Many of them are good, but their sentiments are warped by the lies of centuries. Some day their children's children will at last learn of the truth; until then you and all of us must remember the words of Christ on the Cross, 'Father, forgive them for they know not what they do.' " We learned the lesson as best we could, though oftentimes it was a bitter dose to swallow. It was good discipline for us and even now I realize the truth of her words, "Some day their children's children will bitterly regret all this."

The years flew by amid all those circumstances, grave and gay; we were too brimful of Celtic spirits not to feel the joyousness of youth in those carefree days between five and fifteen. In school, it is true, there was a fearful sense of repression and a subtle sense of antipathy toward us. But the moment school was dismissed, we turned our backs upon all that, and with football and baseball, cricket and hockey, and all the other sports and games in which youth revels, we lived through those days in high hopes that when school days were over, we should be able somehow to enter upon the work of life, and help by every effort we could spend, to make conditions as we had found them a thing only of faint and unpleasant memories. And it is well for Lowell that, by the efforts of her sons and daughters of the immigrant Irish and French Catholics, this whole atmosphere of a stunted Puritanic and provincial spirit is now practically a thing of the past.

FOUR

Ideas and Attitudes from Abroad

The Escape from Paganism

G. K. CHESTERTON

The modern missionary, with his palm-leaf hat and his umbrella, has become rather a figure of fun. He is chaffed among men of the world for the ease with which he can be eaten by cannibals and the narrow bigotry which makes him regard the cannibal culture as lower than his own. Perhaps the best part of the joke is that the men of the world do not see that the joke is against themselves. It is rather ridiculous to ask a man just about to be boiled in a pot and eaten, at a purely religious feast, why he does not regard all religions as equally friendly and fraternal. But there is a more subtle criticism uttered against the more old-fashioned missionary; to the effect that he generalises too broadly about the heathen and pays too little attention to the difference between Mahomet and Mumbo Jumbo. There was probably truth in this complaint, especially in the past; but it is my main contention here that the exaggeration is all the other way at present. It is the temptation of the professors to treat mythologies too much as theologies; as things thoroughly thought out and seriously held. It is the temptation of the intellectuals to take much too seriously the fine shades of various schools in the rather irresponsible metaphysics of Asia. Above all it is their temptation to miss the real truth implied in the idea of Aquinas contra Gentiles or Athanasius contra mundum.

If the missionary says, in fact, that he is exceptional in being a Christian, and that the rest of the races and religions can be collectively classified as heathen, he is perfectly right. He may say it in quite the wrong spirit, in which case he is spiritually wrong. But in the cold light of philosophy and history, he is intellectually right. He may not be right-minded, but he is right. He may not even have a right to be right, but he is right. The outer world to which he brings his creed really is something subject to certain generalisations covering all its varieties, and is not merely a variety of similar creeds. Perhaps it is in any case too much of a temptation to pride or hypocrisy to call it heathenry. Perhaps it would be better simply to call it humanity. But there are certain broad characteristics of what we call humanity while it remains in what we call heathenry. They are not necessarily bad characteristics; some of them are worthy of the respect of Christendom; some of them have been absorbed and transfigured in the substance of Christendom. But they existed before Christendom and they still exist outside Christendom, as certainly as the sea existed before a boat and all round a boat; and they have as strong and as universal and as unmistakeable a savour as the sea.

For instance, all real scholars who have studied the Greek and Roman culture say one thing about it. They agree that in the ancient world religion was one thing and philosophy quite another. There was very little effort to rationalise and at the same time to realise a real belief in the gods. There was very little pretense of any such real belief among the philosophers. But neither had the passion or perhaps the power to persecute the other, save in particular and peculiar cases; and neither the philosopher in his school nor the priest in his temple seems ever to have seriously contemplated his own concept as covering the world. A priest sacrificing to Artemis in Calydon did not seem to think that people would some day sacrifice to her instead of to Isis beyond the sea; a sage following the vegetarian rule of the Neo-Pythagoreans did not seem to think it would universally prevail and exclude the methods of Epictetus or Epicurus. We may call this liberality if we like; I am not dealing with an argument but describing an atmosphere. All this, I say, is admitted by all scholars; but what neither the learned nor the unlearned have fully realised, perhaps, is that this description is really an exact description of all non-Christian civilisation to-day; and especially of the great civilisations of the East. Eastern paganism really is much more all of a piece, just as ancient paganism was much more all of a piece, than the modern critics admit. It is a many-coloured Persian Carpet as the other was a varied and tesselated Roman pavement; but the one real crack right across that pavement came from the earthquake of the Crucifixion.

The modern European seeking his religion in Asia is reading his religion into Asia. Religion there is something different; it is both more and less. He is like a man mapping out the sea as land; marking waves as mountains; not understanding the nature of its peculiar permanence. It is perfectly true that Asia has its own dignity and poetry and high civilisation. But it is not in the least true that Asia has its own definite dominions of moral government, where all loyalty is conceived in terms of morality; as when we say that Ireland is Catholic or that New England was Puritan. The map is not marked out in religions, in our sense of churches. The state of mind is far more subtle, more relative, more secretive, more varied and changing, like the colours of the snake. The Moslem is the nearest approach to a militant Christian; and that is precisely because he is a much nearer approach to an envoy from western civilisation. The Moslem in the heart of Asia almost stands for the soul of Europe. And as he stands between them and Europe in the matter of space, so he stands between them and Christianity in the matter of time. In that sense the Moslems in Asia are merely like the Nestorians in Asia. Islam, historically speaking, is the greatest of the Eastern heresies. It owed something to the quite isolated and unique individuality of Israel; but it owed more to Byzantium and the theological enthusiasm of Christendom. It owed something even to the Crusades. It owed nothing whatever to Asia. It owed nothing to the atmosphere of the ancient and traditional world of Asia, with its immemorial etiquette and its bottomless or bewildering philosophies. All that ancient and actual Asia felt the entrance of Islam as something foreign and western and warlike, piercing it like a spear.

Even where we might trace in dotted lines the domains of Asiatic religions, we should probably be reading into them something dogmatic and ethical belonging to our own religion. It is as if a European ignorant of the American atmosphere were to suppose that each "state" was a separate sovereign state as patriotic as France or Poland; or that when a Yankee referred fondly to his "home town" he meant he had no other nation, like a citizen of ancient Athens or Rome. As he would be reading a particular sort of loyalty into America, so we are reading a particular sort of loyalty into Asia. There are loyalties of other kinds; but not what men in the west mean by being a believer, by trying to be a Christian, by being a good Protestant or a practising Catholic. In the intellectual world it means something far more vague and varied by doubts and speculations. In the moral world it means something far more loose and drifting. A professor of Persian at one of our great universities, so passionate a partisan of the East as practically to profess a contempt for the West, said to a friend of mine: "You will never understand oriental religions, because you always conceive religion as connected with ethics. This kind has really nothing to do with ethics." We have most of us known some Masters of the Higher Wisdom, some Pilgrims upon the Path to Power, some eastern esoteric saints and seers, who had really nothing to do with ethics. Something different, something detached and irresponsible, tinges the moral atmosphere of Asia and touches even that of Islam. It was very realistically caught in the atmosphere of *Hassan;* and a very horrible atmosphere too. It is even more vivid in such glimpses as we get of the genuine and ancient cults of Asia. Deeper than the depths of metaphysics, far down in the abysses of mystical meditations, under all that solemn universe of spiritual things, is a secret, an intangible and a terrible levity. It does not really very much matter what one does. Either because they do not believe in a devil, or because they do believe in a destiny, or because experience here is everything and eternal life something totally different, but for some reason they are totally different. I have read somewhere that there were three great friends famous in medieval Persia for their unity of mind. One became the responsible and respected Vizier of the Great King; the second was the poet Omar, pessimist and epicurean, drinking wine in mockery of Mahomet; the third was the Old Man of the Mountain who maddened his people with hashish that they might murder other people with daggers. It does not really much matter what one does.

.   .   .   .   .

Asia is all humanity; as it has worked out its human doom. Asia, in its vast territory, in its varied populations, in its heights of past achievement and its depths of dark speculation, is itself a world; and represents something of what we mean when we speak of the world. It is a cosmos rather than a continent. It is the world as man has made it; and contains many of the most wonderful things that man has made. Therefore Asia stands as the one representative of paganism and the one rival to Christendom. But everywhere else where we get glimpses of that mortal destiny, they suggest stages in the same story. Where Asia trails away into the southern archipelagoes of the savages, or where a darkness full of nameless shapes dwells in the heart of Africa, or where the last survivors of lost races linger in the cold volcano of prehistoric America, it is all the same story; sometimes perhaps later chapters of the same story. It is men entangled in the forest of their own mythology; it is men drowned in the sea of their own metaphysics. Polytheists have grown weary of the most wonderful of truths. Diabolists here and there have such a hatred of heaven and earth that they have tried to take refuge in hell. It is the Fall of Man; and it is exactly that fall that was being felt by our own fathers at the first moment of the Roman decline. We also were going down that wide road; down that easy slope; following the magnificent procession of the high civilisations of the world.

If the Church had not entered the world then, it seems probable that Europe would be now very much what Asia is now. Something may be allowed for a real difference of race and environment, visible in the ancient as in the modern world. But after all we talk about the changeless East very largely because it has not suffered the great change. Paganism in its last phase showed considerable signs of becoming equally changeless. This would not mean that new schools or sects of philosophy would not arise; as new schools did arise in Antiquity and do arise in Asia. It does not mean that there would be no real mystics or visionaries; as there were mystics in Antiquity and are mystics in Asia. It does not mean that there would be no social codes, as there were codes in Antiquity and are codes in Asia. It does not mean that there could not be good men or happy lives, for God has given all men a conscience and conscience can give all men a kind of peace. But it does mean that the tone and proportion of all these things, and especially the proportion of good and evil things, would be in the unchanged West what they are in the changeless East. And nobody who looks at that changeless East honestly, and with a real sympathy, can believe that there is anything there remotely resembling the challenge and revolution of the Faith.

In short, if classic paganism had lingered until now, a number of things might well have lingered with it; and they would look very like what we call the religions of the East. There would still be Pythagoreans teaching reincarnation, as there are still Hindus teach-

ing reincarnation. There would still be Stoics making a religion out
of reason and virtue, as there are still Confucians making a religion
out of reason and virtue. There would still be Neo-Platonists studying
transcendental truths, the meaning of which was mysterious to other
people and disputed even amongst themselves; as the Buddhists still
study a transcendentalism mysterious to others and disputed among
themselves. There would still be intelligent Apollonians apparently
worshipping the sun-god but explaining that they were worshipping
the divine principle; just as there are still intelligent Parsees apparently worshipping the sun but explaining that they are worshipping
the deity. There would still be wild Dionysians dancing on the mountain as there are still wild Dervishes dancing in the desert. There would
still be crowds of people attending the popular feasts of the gods, in
pagan Europe as in pagan Asia. There would still be crowds of gods,
local and other, for them to worship. And there would still be a great
many more people who worshipped them than people who believed
in them. Finally there would still be a very large number of people
who did worship gods and did believe in gods; and who believed
in gods and worshipped gods simply because they were demons.
There would still be Levantines secretly sacrificing to Moloch as
there are still Thugs secretly sacrificing to Kalee. There would still
be a great deal of magic; and a great deal of it would be black magic.
There would still be a considerable admiration of Seneca and a considerable imitation of Nero; just as the exalted epigrams of Confucius
could coexist with the tortures of China. And over all that tangled
forest of traditions growing wild or withering would brood the broad
silence of a singular and even nameless mood; but the nearest name
of it is nothing. All these things, good and bad, would have an in-
describable air of being too old to die.

    None of these things occupying Europe in the absence of Chris-
tendom would bear the least likeness to Christendom. Since the
Pythagorean Metempsychosis would still be there, we might call it
the Pythagorean religion as we talk about the Buddhist religion. As
the noble maxims of Socrates would still be there, we might call it
the Socratic religion as we talk about the Confucian religion. As the
popular holiday was still marked by a mythological hymn to Adonis,
we might call it the religion of Adonis as we talk about the religion
of Juggernaut. As literature would still be based on the Greek mythology, we might call that mythology a religion, as we call the Hindu

mythology a religion. We might say that there were so many thousands or millions of people belonging to that religion, in the sense of frequenting such temples or merely living in a land full of such temples. But if we called the last tradition of Pythagoras or the lingering legend of Adonis by the name of a religion, then we must find some other name for the Church of Christ.

· · · · ·

There will be no end to the weary debates about liberalising theology, until people face the fact that the only liberal part of it is really the dogmatic part. If dogma is incredible, it is because it is incredibly liberal. If it is irrational, it can only be in giving us more assurance of freedom than is justified by reason. The obvious example is that essential form of freedom which we call free-will. It is absurd to say that a man shows his liberality in denying his liberty. But it is tenable that he has to affirm a transcendental doctrine in order to affirm his liberty. There is a sense in which we might reasonably say that if man has a primary power of choice, he has in that fact a supernatural power of creation, as if he could raise the dead or give birth to the unbegotten. Possibly in that case a man must be a miracle; and certainly in that case he must be a miracle in order to be a man; and most certainly in order to be a free man. But it is absurd to forbid him to be a free man and do it in the name of a more free religion.

· · · · ·

What the denouncer of dogma really means is not that dogma is bad; but rather that dogma is too good to be true. That is, he means that dogma is too liberal to be likely. Dogma gives man too much freedom when it permits him to fall. Dogma gives even God too much freedom when it permits him to die. That is what the intelligent sceptics ought to say; and it is not in the least my intention to deny that there is something to be said for it. They mean that the universe is itself a universal prison; that existence itself is a limitation and a control; and it is not for nothing that they call causation a chain. In a word, they mean quite simply that they cannot believe these things; not in the least that they are unworthy of belief. We say, not lightly but very literally, that the truth has made us free. They say that it makes us so free that it cannot be the truth. To them it is like believing in fairyland to believe in such freedom as we enjoy. It is

like believing in men with wings to entertain the fancy of men with
wills. It is like accepting a fable about a squirrel in conversation with
a mountain to believe in a man who is free to ask or a God who is
free to answer. This is a manly and a rational negation for which I
for one shall always show respect. But I decline to show any respect
for those who first of all clip the wings and cage the squirrel, rivet
the chains and refuse the freedom, close all the doors of the cosmic
prison on us with a clang of eternal iron, tell us that our emancipation
is a dream and our dungeon a necessity; and then calmly turn round
and tell us they have a freer thought and a more liberal theology.

The moral of all this is an old one; that religion is revelation.
In other words, it is a vision, and a vision received by faith; but it is
a vision of reality. The faith consists in a conviction of its reality.
That, for example, is the difference between a vision and a day-
dream. And that is the difference between religion and mythology.
That is the difference between faith and all that fancy-work, quite
human and more or less healthy, which we considered under the head
of mythology. There is something in the reasonable use of the very
word vision that implies two things about it; first that it comes very
rarely, possibly that it comes only once; and secondly that it probably comes once and for all. A day-dream may come every day. A
day-dream may be different every day. It is something more than the
difference between telling ghost-stories and meeting a ghost.

But if it is not a mythology neither is it a philosophy. It is not
a philosophy because, being a vision, it is not a pattern but a picture.
It is not one of those simplifications which resolve everything into an
abstract explanation; as that everything is recurrent; or everything
is relative; or everything is inevitable; or everything is illusive. It is
not a process but a story. It has proportions, of the sort seen in a
picture or a story; it has not the regular repetitions of a pattern or
a process; but it replaces them by being convincing as a picture or a
story is convincing. In other words, it is exactly, as the phrase goes,
like life. For indeed it is life. An example of what is meant here might
well be found in the treatment of the problem of evil. It is easy enough
to make a plan of life of which the background is black, as the
pessimists do; and then admit a speck or two of star-dust more or
less accidental, or at least in the literal sense insignificant. And it is
easy enough to make another plan on white paper, as the Christian
Scientists do, and explain or explain away somehow such dots or

smudges as may be difficult to deny. Lastly it is easiest of all, perhaps, to say as the dualists do, that life is like a chessboard in which the two are equal; and can as truly be said to consist of white squares on a black board or of black squares on a white board. But every man feels in his heart that none of these three paper plans is like life; that none of these worlds is one in which he can live. Something tells him that the ultimate idea of a world is not bad or even neutral; staring at the sky or the grass or the truths of mathematics or even a new-laid egg, he has a vague feeling like the shadow of that saying of the great Christian philosopher, St. Thomas Aquinas, "Every existence, as such, is good." On the other hand, something else tells him that it is unmanly and debased and even diseased to minimise evil to a dot or even a blot. He realises that optimism is morbid. It is if possible even more morbid than pessimism. These vague but healthy feelings, if he followed them out, would result in the idea that evil is in some way an exception but an enormous exception; and ultimately that evil is an invasion or yet more truly a rebellion. He does not think that everything is right or that everything is wrong, or that everything is equally right and wrong. But he does think that right has a right to be right and therefore a right to be there; and wrong has no right to be wrong and therefore no right to be there. It is the prince of the world; but it is also a usurper. So he will apprehend vaguely what the vision will give to him vividly; no less than all that strange story of treason in heaven and the great desertion by which evil damaged and tried to destroy a cosmos that it could not create. It is a very strange story and its proportions and its lines and colours are as arbitrary and absolute as the artistic composition of a picture. It is a vision which we do in fact symbolise in pictures by titanic limbs and passionate tints of plumage; all that abysmal vision of falling stars and the peacock panoplies of the night. But that strange story has one small advantage over the diagrams. It is like life.

.   .   .   .   .

The Catholic faith is the reconciliation because it is the realisation both of mythology and philosophy. It is a story and in that sense one of a hundred stories; only it is a true story. It is a philosophy and in that sense one of a hundred philosophies; only it is a philosophy that is like life. But above all, it is a reconciliation because it is something that can only be called the philosophy of stories. That normal

narrative instinct which produced all the fairy tales is something that
is neglected by all the philosophies—except one. The Faith is the
justification of that popular instinct; the finding of a philosophy for
it or the analysis of the philosophy in it. Exactly as a man in an
adventure story has to pass various tests to save his life, so the man
in this philosophy has to pass several tests and save his soul. In both
there is an idea of free will operating under conditions of design; in
other words, there is an aim and it is the business of a man to aim at
it; we therefore watch to see whether he will hit it. Now this deep and
democratic and dramatic instinct is derided and dismissed in all the
other philosophies. For all the other philosophies avowedly end where
they begin; and it is the definition of a story that it ends differently;
that it begins in one place and ends in another. From Buddha and his
wheel to Akhen Aten and his disc, from Pythagoras with his abstraction of number to Confucius with his religion of routine, there is not
one of them that does not in some way sin against the soul of a story.
There is none of them that really grasps this human notion of the
tale, the test, the adventure; the ordeal of the free man. Each of them
starves the story-telling instinct, so to speak, and does something
to spoil human life considered as a romance; either by fatalism
(pessimist or optimist) and that destiny that is the death of adventure;
or by indifference and that detachment that is the death of drama;
or by a fundamental scepticism that dissolves the actors into atoms;
or by a materialistic limitation blocking the vista of moral consequences; or a mechanical recurrence making even moral tests
monotonous; or a bottomless relativity making even practical tests
insecure. There is such a thing as a human story; and there is such a
thing as the divine story which is also a human story; but there is no
such thing as a Hegelian story or a Monist story or a relativist story
or a determinist story; for every story, yes, even a penny dreadful or
a cheap novelette, has something in it that belongs to our universe
and not theirs. Every short story does truly begin with creation and
end with a last judgment.

And *that* is the reason why the myths and the philosophers were
at war until Christ came. That is why the Athenian democracy killed
Socrates out of respect for the gods; and why every strolling sophist
gave himself the airs of a Socrates whenever he could talk in a
superior fashion of the gods; and why the heretic Pharoah wrecked
his huge idols and temples for an abstraction and why the priests

could return in triumph and trample his dynasty under foot; and why Buddhism had to divide itself from Brahminism, and why in every age and country outside Christendom there has been a feud for ever between the philosopher and the priest. It is easy enough to say that the philosopher is generally the more rational; it is easier still to forget that the priest is always the more popular. For the priest told the people stories; and the philosopher did not understand the philosophy of stories. It came into the world with the story of Christ.

And this is why it had to be a revelation or vision given from above. Anyone who will think of the theory of stories or pictures will easily see the point. The true story of the world must be told by somebody to somebody else. By the very nature of a story it cannot be left to occur to anybody. A story has proportions, variations, surprises, particular dispositions, which cannot be worked out by rule in the abstract, like a sum. We could not deduce whether or no Achilles would give back the body of Hector from a Pythagorean theory of number or recurrence; and we could not infer for ourselves in what way the world would get back the body of Christ, merely from being told that all things go round and round upon the wheel of Buddha. A man might perhaps work out a proposition of Euclid without having heard of Euclid; but he would not work out the precise legend of Eurydice without having heard of Eurydice. At any rate he would not be certain how the story would end and whether Orpheus was ultimately defeated. Still less could he guess the end of our story; or the legend of our Orpheus rising, not defeated, from the dead.

To sum up; the sanity of the world was restored and the soul of man offered salvation by something which did indeed satisfy the two warring tendencies of the past; which had never been satisfied in full and most certainly never satisfied together. It met the mythological search for romance by being a story and the philosophical search for truth by being a true story. That is why the ideal figure had to be a historical character, as nobody had ever felt Adonis or Pan to be a historical character. But that is also why the historical character had to be the ideal figure; and even fulfil many of the functions given to these other ideal figures; why he was at once the sacrifice and the feast, why he could be shown under the emblems of the growing vine or the rising sun. The more deeply we think of the matter the more we shall conclude that, if there be indeed a God, his creation could hardly have reached any other culmination than this granting of a real romance to the world. Otherwise the two sides of the human mind could never have touched at all; and the brain of man would have remained cloven and double; one lobe of it dreaming impossible dreams and the other repeating invariable calculations. The picturemakers would have remained forever painting the portrait of nobody. The sages would have remained for ever adding up numerals that came to nothing. It was that abyss that nothing but an incarnation could cover; a divine embodiment of our dreams; and he stands above that chasm whose name is more than priest and older even than Christendom; Pontifex Maximus, the mightiest maker of a bridge.

But even with that we return to the more specially Christian symbol in the same tradition; the perfect pattern of the keys. This is a historical and not a theological outline, and it is not my duty here to defend in detail that theology, but merely to point out that it could not even be justified in design without being justified in detail—like a key. Beyond the broad suggestion of this chapter I attempt no apologetic about why the creed should be accepted. But in answer to the historical query of why it was accepted, and is accepted, I answer for millions of others in my reply; because it fits the lock; because it is like life. It is one among many stories; only it happens to be a true story. It is one among many philosophies; only it happens to be the truth. We accept it; and the ground is solid under our feet and the road is open before us. It does not imprison us in a dream of destiny or a consciousness of the universal delusion. It opens to us not only incredible heavens, but what seems to some an equally incredible earth, and makes it credible. This is the sort of truth that is hard to explain because it is a fact; but it is a fact to which we can call witnesses. We are Christians and Catholics not because we worship a key, but because we have passed a door; and felt the wind that is the trumpet of liberty blow over the land of the living.

The Faith and Industrial Capitalism
HILAIRE BELLOC

If there is one mark more striking than another about the Catholic Church it is its intellectual freedom.

The moment a Catholic goes outside and lives with people not under the influence of the Church he finds himself in an atmosphere of intellectual convention which to a man of Catholic habit is stifling. Perhaps I ought to call it "intellectual faith" rather than "intellectual convention," for the simplicity and tenacity with which intellectual doctrines are taken for granted outside the Catholic Church much more resembles the simpler and more childlike forms of faith than a social convention.

People outside the Catholic atmosphere seem to take as a matter of course the intellectual fashion of their time; and never, within my experience, at least, go to first principles and ask themselves why they accept that fashion. One comes across this tiresome petrifying of the intellect in all directions. In the acceptation of majorities, for example; in the swallowing whole of official history; in the blind acquiescence in the right of the State to take control of education; in the bland repetition of newspaper science and newspaper politics. An excellent instance is the attitude towards miracle. Mention an historical miracle, and the man unfamiliar with Catholic truth denies it at once: without consideration of the evidence. But when you are discussing with Catholics an historical event in which the marvellous *may* have entered you get free discussion, one man saying he believes in the miracle and giving his reasons, another saying he does not and giving *his* reasons; while for the most part those who take one side or the other at least imply their first principles and often state them.

It is all part of the modern process which others than Catholics are beginning to realise, that, outside the Faith, men are abandoning reason.

Now one of the consequences of this intellectual freedom produced in the mind by the influence of the Faith is that Catholics may and do hold an infinity of positions upon matters where the general trend of Catholicism is manifest, but where there has been as yet no theological definition, or where in the nature of things there can be none.

The most important of these in temporal matters to-day is the attitude of the Catholic towards Industrial Capitalism.

There is and can be no doctrinal decision either for or against the morality of Industrial Capitalism. On the other hand, no one will doubt that Catholicism is in spirit opposed to Industrial Capitalism; the Faith would never have produced Huddersfield or Pittsburg. It is demonstrable that historically Industrial Capitalism arose out of the denial of Catholic morals at the Reformation. It has been very well said by one of the principal enemies of the Church, and said boastfully, that Industrial Capitalism is the "robust child" of the Reformation and that the vitality of the effect proves the enduring strength of the cause. It is equally clear that the more Catholic a country is the less easily does it accommodate itself to the social arrangement of a proletariat subjected to millionaire monopolists.

Yet not only is there no doctrine which can be quoted to contradict any one of the necessary parts of Industrial Capitalism, but there are a sufficient number of excellent Catholics who will actively defend it.

No one can say that it stands condemned specifically by Catholic definition, for what is there in Catholic morals to prevent my owning a machine and stores of livelihood? What is there to prevent my offering these stores of livelihood to destitute men on condition they work my machine, and what is there in Catholic morals to forbid my taking a profit upon what they produce, receiving from such production more than I lay out in the sustenance of the labourers? And as for individual Catholics supporting Industrial Capitalism, nine well-to-do Catholics out of ten do so in practice by the way they live and by the way they make their investments, while at least one wealthy Catholic out of ten (I should guess a much larger proportion) is ready to defend Industrial Capitalism and even to grow eloquent about it, rightly contrasting it with the other evils of anarchy or insufficient production, or the menacing tyranny of Communism.

What is even more significant—when, in a nation of Catholic culture such as France or Italy, Industrial Capitalism takes root, then the fiercest revolt against it on the part of the poor does not spring from the more Catholic workmen but from the less Catholic. The masses of a Catholic proletariat—where such masses exist—are upon the whole docile to Industrial Capitalism. They are not in such active revolt against it as their anti-Catholic fellows. Upon the Continent they actually form Trade Unions proud to call themselves Catholic and specially distinguished by their refusal to admit class conflict between employer and employee. Moreover take the modern world at large and you will see that on whatever portions of a Catholic country Industrial Capitalism has laid its hands, the capitalist class and the system which it maintains defends the Catholic Church as a bulwark of its power, and conversely that in those places (Barcelona for instance) the Catholic Church is particularly attacked by those who wish to destroy Industrial Capitalism.

So far, so good. We all admit that in theory there is no precise logical definable conflict between Industrial Capitalism and the Church. In practice we all tolerate, and many of us praise, Industrial Capitalism in its effects, while none of us can join its modern organised enemies, because its modern organised enemies proclaim a doctrine—to wit, the immorality of private property—which is in direct contradiction to Catholic morals.

Now look at the other side of the picture. Not only is Industrial Capitalism as a point of historical fact the product of that spirit which destroyed the Faith in men's hearts and eradicated it from society—where they could—by the most abominable persecutions; but, also in point of historical fact, Industrial Capitalism has arisen late in societies of Catholic culture, has not flourished therein, and, what is more, in proportion as the nation is affected by Catholicism, in that proportion did it come tardily to accept the inroads of Industrial Capitalism and in that proportion does it still ill agree with Industrial Capitalism. That is why the more Catholic districts of Europe have in the past been called "backward"; and that is why there is a fiercer class war in the industrial plague spots of Catholic Europe than in the great towns of Protestant Europe.

In France, one of the main reasons why the anti-Catholic minority, especially the anti-Catholic of the Huguenot type, plays so great a part in the economic control of the country is that he has been the pioneer in introducing the mechanics of Industrial Capitalism. In Spain Industrial Capitalism halts and occasions fierce revolts. It came very late to Italy; it has taken no strong root in Catholic

Ireland; its triumphs have been everywhere the triumphs of the Protestant culture—in Prussianized Germany, in Great Britain, in the United States of America. The Calvinist has fitted in with it admirably and has indeed actively fostered it.

If we go behind the external phenomena and look at the workings of the mind we find the disagreement between Catholicism and Industrial Capitalism vivid and permanent. There is something irreconcilable between the one and the other. There is the point of Usury, which I have dealt with elsewhere, there is the all important point of the Just Price, there is the point of the "*Panis Humanus*,"— man's daily bread, the right possessed by the human being according to Catholic doctrine to live, and to live decently. There is the whole scheme of Catholic morals in the matter of justice, and particularly of justice in negotiation. There is even, if you will consider the matter with an active intelligence, underlying the whole affair the great doctrine of Free Will. For out of the doctrine of Free Will grows the practice of diversity, which is the deadly enemy of mechanical standardisation, wherein Industrial Capitalism finds its best opportunity; and out of the doctrine of Free Will grows the revolt of the human spirit against restraint of will by that which has no moral authority to restrain it; and what moral authority has mere money? Why should I reverence or obey the man who happens to be richer than I am?

And, with that word "authority," one may bring in that other point, the Catholic doctrine of authority. For under Industrial Capitalism the command of men does not depend upon some overt political arrangement, as it did in the feudal times of Catholicism or in the older Imperial times of Catholicism, as it does now in the peasant conditions of Catholicism, but simply upon the ridiculous, bastard, and illegitimate power of mere wealth. For under Industrial Capitalism the power which controls men is the power of arbitrarily depriving them of their livelihood because you have control, through your wealth, of the means of livelihood and they have it not. Under Industrial Capitalism the proletarian tenant can be deprived of the roof over his head at the caprice or for the purely avaricious motives of a so-called master who is not morally a master at all; who is neither a prince, nor a lord, nor a father, nor anything but a credit in the books of his fellow capitalists, the banking monopolists. In no permanent organised Catholic state of society have you ever had citizens thus at the mercy of mere possessors.

Everything about Industrial Capitalism—its ineptitude, its vulgarity, its crying injustice, its dirt, its proclaimed indifference to morals (making the end of man an accumulation of wealth, and of labour itself an inhuman repetition without interest and without savour) is at war with the Catholic spirit.

What, then, are we to make of all this? Here is a conflict of spirits irreconcilable by their very nature. But we cannot engage in this conflict as it is now fought; we cannot take up the weapons ready to hand against Industrial Capitalism, because the weapons against Industrial Capitalism have been forged by men whose minds were of exactly the same heretical or anti-Catholic sort as those who framed Industrial Capitalism itself. What is called vaguely "Socialism," of which the only logical and complete form worthy of notice in practice is Communism, directly contradicts Catholic morals and is at definable and particular issue with them in a more immediate way than is capitalism. Communism involves a direct and open denial of free will; and that it has immediate fruits violently in opposition to the fruits of Catholicism there can be no doubt. To put it more plainly, a Catholic supporting Communism is committing a mortal sin.

Further, to promote conflict between citizens, to engage in a class war with the destruction of capitalism *as the main end* is also directly in contradiction with Catholic morals. We may make war in defence of the Faith; we may make war against a direct denial of definable justice in a particular instance; but we may not say to the poor: "You have a right to fight the rich merely because they are rich and in order to make yourselves less poor." We may say: "You have a right to fight to prevent the conditions of your life becoming inhuman," but we may not say "you have a right to fight merely because you desire to have more and your opponent to have less." It has been wittily and truly said that there has been only one Christian Socialist in history, and that even he did not try to be Christian and Socialist at the same time—the said individual being the penitent thief. He had the good fortune to be, while he was yet alive, promised Paradise by God Himself—but that was only after he had given up his Socialism. A very striking piece of recantation.

Nevertheless, Catholics are for ever in our time—or at least the more intelligent of them—seeking a way out. They are like men who find themselves in prison, who are forbidden by their very nature to break through the walls of that prison, but who grope for an exit of some kind, who are sure that somewhere they can find a door. Over and over again through the nineteenth and early twentieth centuries there have been Catholic efforts of this kind to escape from the injustice and degradations of Industrial Capitalism. Hitherto they have led to nothing.

One of the most remarkable was that propounded in some detail by Mr. Arthur Hungerford Pollen in a paper he read to the Wiseman society a few years ago. He put forth a detailed scheme which, as it is his and not mine, I will not here recapitulate, but of which the gist was the recognition of two things necessary to the reformation of our industrial society: (1) the sharing of the profits by the worker, and (2) the achievement of security by him; the stabilisation of his economic position under such profit sharing. And the same authority has put forward privately in my hearing a very interesting form of this scheme under a particular name—"The Carpenter's Shop." All those who are making such attempts naturally rally round the "*Rerum Novarum*" of the great Pope Leo XIII, a document of great force to which our posterity will return and which was itself the product of the most eminent of Catholic minds and the chief authority of the Church approaching the problem.

In my judgment (and as this book is no more than a book of personal essays I may be excused for putting forth a personal judgment), the essential of the effort must lie in our recognition of the true order of cause and effect. If we are to attack Industrial Capitalism we must do so because we are keeping in mind very clearly and continually the truth that religion is the formative element in any human society. Just as Industrial Capitalism came out of the Protestant ethic, so the remedy for it must come out of the Catholic ethic. *In other words, we must make the world Catholic before we can correct it from the evils into which the denial of Catholicism has thrown it.*

Consider what happened to the institution of slavery. The Church, when it began on earth its militant career, found slavery in possession. The antique world was a servile state; the civilized man of the Graeco-Roman civilization based his society upon slavery; so did (this must always be insisted upon because our text-books always forget it) the barbarian world outside.

There were plenty of revolts against that state of affairs; there was to our knowledge one huge servile war, and there was protest of every kind by the philosophers and by individuals. But they had no success. Success in this field, though it came very slowly, was due to the conversion of the Roman Empire to Catholicism.

The Church did not denounce slavery, it accepted that institution. Slaves were told to obey their masters. It was one of their social duties, as it was the duty of the master to observe Christian charity towards his slave. It was part of good works (but of a rather heroic kind) to give freedom in bulk to one's slaves. But it was not an obligation. Slavery only disappeared after a process of centuries, and it only disappeared through the gradual working of the Catholic doctrine upon the European mind and through the incompatibility of that doctrine with such treatment of one's fellow men as was necessary if the discipline of servitude were to remain efficient. The slave of Pagan times was slowly transformed into the free peasant, but he was not declared free by any definite doctrine of the Church, nor at any one stage in the process would it have entered into the Catholic mind of the day to have said that slavery was in itself immoral. The freedom of the peasant developed as the beauty of external art developed in its Christian form, through the indirect working of the Catholic ethic.

In the absence, the gradual decline (where it is declining) of the Catholic ethic, slavery is coming back. Anyone with eyes to see can watch it coming back slowly but certainly—like a tide. Slowly but certainly the proletarian, by every political reform which secures his well-being under new rules of insurance, of State control in education, of State medicine and the rest, is developing into the slave, leaving the rich man apart and free. All industrial civilization is clearly moving towards the re-establishment of the Servile State, a matter I have discussed at greater length under the title of "the new Paganism."

To produce the opposite of the Servile State out of the modern inhuman economic arrangement, the Church, acting as a solvent, is the necessary and the only force available. The conversion of society cannot be a rapid process, and therefore not a revolutionary one. It is therefore also, for the moment, an unsatisfactory process. But it is the right process. There is a very neat phrase which expresses the whole affair, "in better words than any poor words of mine," as the parson said in the story. These words are to be found in the vernacular translation of the New Testament. They are familiar to many of us. "Seek ye first the kingdom of God and its justice and all the rest shall be added unto you."

Begin by swinging society round into the Catholic course, and you will transmute Industrial Capitalism into something other, wherein free men can live, and a reasonable measure of joy will return to the unhappy race of men. But you must begin at the beginning.

The New Sin

RONALD A. KNOX, S. J.

The first advertisement didn't attract much attention. It was quite unclassified, and the advertisement editors, after a single glance, immediately put it down under Theatre Engagements. It ran simply, "Look out for the New Sin: Professor Laileb's remarkable discovery: Satisfaction Guaranteed." Naturally, the public merely supposed it to be the title of a new *revue,* and—already somewhat jaded—awaited the appearance of Press notices. But the next was far more formidable, appearing in the most expensive pages of the daily Press, and in very large letters all over the underground stations: "Professor Laileb's Great Discovery. On Tuesday, September 27 (the date was about a month and a half ahead), Professor Laileb will lecture in the Albert Hall at 3 P.M. on The New Sin, recently discovered by him and now for the first time brought to the notice of the public. All seats free." The mention of free seats and the Albert Hall made it clear that the Professor had money behind him, and was a person to be reckoned with; he was also a generous advertiser, and the leading daily papers lost no time in fishing out all they could in the way of information and writing him up as a Silly Season column. The public, though gravely afraid (from the use of the word "lecture") that this particular form of transgression must be a System, needing

"The New Sin," from *Essays in Satire,* by Ronald A. Knox (London: Sheed & Ward, 1928). Reprinted by permission of the Literary Executor and Messrs. Sheed & Ward, Ltd.

(like the Physical Development and Memory-training Systems) stern months of self-discipline for its acquisition, nevertheless pricked up its ears, and was ready to know all about Professor Laileb that there was to be known.

There was singularly little. He was staying at the Langham, which found its gates uncomfortably thronged with enquirers, and its staff being replaced at an alarming rate by enterprising journalists in disguise. On the rare occasions when the Professor went out, he was attended by a horde of photographers, and their results figured boldly in the illustrated papers under a variety of titles, of which "Thinking out Another" and "Professor Laileb at it again" were among the least sportive. But actual information of any interesting kind was hopelessly wanting. Professor Laileb kept regular hours, drank only in moderation, indulged in no mysterious occupations, seemed to partake no more and no less than his neighbors in the more hackneyed imperfections of human nature. Of his origin, nothing was known, nothing revealed to interviewers. The British public, always impressed by a foreign name in matters of learning, and always ready to take the title of "Professor" on trust, without examining the details of graduation, was prepared to accept him at his own estimate. So was the Press, unless we accept the *New Witness,* which was immediately in a position to give the name of the actual street in Vienna where he was born, and the actual synagogue which gave its cast to his early theological training.

On the subject of the Sin itself, the Professor was pardonably reticent. No, it was not a mere by-form or adaptation of any existing sin; it was not a matter of circumstances or of method that constituted its novelty. It was, he proudly said, as if someone had added a new colour to the rainbow. It reacted properly on all the usual tests of a sin; it was harmful to society in the long run, it gave a pleasing twinge of regret to the conscience, it definitely lowered the general moral level of its votaries. It was a purely original discovery, not a lost art unearthed from the Renaissance or any other forgotten period. And so Professor Laileb would bow the interviewer out, as mystified as ever, not failing to assure him of the high respect he entertained for the Press as an institution, and the deep conviction he had of its supreme mission as an educative influence.

But where interest is sufficiently aroused, lack of precise knowledge makes an agreeable stimulant to speculation. Thus the *Daily*

Mail, after its inevitable articles on "Sins of the Century" and "The World's Great Sinners," left the discussion to its readers, who fell upon it eagerly from a variety of standpoints. "A Britisher" wrote from Walthamstow demanding that, in the interests of our all-round supremacy, the secret should not be allowed to travel outside these islands. A certain Mr. Borthwick Stapleton, writing from Newport Pagnell, engineered a crusade against it, which only lasted three numbers. "An Anxious Mother" tried to organize a fund for inducing Professor Laileb to keep his mouth shut. "A Sinner of Forty Years' Standing" pooh-poohed the whole story, and argued that the sin was perfectly familiar to himself, and as old as the Fall. Challenged, he professed himself disinclined to furnish any particulars. Next day, however, the Vicar of Much Boosting was almost certain that its nature had been disclosed to his grandfather by Lord Chesterfield. (This led to some rather irrelevant side-controversies on Memory, Longevity, and British Sea Power.) Somebody dreamt that he had discovered the secret, but forgotten it, and there was a full tide of letters on Occultism and Thought-transference. There were proposed Memorials to the Government in favour of the sin and against it, attacks on Professor Laileb, followed by hasty retractations, and several Deans earned a reputation for broad-mindedness by appealing to the public not to condemn him unheard.

.   .   .   .   .

Meanwhile the public naturally talked of nothing else. Statisticians reported that more bets had been laid on this than on any other event within living memory; the Stock Exchange, in particular, had a most popular sweepstake as to which precept in the Decalogue would prove to be most nearly infringed. Numerous enthusiasts insured themselves at Lloyds' against any possible form of disappointment on September 27th. The theatres languished, even in the provinces; the managers complained that the public was all out for novelty, and nothing they could do would satisfy it. Even the pictures were unfrequented, since the Professor had sold his film rights to a forthcoming enterprise of his own which described itself as the New Cinema. Money was tight, for he had dropped a hint about floating, in October, a New Syndicate. Parliament congratulated itself heartily on the recess, but a by-election in a Northern constituency looked as if it might be fought on this sole issue. Both candidates tried to hedge by saying that it was not a party question, and neither side of the House had (ha!) a monopoly of these things; but before long both found themselves pledged to expel Professor Laileb from the country, to secure him a peerage, to take the chair at his meeting, to get his meeting stopped, to suppress his discovery, to promote it in every possible way, and to make sure that it was immediately taken over by the Nation. The election was finally decided in favour of a candidate who had once unsuccessfully defended in court a pawn-broker of the name of Laibach.

Ecclesiastical circles viewed the whole affair not, of course, with a personal, but with a thoroughly professional interest. The *Church Times,* with its keen eye for the latest development, led the way. It even seems to have hesitated for a moment as to the propriety of reproducing the great advertisement, but compromised in the end by printing it, and coming out in the same issue with a pulverizing leader, calculated to extirpate Professor Laileb's sin, whatever it should prove to be. It warned churchpeople against attending the Albert Hall meeting, which could not possibly do good, and might very well do harm. The Professor's doctrines were, it appeared, the logical outcome of Archbishop Cranmer's. It would do good if Dedication Festival services, occurring about that time, were specially well attended as a sort of protest. Accepting a current rumour that the Professor was a Serbian by origin, it conjectured that he had been expelled from his own country as a heresiarch, and deplored the anomalous state of things which made it impossible for Convocation to follow the example of the Serbian authorities. The clergy of the corresponding school, in their parish magazines, put down all the trouble to the weak and ineffective attitude of the Bishops; why could not the Bishops, at the eleventh hour, put themselves at the head of a great movement? But Bishops do not read parish magazines, and (to do them justice) were mostly enjoying a well-deserved holiday.

.   .   .   .   .

The Catholic theologians were a good deal exercised over the theoretical aspect of the question. The Dominicans maintained that, if the course of action recommended by Professor Laileb was contrary to any existing precept, divine or ecclesiastical, it was not new; if it was not, it could not properly be called a sin. "The New Sin" was therefore a contradiction in terms. But a school of moral theologians, who perhaps looked forward to new appendices and new cases of conscience, dissented from the verdict; if the sin was all its inventor said it was, there must clearly be something in it contrary to the natural law, and consequently no direct precept on the subject was necessary. Finally, it was generally agreed that the new sin was in all probability only new *quoad nos,* and only a sin *secundum quid.* But the controversy only agitated the pundits; the Catholic public in general was not going to excite itself over a single addition to the numerous existing forms of Satanism. . . .

Early in the morning of Monday, September 26th, there was a fair-sized *queue* outside the Albert Hall. The police moved it on; it reassembled. By the middle of the afternoon there was a picket of horse-policemen, who kept order with difficulty. There was a thin drizzle during the night, but thousands under umbrellas held their own against it. From the dawning hours of Tuesday, traffic was out of the question. The Park Gates had to be closed at several places. All down Knightsbridge you could not see an inch of the pavement. The Langham cut off its telephone communication: it could not cope with the inquiries. The day was fine, but, as it wore on, a threatening bank of cloud rose from the West; the air was electric and over-charged. An aeroplane appeared from nowhere in particular, and gently moulted Anti-New-Sin Society pamphlets. . . .

For my accounts of the proceedings inside the Hall I depend, alas, on hearsay. The doors opened at one o'clock, and the building filled up like a lock in flood-time. There was a band which played ragtime airs, that seemed strangely old-fashioned and pathetic; the meeting was dissatisfied with the effect, and various irrelevant demonstrations rose from different parts of the building, "The Red Flag" mingling inharmoniously with "Round the sacred city gather." Two or three times attendants appeared on the platform, and were applauded by mistake. The cloud-bank mounted higher outside, and the sunlight paled and grew ominous.

Professor Laileb, whom no one has ever accused of disregarding the conventions, was punctual to the minute. He was short, fashionably dressed, slightly grizzled: a suspicion of side-whiskers made him seem vaguely old-fashioned; you would have put him down for a professional man rather than a research student. He looked straight in front of him, as if he took in the whole of that vast audience. His chairman, a most insignificant M.P., intoned the prescribed ritual of oratorical patter—would not keep them long—thought they all knew why they had come there—no introduction necessary—he himself as eager as anyone else to get on to business—he believed in every man having a fair hearing, without committing himself beforehand to all the Professor might have to say—there, he would not detain them any longer.

The shadow of the cloud crept over the last of the windows, and Professor Laileb stood up. There was applause, but it was almost drowned in impatient Hushes.

"The pioneers of any movement," began the Professor, "are proverbially liable to detraction. Habit, lack of initiative, the love of the rut—these factors, so powerful in deterring the individual from stepping outside the beaten path, reflect themselves, in the case of the mob, in a singular reluctance to see another set foot on the mountain-track which we have declared unsafe for our own passage. The dead-weights which clog all independent human action are the material we use for stoning the prophets. I was not unaware, when I began to institute researches into a branch of science hitherto comparatively undeveloped, that I was exposing myself in so doing to the opprobrium of small minds. I am not without experience of the fate that awaits the innovator. Indeed"—a smile of singular melancholy passed over the Professor's features as he said this—"years ago I lost a very good position myself, simply through my dislike of always following with the herd.

"For longer time now than I care to remember, I have been strongly impressed with the absence of any scientific inquiry into a subject which interests us all so deeply and concerns us all so nearly as that of sin. Picture it to yourselves: the pursuit to which we devote more than half our lives, for which we are ready to postpone so many opportunities of leisure and contentment, so much of our tranquillity of mind; the factor which has so profoundly affected every development of human history; the ideal which has been the sole inspiration of so much that is most remarkable in the recent literature of Europe—this pursuit, this factor, this ideal, still neglected everywhere as a subject of organized research. Philosophers have filled libraries with their inquiries into the study of ethics—the problem of how to act rightly; they have never dared to look facts in the face, and, recognizing the hopelessness of a struggle against human progress, resigned themselves to the problem of how we are to act in a manner more accurately, more fully, more deliberately wrong.

"I will not weary you, for the present at any rate, with the history of my early struggles. Suffice it to say that I found myself, after years of endeavour, in a position to add substantially to the opportunities of mankind for developing this most characteristic side of its nature. It will be asked why I determined to choose England, to choose London, to choose this particular building and these particular circumstances, for the disclosure of my results. My reason was simple. I knew that for purposes of publicity London is the world's best centre, and that the thing which impresses it most is a meeting of a half-scientific, half-political character such as the present. As I stand here, I feel that I am speaking through a megaphone to the civilized world.

"I was determined to give the fruits of my study to humanity. If, in all these years, no one had hit upon my discovery by accident, it might well be that the secret, unless I revealed it, would remain for ever unguessed. It did, of course, occur to me to wonder whether my fellow-creatures were worthy of the revelation; but the doubt did not seriously give me pause. In the case of a boy's education, or in the testing of a confidential servant, we begin by entrusting the neophyte with business of little importance, and advance him further in proportion as he has shown faithfulness and aptitude already. Gentlemen, it seemed to me that the human race, to judge by the use it made of its existing opportunities for wrongdoing, had shown itself full worthy of initiation into a higher degree. Every day I have spent in London, every observation I have made during my brief stay in your city, has fortified me in my opinion and encouraged me to carry out my decision. I studied your legal institutions, your business methods, your ambitions, your pleasures, and said to myself that London would look back on all this as an age of innocence before I had done with it. My share in the transformation might be forgotten, history might be silent about me, but generation upon generation of your descendants would live by my precept, perhaps hardly even paying me the compliment of remembering that it was wrong.

"And now, let us get to business." The Professor's voice, which had hitherto been of a silvery quality, admirable for its rhetorical value, rang out sharply and crisply at these words like the crack of a whip. At the same time he looked round, hostess-like, at his four supporters on the platform, and these, as by some previous arrangement, retired by a side door, leaving the Professor face to face with his audience, alone on the platform. The light in the Hall was now still more ominously pallid, and there was an occasional roll of distant thunder; everybody in the audience felt, I am told, an extraordinary sense of close contact with the distinguished forceful figure that now loomed solitary in front of them.

"As I said," continued the Professor, "I had determined to make known my discovery to the world. I had reckoned on opposition; for reasons which I need not go into, I had nothing to fear from that. I had reckoned, I must say, on incredulity; I was gratified to find that, on this head, I had done the British public an injustice. In a word, until the moment when I came on to this platform, I thought that I had counted the cost, and was prepared to go through with it.

"It was only when I looked round on my audience that I realized something was wrong. Gentlemen, I regret to say that you are not the stuff sinners (I use the term in its higher sense) are made of. You did not come here because you wanted to do something naughty: you came here because you wanted to know about something naughty, to get wind of it and be able to talk intelligently about it before other people could, to make sure that it should be your wives who explained it to your neighbours' wives, and not the other way about. You would flatter yourselves with being men of the world, with no nonsense about you, broad-minded enough to understand the attitude of people who did not see eye to eye with you. You were not vicious, as I had hoped, you were just monumentally inquisitive. And there is about your inquisitiveness a quality—something I do not find it easy to define in terms—a quality which is simply revolting to me. Curiosity is the easiest of all sins to punish, for it carries with it its own worst punishment when it is ungratified. Gentlemen, the New Sin is not a mere fraud; I could explain it to you in half a dozen sentences. But I am not going to tell you about it. I shall go back to the place I came from, and leave you to go to hell as best you may with the assistance of those dreary, hackneyed sins whose familiarity almost sickens you of them. Gentlemen, good night."

The wave of a single impulse moved over the vast audience, and swept them onwards, as if they had been drilling for it for weeks, towards the platform. They did not want any New Sin now; they just wanted the old, conventional sin of murder. And then the storm broke, and the hall was suddenly illuminated by a brilliant lightning flash, which showed each man the face of his neighbour, drawn with insatiable hatred. And with the flash, Professor Laileb suddenly disappeared from the platform, and all inquiries (conducted, you may be sure, with the utmost thoroughness and good-will) failed to reveal any clue to his existence.

You blame the public, reader, as the Professor did, for its inquisitiveness? Truly, curiosity is the most odious of vices. But, confess now, when you began to read this history yourself, had you not a faint hope that, before reaching the end of it, you would find out what the New Sin really was?

FIVE

Essays Informal and Critical

Reminiscences of a Fine Gentleman
LOUISE IMOGEN GUINEY

My friend was of illustrious ancestry. While so many trace their lifestream to pirates or usurpers who shed their brothers' blood to possess their brothers' power, it is a distinction worth recording, that this Fine Gentleman was descended from a princely person in Switzerland who saved some sixty lives, and whose ancient portrait is loaded like a French marshal's, with the ribbons and medals of recognition. Though of foreign origin, he did an American thing at my introduction to him: he shook hands. I dropped the white pebble of the Cretans to mark the day he arrived. It is needless to say I loved and understood him, blond, aggressive, wilful, from the first. He had then, despite his extreme youth, the air of a fighting aristocrat, a taking swashbuckler attitude, as he stood at the open door: the look of one who has character, and a defined part to play, and whose career can never reach a common nor ignoble end. Comely in the full sense he was not; but impressive he was, despite the precocious leanness and alertness which come of too rapid growth.

He had every opportunity, during his babyhood and later, of gratifying his abnormal love of travel; he managed to see more of city life than was good for him, thanks to many impish subterfuges. His golden curiosity covered everything mundane, and he continued his private studies in topography until he was kidnapped, and restored by the police: an abject, shamefaced little tourist, heavy with conscience, irresponsive to any welcomes, who sidled into his abandoned residence, and forswore from that day his unholy peregrinations. But

"Reminiscences of a Fine Gentleman," from *Patrins*, by Louise Imogen Guiney (Boston: Copeland & Day, 1897).

he had a roaming housemate, and grew to be supremely happy, journeying under guidance.

His temper, at the beginning, was none of the best, and took hard to the idea of moral governance; he overcame obstacles after the fashion of a catapult. His sense of humor was always grim: he had a smile, wide and significant, like a kobold's; but a mere snicker, or a wink, was foreign to his nature. With certain people he was sheer clown; yet he discriminated, and never wore his habitual air of swaggering consequence before any save those he was pleased to consider his inferiors. The sagacious and protective instincts were strong in him. For children he had the most marked indulgence and affection, an inexhaustible gentleness, as if he found the only state-craft he could respect among them. For their delight he made himself into a horse, and rode many a screaming elf astride of his back for a half-mile through the meadow, before coming to the heart of the business, which was to sit or kneel suddenly, and cast poor Mazeppa yards away in the wet grass: a proceeding hailed with shouts of acclaim from the accompanying crowd of play-fellows. And again, in winter, he became an otter, and placing himself upon his worthy back at the summit of a hill, rolled repeatedly to the bottom, drenched in snow, and buried under a coasting avalanche of boys.

He never found time, in so short a life, to love many. Outside his own household and his charming cat, he was very loyal to one lady whose conversation was pleasingly ironical, and to one gentleman whose character was said to resemble his own. Several others were acceptable, but for these two visitors he had the voice and gesture of joyful greeting. He had so arrant an individuality that folk loved or hated him. One could not look with indifference on that assertive splendid bearing, or on the mighty muscles as of a Norse ship. A civil address from you made him your liegeman. But the merest dis-regard or slight, no less than open hostility, sealed him your foe. And there were no stages of vacillation. A grudge stood a grudge, and a fondness a fondness. He was a famous retaliator; none ever knew him to ride first into the lists. Battle he loved, but he had a gentlemanly dislike of "scenes": when a crisis came, he preferred to box or wrestle; and what he preferred he could do, for no opponent ever left a scar upon him. A rival less in size, or impudent solely, he took by the nape of the neck and tossed over the nearest fence, resuming his walk with composure. Training and education helped him to the pacific solving of many problems. His good dispositions, all but established, were once badly shaken by a country sojourn; for he had been taught there a bit of cabalistic boys' Latin whose slightest whisper would send him tiptoeing to every window in the house, scanning the horizon for a likely enemy, with a rapture worthy of another cause.

He was rich in enemies, most of them of the gentler sex. Upon a civic holiday, three villageous women were seen to bear down upon him, as he was calmly inspecting the outposts of their property, laden with weapons (*timor arma ministrat!*) no less classic than a pail, a broom, and an axe. Not Swift's self could have added to the look of withering comment with which he turned and confronted his assailants: a single glance which dispersed the troops, and held in itself the eloquence of an Aristophaneian comedy. Eternal warfare lay between him and the man who had peevishly flapped that haughty nose with a glove, before his first birthday-anniversary, and revenge boiled in his eye, long after, at sight of a citizen who had once addressed to him a word unheard in good society. A loud tone, a practical joke, a teasing reminder of a bygone fault, disconcerted him wholly. Sensitive and conservative of mood, my Fine Gentleman could never forget a rudeness, nor account satisfactorily for such a thing as a condescension. All his culture and his thinking had not taught him to allow for the divers conditions and dispositions of mankind. To the last he looked for courtesy, for intelligence, and, alas, for fashionable clothes, in his ideal. For the Fine Gentleman was a snob. Hunger and nakedness, even honest labor, had for him no occult charm. Throughout his youth, he courted patrician acquaintances, and on the very highway ached to make worse rags yet of the floating rags of a beggar's coat; but the experience of friendship with a kindly butcher-lad made inroads upon his exclusiveness; and I know that, had he outlived his years, there would have been one more convert democrat. His own personal appearance was of the nicest; by scrupulous superintendence of his laundry, chiefly by night, he kept himself immaculate and imposing. His colors were those of the fallen leaves and the snow; the November auburn falling away on either side from the magnificent brow and eyes, and from the neck in its triple white fold: a head to remind you of Raleigh in his ruff.

He must have been patriotic, for he revelled in the horns, gunpowder, rockets, and smoke of the Fourth of July. Archery and rifle-practice seemed to strike him as uncommonly pleasant devices to kill time. In all games which had noise and motion, he took the same strong vicarious interest. He had heard much music, and learned something of it; he was once known to hum over an august recitative of the late Herr Wagner. Singular to relate, he had an insuperable objection to books, and protested often against the continued use of the pen by one he would fain esteem. Yet he seemed greatly to relish the recital of a tribute of personal verse from a United States Senator, and the still more elaborate lines of a delightful professional satirist.

His health, aside from his great size, his spirit and nervous vigor, was never steady nor sound. Every chapter of the Fine Gentleman's biography is crammed with events, perils, excitements, catastrophes, and blunders, due in great part, by a scientific verdict, to this tremendous vitality balancing on too narrow a base. With years, there began to come the "philosophic mind." His sweetness and submission grew with his strength; never was there a sinner so tender of conscience, so affected by remonstrance, so fruitful, after, in the good works of amended ways. New virtues seemed to shoot on all sides, and the old ones abided and flourished. He had never tried to deceive, nor to shirk, nor to rebel, nor to take what was not his, nor to appear other than he was. In the country town where he had many a frolic, and where he lies buried, he found congenial circumstances. There were no gardens there, no timid neighbors; he had opportunity, being allowed to inspect everything that stirred in air, or upon the earth, or in the waters under, for the pursuit of natural history, which was his passion; he ate what he pleased, he lorded it as he liked, he shifted his responsibilities, he won endless flattery from the inhabitants. His frank acknowledgment of all this was unique. On his return, while his escort was still in the room, the Fine Gentleman was asked whether he would rather remain now at home, or spend a week longer in the fascinating precincts of Cambrook. He arose briskly, bestowed on the questioner, whom he professed to adore, his warmest embrace (a thing unusual with him), and immediately, pulling his escort by the sleeve, placed himself at the door-knob which led into the more immoral world. His last accomplishment was to acquire an accurate sense of time, to make his quarter-hour calls, his half-hour walks, when sent out alone: "as wise as a Christian," an honest acquaintance was wont to say of him, perhaps on the suspicion that the Fine Gentleman, after he reached his majority, was a free-thinker.

He was in his perfect prime when a slight seeming disgrace fell upon him, though an incident never clearly understood. His believers believed in him still; but, for the need of quiet and impartial adjustment of matters, persuaded him to stay an indefinite while in the beloved farming district where many of his earlier vacations were spent. So that, after all his tender rearing, he was at last abroad and divorced: with a mist, such as we recognized immortals call sin, upon his spirit, and, because of that, a scruple and a doubt upon mine, answerable for much of what he was. Before the eventual proof came that he was clear of blame, there were thoughts even of an imperative parting, and a reaching for the rectification towards the Happy Hunting-Grounds, where, at an era's end, we could be joyous together; and where under the old guiding then never unskilful, the old sympathy then never erring, the Fine Gentleman could be to his virtue's full, and in no misapprehending air, his innocent, upright, loving self again. But instantly, as if to wipe out forever that possible evil of which men could dream him guilty, came the moving and memorable end. Amid the tears of a whole town, and the thanksgiving of some for a greater grief averted, very quietly and consciously, under the most painful conditions, the Fine Gentleman laid down his life for a little child's sake. The fifth act of his tragedy had a sort of drastic consistency, to those who knew him; it was in line with his odd, inborn, unconventional ways: the fate one would have chosen for him, and the fittest with which to associate his soldierly memory. In exile and cashiered, he had overturned his defamers at a stroke.

It is not too proud a sentence to write over him, that this world, for the most part, was jealous of his nobility. Human society was some sort of huge jest to him; he did not always do his best there, as if the second-best were the shrewder policy, and the neater adaptation to the codes of honor he found established. His main concern was certainly the study of mankind, and he stood to it, a free and unbookish philosopher, looking on and not partaking, with his reticent tongue, his singularly soft foot-fall, his "eye like a wild Indian's, but cordial and full of smothered glee." To his own race he must be an epic figure and a precedent, and to ours something not undeserving of applause.

> "Go seek that hapless tomb, which if ye hap to find,
> Salute the stones that keep the bones that held so good
> a mind."

Such are the only annals of the Fine Gentleman, a Saint Bernard dog, faithful and forgotten, who bore a great Bostonian's name nearly five years without a stain, and who is, to one or two of us, not alone a friend lost, but an ideal set up: Perseus become a star.

Review of Eugene O'Neill's
"Strange Interlude"
R. DANA SKINNER

Two years ago Eugene O'Neill startled us somewhat by reverting to the use of masks in his play *The Great God Brown*. Of course he did not go back to any known tradition in the use of masks, and adopted the interesting if somewhat confusing method of having the masks follow the outlines of the actors' faces. Moreover the masks were used only on occasions to indicate the difference between one's outward attitude toward the world and reality and one's inner state of mind. In his latest play, *Strange Interlude*, O'Neill has startled us in somewhat similar fashion by reverting to the use of the aside. His stage characters enjoy the privilege of a double dialogue, part of it expressing the thoughts they are willing to show to the world, and part of it expressing only their innermost feelings. This is a technical novelty which, in the opinion of many of the critics, adds enormously to the scope of the drama, giving to the play the benefit, generally reserved only to novels, of describing motives as well as speech and action. On the other hand there are many who believe that really skilful playwrighting and acting enable an audience to grasp inner motives quite as clearly as when they are enunciated after this O'Neill method.

This much is certain, that Mr. O'Neill has managed to contrive a dramatic story of absorbing interest, and that he has no difficulty in holding the attention of the audience for five hours, and across the

Review of Eugene O'Neill's *Strange Interlude*, by R. Dana Skinner, reprinted from *The Commonweal*, February 22, 1928, by permission of The Commonweal Publishing Co.

stretch of a dinner intermission, as against the two and one-half hours permitted to the average playwright. In spite of this, I am not convinced that he has achieved, in the full sense, a great play. *Strange Interlude* probes deeply and terribly into the recesses of a neurotic mind, as summed up in the character of Nina Leeds. It probes also into many other types of mind, and as a work of intuitive psychology, it is undoubtedly a monumental achievement. But to regard it as a great play, stated in the terms of the theatre, is somewhat like regarding a piece of statuary as a great piece of sculpture because the brush of a painter had added to it the color of life. Such a statue might be a great work of art, in the sense that it combines the finest qualities of two of the arts, but it might be neither a great statue nor a great painting.

We admit this distinction readily enough in the case of opera. Richard Wagner attempted to fuse the arts of the drama and of music and, being unwilling to have his works spoken of as opera, solved the problem simply by calling them "music dramas." Under this name we are often willing to call them great works of art, with a general inclination to admit that the music is greater than the dramas themselves. But we do not say, for example, that Parsifal is a great play, although its interest and its emotional intensity are vastly heightened by the musical score. For this reason I think it is a great mistake and a distinct injustice to other dramatists to speak of Mr. O'Neill's combination of two separate arts as a great play—to call it possibly the greatest play produced by the American theatre. He has combined the arts of the novelist and the playwright and given us what, for want of a better description, we can only call a dramatic novel. And in this particular example, the element of the novel achieves higher and greater proportions than the element of the play, just as the music of Wagner achieves a greatness lacking in his dramas alone.

Certainly there can be no objection to creating this new form of expression, and when it is handled with the power and ruthless searching of O'Neill's mind, the resultant whole deserves presentation. But although the fusion of the arts can be a fine thing in itself, it is very misleading to assume that the separate arts have ceased to exist, or that henceforth no play can be truly great which does not make use of the art of the novel as well. The bald truth is that Mr. O'Neill has covered a great deal of second-rate playwrighting by some very intensive use of the novelist's privileges. In spite of certain obvious faults, Sidney Howard's *The Silver Cord* is a far finer play than the dramatic elements of *Strange Interlude* considered alone. Yet the final product of O'Neill's pen, provided you do not think of it solely as a play, is vastly more absorbing and exciting than anything Sidney Howard has written.

What O'Neill has really done is to take a rather morbid story of mediocre people and give it an almost universal importance by a careful side exposition of the motives, conscious and unconscious, that are guiding his characters. These asides are vastly more interesting than anything in the dialogue proper of the play. They touch upon experiences common to nearly all mankind. It is as if O'Neill were applying a sort of X-ray to the souls of his characters. To do this it is necessary for the characters, every few moments, to remain absolutely stationary and, in a tone quite different from the ordinary dialogue, speak out the truth which they are concealing from each other. A good actor would probably tell you that at least half of these concealed emotions could be expressed through gesture, or manner, or through the hundred and one tricks known to the artist. An actor might even make the suggestion that the play, with a little skilful rewriting of the main dialogue, could convey in conventional form everything which Mr. O'Neill has now placed in the asides. This, however, is rather unfair to Mr. O'Neill's intention and also to what he has actually accomplished. For in many of the asides Mr. O'Neill has made the characters reveal certain hidden depths of which they themselves are probably almost unconscious.

The human mind seems to work on at least three main levels— the thoughts it shares with the world in speech or writing, the private thoughts it reserves, and the deeper sources of action or feeling which it often strives to keep from its own consciousness because of the cruelty or the selfishness of the pride which they seem to reveal. The old-fashioned aside merely gave the audience the advantage of touching the second level. Mr. O'Neill's asides dive to the depths of the third level, the repressed thoughts, the unworthy emotions, the egotism, the pride or the possessiveness that so often stimulate us to apparently unaccountable action. It is this revelation of the semiconscious or sub-conscious which constitutes Mr. O'Neill's unique achievement, and which will undoubtedly stand to many for the greatness of his play, whereas in fact it stands only for the keenness of his intuition as an analyst of human emotions and actions.

There is a great deal of Jung and a certain amount of Freud mixed up with the intuitions which are purely those of Mr. O'Neill. His explanation of the curious action of Nina Leeds would not find universal acceptance among all schools of modern psychology. We can imagine a cynical behaviorist remarking to himself, "Interesting if true." Thus when Nina's father dies, Mr. O'Neill assumes that the curious and unimpassioned love which she bestows upon the novelist, Charles Marsden, is a psychological transference of the love previously given to her father. On the other hand, this particular attachment might be explained on the ground that every human being desires at certain times the comfort of a love which does not ask too much in return. Or again, it might be said that Nina is merely exhibiting an automatic reaction from the intensity of her other emotional experiences. And so it is that throughout the play you have a hundred varied explanations for events, through motives which, while intensely interesting to unravel and often approaching universal truths, are so limited by a particular psychological creed as to lose much of their general importance. In some recent popular murder trials we were regaled with interpretations supplied by various schools of psychologists. Each one was interesting in its own way, but they often differed radically in their deductions from known facts. Mr. O'Neill's asides, then, vary greatly in importance according to the particular prejudices of the audience and according to which way you happen to account for the vagaries of human actions under given conditions.

The story of the play itself is comparatively simple. Nina Leeds is engaged to a young aviator who is killed. She might have married him but for the opposition of her father. She then decides to go into hospital nursing and gives her love promiscuously to various crippled soldiers in the belief that she is somehow making reparation to her dead hero. She discovers her mistake and marries Sam Evans, a likely young man with whom she believes she can lead a normal life undisturbed by any great passion. To her horror, however, she discovers there is a history of peristent insanity in the Evans family. Rather than bring another child of this tainted blood into the world, she destroys the life that is already started and, with the idea of satisfying Sam's craving for fatherhood, arranges to have another child by another man named Darrell. Sam, knowing nothing of this, and inspired by his sense of fatherhood, progresses rapidly in material things and becomes a highly successful business man, of rather mediocre mentality. Nina, in the meantime, has fallen in love with Darrell and years of her life thereafter are spent in trying to resolve the conflict between her love for him and her determination to make Sam Evans happy at all costs. The child grows up having a distinctive hatred for his own father and a genuine devotion for Sam Evans, his supposed father. During all of this time Charles Marsden, the novelist, has been always on hand, ready with comfort and unselfish devotion, but quite unable to inspire in Nina any more complete sense of love. In the end, Sam Evans dies from a stroke, Nina and Darrell find that the passion of their youth has gone, and Nina settles down in the sunset of her life in the tranquil companionship of Marsden, her son having left her to marry, in spite of her frantic efforts to hold him.

Nina is thus meant to typify in herself the possessive and absorbing type of woman who draws to herself, and involves in her own neurotic cravings, the lives of all she touches. It is not until the very end of her days that she fully relinquishes the desire to gather to herself every form of male love. The explanation which Mr. O'Neill affords by means of the asides to this curious human entanglement, is the outstanding interest of this obviously unpleasant theme. The Theatre Guild, as usual, has bestowed the utmost skill upon the production of this dramatic novel. Lynn Fontanne, in re-creating the character of Nina, has achieved a height of artistry quite beyond anything now current in the American theatre.

The Lady Anchoress

KATHERINE BRÉGY

It is often difficult, of course, in studying any medieval story, to tell where literature ends and life begins—or where life ends and literature begins. The soap and water of fact get themselves habitually

"The Lady Anchoress," from *From Dante to Jeanne D'Arc*, by Katherine Brégy (Milwaukee: The Bruce Publishing Company, 1933), 77–85, 86–89. Reprinted by permission of the publisher.

transposed into the large and luminous bubble of imagination. Still, there *was* this essence of fact at the root of even the most glamorous and extravagant bubbles. People—all kinds of people, just as Chaucer pictures them—really did go on pilgrimages: did they not, for better or worse, even go on crusades? Knights really fought in tourneys, minstrels carried their treasure of song and story from court to court, and for centuries men and women honestly reaching out after justice believed in the possibility of establishing truth by single combat and even by various kinds of painful ordeals. It seems incredible; yet something of the same belief must underlie the persistent human resort to war—just as something of the old cruel fallacy that human beings speak truth under torture underlies modern police methods.

Probably one can safely take for granted the general background of life in any given romance; it is the details of the story which gallop off incontinently upon the high-road of imagination. For instance, there is the anchoress. Fugitive references to these solitary ladies—as to the hermits of the woods—often stray into the various romances, one of the most piquant occurring at the end of the thirteenth and the beginning of the fourteenth books of Malory's *Morte d'Arthur*. Here Launcelot and Percivale, in one of the detours of the Grail quest, meet Galahad riding through a forest, and not recognizing him, promptly draw him into a combat in which they are both worsted. This jousting happened, we are told, "tofore the hermitage where a recluse dwelled." But she, no doubt drawn to her window by the all-too-familiar sound of fighting, cries out to Galahad: "God be with thee, best knight of the world!"—adding, loud enough for the others to hear: "An yonder two knights had known thee as well as I do they would not have encountered with thee." Thereupon Sir Galahad spurs off "at a great pace" for fear of further recognition; while his harassed father, riding in another direction, comes upon the adventure of the ruined chapel, of the vision of the sick knight healed by a visitation of the Grail—and subsequently to his own confession and shriving by a near-by hermit-priest. But Percivale, determined to know more of the anchoress' clairvoyance, turns back to the recluse's cell and kneeling at the window tells her his name. And the lady, filled with great joy, commands the gates to be opened (Malory does not explain just what gates, but they were probably those of her little garden), while the knight is offered "all the cheer that she might make him"; for as she soon explains to Percivale: "I well ought to know

you, for I am your aunt although I be in a priory place." Then follows
a scene of deliciously domestic intimacy in which the knight, who
confesses that he has recently dreamed much about his mother, is
told of her death. His "fair aunt" comforts him well, and she who was
once Queen of the Waste Lands reveals to him Galahad's unique
vocation and how Merlin once fashioned the Round Table and the
Siege Perilous: adding for herself—"I was called the Queen of most
riches in the world; and it pleased me never my riches so much as
doth my poverty."

As usual, Malory and the earlier romancers from whom he drew
were using as a *décor* or setting the actual conditions of life in the
later *Moyen Age*. Dipping into that delightful and scholarly summary,
Hermits and Anchorites of England, by Rotha Mary Clay, we find that
before the sixteenth-century cleavage English soil was fairly dotted
by recluses' cells. There were many types: solitaries of forest and
glen, light-keepers on the coast, hermits upon bridges, and the more
conservative anchorites of "church and cloister"—among these last
being many women of high birth, particularly widows. Apparently
from the beginning of the world there have been two types of philosopher: those who believe it is "not good for man"—still less for
woman!—"to be alone," and those who insist they are "never less
alone than when alone." The Church's answer to the spiritual indi-
vidualist or solitary was the life of the hermit. And although her
preference was increasingly for the safe and more easily disciplined
group of the religious community, she provided a special office for
the blessing and inclosing of anchorites; who might not enter upon
their life without permission from the bishop—he, in the last resort,
being responsible for their support—and who even then were generally subjected to some sort of probation. There were hundreds of
approved anchorages in England alone—many of them attached to
the side of a church or monastery, like the "priory" of Percivale's
aunt—evidently handed on after the incumbent's death almost as a
title to nobility. Legend linked the name of King Harold with a certain cell at Chester, declaring that after Hastings he had lived there
"holily" and "made a gracious end." And there was a charming story
—which Wordsworth incorporated into one of his sonnets—of how
Katherine, Lady Audley (born in 1272) determined to travel on after
her lord's death until she heard bells ringing without hands. This
rather familiar miracle happened at the church of Ledbury, where,

with her faithful maid Mabel, she remained as an anchoress until death came.

These little anchorages were generally of two rooms—although there were apparently some "duplex apartments" with two rooms on each floor, occasionally surrounded by a tiny garden. There was nearly always one window looking toward the outside, where more worldly Christians dearly loved to stop for advice or "tydings," and the most important one of all looking into the sanctuary of the adjoining church or chapel—through which the recluse might assist at Mass and other devotions, and receive Holy Communion fifteen times a year. No doubt, since we find them occasionally rebuked by their spiritual directors, some of the solitaries inclined toward excessive asceticism; but in the main an atmosphere of remarkable sweetness and sanity seems to have pervaded these anchorites' cells. "Men wit that we are in pain and penance," wrote the great mystic, Richard Rolle of Hampole, to his friend Dame Margaret: "but we have more joy in a day than they have all their life. They see our body, but they see not our heart, where is our solace." From this fourteenth-century message, as from Hilton's *Scale* or *Ladder of Perfection,* or perhaps best of all the thirteenth-century *Ancren Riwle,* it is possible to build up a very illuminating picture of the anchoress' discipline and way of life. It is a noble and serene piece of spiritual instruction, this *Regulae Inclusarum,* generally supposed to have been written by Bishop Poore for three sisters living together as anchoresses at Tarrent in Dorsetshire. They were permitted, we find, to keep no animal but a cat— or if necessary, a cow; and much direction is given concerning that important corollary of the anchoress' life, the serving women who went in and out on needful errands. "It is very necessary for you both that you take much care of them," writes the author of the *Ancren Riwle,* "for ye may be much benefited by them; and on the other hand made worse. If they sin through your negligence ye shall be called to give account of it before the Supreme Judge. Therefore it is very necessary for you, and still more for them, that ye teach them to keep their rule . . . in a gentle manner, however, and affectionately; for such ought the instructing of women to be—affectionate and gentle, and seldom stern."

This Salesian gentleness is indeed the keynote of his work. "Do you now ask what rule you anchoresses should observe?" he continues. "Ye should by all means, with all your might and all your strength, keep well the inward rule, and for its sake the outward. The inward rule is always alike. The outward is various, because everyone ought so to observe the outward rule as that the body may therewith serve the inward. . . . My dear sisters, in like manner as ye guard well your senses externally, so above all things see that ye be gentle within; and mild and meek, affectionate and kind-hearted and patient of any word—if anyone speaks ill of you—or of any deed, if anyone harms you—lest you lose all." Every state of life has, of course, its besetting temptations, and those against which the anchoress is chiefly warned are precisely those we might expect—love of gossip or of idleness, melancholy, and spiritual pride. "Let not anyone of remarkably pious life think that she may not be tempted. The good, who have reached a high degree of virtue, are more tempted than the frail . . . for the greater and higher the hill is, there is the more wind upon it. . . . I firmly believe that neither carnal nor spiritual temptation shall ever master thee if thou art kind-hearted and humble and meek, and lovest so sincerely all men and women, and especially anchoresses, that thou art as sorry for their evil and glad of their good as of thine own." Then Bishop Poore, or whoever it was who wrote these golden words, breaks into a striking metaphor: "If the chalice could speak, which was molten in the fire and made to boil vehemently, and then with much beating and polishing made into so very beautiful a form for the service of God, would it curse the purifying fire and the hands of its artificer? The whole world is God's smithy, in which He forgeth His elect. Wouldst thou that God had no fire in His smithy, nor bellows, nor hammers?" . . . And the volume ends with the naive plea: "As often as ye read anything in this book, greet the Lady with an Ave Mary for him who made this rule, and for him who wrote it and took pains about it. Moderate enough I am, who ask so little."

But what was to be the flower, the fruit, of all this intensive gardening? What, besides good advice, did the anchoress give to the world she had forsaken? It is interesting to remember how the thirteenth-century Belgian recluse, Eve, sheltered in her cell St. Juliana of Liège when the latter was driven from her convent, both sharing and encouraging the efforts by which that valiant Benedictine was largely responsible for introducing—or shall one say, for imploring?—the joyous feast of Corpus Christi into the Church. But possibly the spiritual achievement may best be gauged by its high-water mark in the highly personal work of another Juliana, the *Revelations* of that true and tender mystic known as Blessed Julian of Norwich. We know rather little externally about this remarkable woman except that she occupied an anchorage at the east end of the old Norman church at Norwich, that she was probably of noble birth, and possibly educated at the near-by Benedictine convent of Carrow; where, in spite of the fact that she habitually speaks of herself as "a simple creature, unlettered," she may or may not have taken vows as a Benedictine nun. Clearly she possessed a fine and well-trained mind, capable of drawing delicate distinctions in theology and psychology, along with a heart full of compassion and fellowship toward our faulty world and a soul absorbed in devotion to God and fealty to the Catholic faith. It was during the May of 1373 when she was "thirty years old and a half," and transported by the combination of severe physical illness and spiritual ardor into a psychic state in which she at first thought her soul had really left her body in death, that there were revealed to her fifteen distinct "Shewings" or "Revelations" of God's love. Afterwards, as pain again submerged body and mind, came a reaction of doubt, almost of despair. Then on the following night was granted the Sixteenth Revelation, a confirmation of all the others. And the rest of Lady Julian's life—she was "esteemed one of the greatest holiness" in 1393 and seems to have lived on until 1413—was spent in meditating upon the message of "wisdom and truth and love," and in expounding it for the consolation of her "even-Christians." For this woman, who had separated herself from everyday life, was singularly untouched by Pharisaism. "Because of the Shewing I am not good but if I love God the better," she writes. "For I am certain that there be many that never had Shewing nor Sight but of the common teaching of Holy Church, that love God better than I." And her immediate impulse after that first revelation was to be "greatly stirred in charity to mine even-Christians, that they might see and know the same that I saw: for I would it were comfort to them." Comfort, indeed, it must have been for the fellow-Christians of her own day—and may well be for her fellow-Christians today—to realize vividly the "courtesy," the "marvelous homeliness" of God to man. His tender, brooding care, the "goodness which cometh down to the lowest part of our need," His unfailing Light and Life and Love.

Julian's revelations seem to have had two sides; a concrete *vision* and an abstract *teaching*—similar to the familiar "preludes" and "considerations" still recommended for meditation or mental prayer. The visions represented for the most part some phase of Christ's Passion upon which the anchoress was accustomed to meditate, such as the Crowning with Thorns, the Scourging, the Paling of the Face in Death. She had "Shewing" also of Our Lady, first as "a simple maid and meek, in the stature that she was when she conceived," later in her exalted "truth, her wisdom, her charity"; after which Christ asks: *"Wilt thou see in her how thou art loved? For thy love I made her so high, so noble, so worthy."* Equally comforting and characteristic is this little colloquy following the Passion scenes: *"Art thou well pleased that I suffered for thee?* I said, Yea, good Lord, I thank Thee; yea, good Lord, blessed mayst Thou be. Then said Jesus, our Kind Lord: *If thou art pleased I am pleased; it is a joy, a bliss, and endless satisfying to me that ever suffered I Passion for thee; and if I might suffer more, I would suffer more."* And Julian understands that "the love that made Him to suffer passeth so far all His Passion as Heaven is above Earth." Soon afterward the anchoress finds herself transported from great "sureness" and joy to depths of spiritual desolation and weariness where scarcely she can "have patience to live"—in order that she may realize how "He keepeth us even alike secure in woe and weal." Then, in the exquisite Sixth Revelation, there is sounded a note of consoling beauty not too common even in the most beautiful of spiritual writings. For Julian sees her Lord reigning as it were in His own house, "fulfilling it with joy and mirth," welcoming His "dearworthy friends," and giving to her her own humility the tremendous message: *"I thank thee for thy travail, and especially for thy youth. . . ."*

Dame Julian's teaching about prayer, the Fourteenth Revelation, is of most exalted spirituality—but it will not be of much comfort to those of us who would be too *particular* in our supplications. "This," she declares, "is our Lord's will, that our prayer and our trust be both alike large"; and if after long prayer we have not our asking, she is confident that "either we abide a better time, or more grace, or a better gift." After all, she seems to say, what does it matter? The *greatest deeds*—our Creation, our Redemption, the ordering of Faith and of Nature—are *already* done: we have but to bring ourselves into harmony with God's will to attain His bliss. *"Prayer oneth the soul to God."* She would have us realize that this union is its glory and its chief end. There is the simplicity of genius also in her words upon the mystery of Death. "It is the more blissful that man be taken from pain, than that pain be taken from man," she cries; telling her vision of the prostrate, shapeless body lying upon the earth, from which sprang suddenly "a full fair creature, a little child . . . nimble and lively, whiter than a lily," returning where there shall be "no manner of pain, no manner of misliking, no wanting of will" . . . only God!

It seems curious, but after all it is frightfully human, that after having soared so high Julian should have been temporarily cast down again to the depths, as she herself puts it, of "feebleness, wretchedness and blindness." At the beginning of those fifteen mysterious Revelations, she tells us how all the long pain of her illness was suddenly taken away; at their close it seems to have returned with renewed agony, and for a few hours the weak body so prevailed over the strong spirit that she not only doubted the reality of her visions but was even swept into a nightmare dream (she is careful to tell us the heavenly "Shewings" never came in sleep) of being overcome by the Fiend or Satan himself. Then "our courteous Lord gave me grace to waken . . . and I was brought to great rest and peace, without sickness of body or dread of conscience." During the next night "our Lord opened my spiritual eye and shewed me my soul in midst of my heart"—with God, "clad majestically," sitting as king in this soul. And it was, says the anchoress, a singular joy and bliss that she saw Him sitting rather than standing; "for the secureness of sitting sheweth endless dwelling." As on the first Pentecost the Paraclete came to the Apostles, "teaching them and bringing all things to their remembrance," so now the "good Lord" comforts this devoted woman, assuring her that the former visions were true, explaining their meaning, and promising her the grace of final perseverance. "He said not: *Thou shalt not be tempested, thou shalt not be travailed, thou shalt not be afflicted;* but He said, *Thou shalt not be overcome.* . . . And soon after, all was close and I saw no more. . . ."

There were to be no more visions in Julian's life—and indeed, no more were needed. She had sought and found the "one thing needful," and had but to savor it, to absorb its beauty as one absorbs the beauty of a rose or of a jewel, for her own enrichment and that of her "even-Christians." Also, and in spite of what a sophisticated critic might incline to call sentimentality, this anchoress of Norwich attained rare balance; for if on one hand she perceived God as Father and Mother and Spouse—as Trinity and Unity and "endless fulfilling

of all true desires"—on the other she was never weary of insisting
that "though we be highly lifted up into contemplation," it is none
the less necessary to keep "meek remembrance of our frailties" and
firm hold upon the Church and her Sacraments.

But it is the very nature of a revelation that it shall be *particular*
—coming to a particular soul and teaching a particular lesson. And
even as the stars, one revelation differs from another in glory. For
fifteen years Julian meditated upon the special reason and interpretation of the Shewings once granted to her. Finally she was
answered "in ghostly understanding: *Wouldst thou learn thy Lord's
meaning in this thing? Learn it well: Love was His meaning. Who
shewed it thee? Love. What shewed He thee? Love. Wherefore shewed
it He? For love. Thou shalt never know nor learn therein other thing
without end.*" After all, it was matter enough for one little book, or
one little life!

The anchoress has gone from us, it seems. She has no place in
our modern world and is scarcely remembered in our modern literature. Miss Willa Cather does, indeed, point out the shadow of the
saintly recluse of seventeenth-century Montreal. But there is something a little frigid and formidable in that indomitable young Canadian girl who hid herself away to converse with the angels. The
medieval anchoress did not scorn to talk familiarly through her little
window with the men and women passing by. She seemed less like an
exotic than a fragrant and friendly perennial. And the message she
has handed down for our comfort may well be that simple, universal
sentence of the *Ancren Riwle*—"Nothing is ever so hard that love
doth not make it tender and sweet."

⊱ SIX ⊰

In the Forum of Public Opinion

Catholic and Patriot
GOVERNOR ALFRED E. SMITH

Charles C. Marshall, Esq.
Dear Sir:

In your open letter to me in the April *Atlantic Monthly* you "impute" to American Catholics views which if held by them, would leave open to question the loyalty and devotion to this country and its Constitution of more than twenty million American Catholic citizens. I am grateful to you for defining this issue in the open and for your courteous expression of the satisfaction it will bring to my fellow citizens for me to give "a disclaimer of the convictions" thus imputed. Without mental reservation I can and do make that disclaimer. These convictions are held neither by me nor by any other American Catholic, as far as I know. Before answering the argument of your letter, however, I must dispose of one of its implications. You put your questions to me in connection with my candidacy for the office of President of the United States. My attitude with respect to that candidacy was fully stated in my last inaugural address as Governor when, on January 1, 1927, I said:

"I have no idea what the future has in store for me. Every one else in the United States has some notion about it except myself. No man could stand before this intelligent gathering and say that he was not receptive to the greatest position the world has to give any one. But I can say this, that I will do nothing to achieve it except to give to the people of the State the kind and character of service that will make me deserve it."

"Catholic and Patriot," by Alfred E. Smith. Reprinted by permission from *The Atlantic Monthly*, May, 1927.

I should be a poor American and a poor Catholic alike if I injected religious discussion into a political campaign. Therefore I would ask you to accept this answer from me not as a candidate for any public office but as an American citizen, honored with high elective office, meeting a challenge to his patriotism and his intellectual integrity. Moreover, I call your attention to the fact that I am only a layman. The *Atlantic Monthly* describes you as "an experienced attorney" who "has made himself an authority upon canon law." I am neither a lawyer nor a theologian. What knowledge of law I have was gained in the course of my long experience in the Legislature and as Chief Executive of New York State. I had no such opportunity to study theology.

My first thought was to answer you with just the faith that is in me. But I knew instinctively that your conclusions could be logically proved false. It seemed right, therefore, to take counsel with some one schooled in the Church law, from whom I learned whatever is hereafter set forth in definite answer to the theological questions you raise. I selected one whose patriotism neither you nor any other man will question. He wears upon his breast the Distinguished Service Cross of our country, its Distinguished Service Medal, the Ribbon of the Legion of Honor, and the Croix de Guerre with Palm of the French Republic. He was the Catholic Chaplin of the almost wholly Catholic 165th Regiment in the World War—Father Francis P. Duffy, now in the military service of my own State.

Taking your letter as a whole and reducing it to commonplace English, you imply that there is conflict between religious loyalty to the Catholic faith and patriotic loyalty to the United States. Everything that has actually happened to me during my long public career leads me to know that no such thing as that is true. I have taken an oath of office in this State nineteen times. Each time I swore to defend and maintain the Constitution of the United States. All of this represents a period of public service in elective office almost continuous since 1903. I have never known any conflict between my official duties and my religious belief. No such conflict could exist. Certainly the people of this State recognize no such conflict. They have testified to my devotion to public duty by electing me to the highest office within their gift four times. You yourself do me the honor, in addressing me, to refer to "your fidelity to the morality you have advocated in public and private life and to the religion you have revered; your

great record of public trusts successfully and honestly discharged."
During the years I have discharged these trusts I have been a com-
municant of the Roman Catholic Church. If there were conflict, I, of
all men, could not have escaped it, because I have not been a silent
man, but a battler for social and political reform. These battles would
in their very nature disclose this conflict if there were any.

I regard public education as one of the foremost functions of
government and I have supported to the last degree the State Department of Education in every effort to promote our public-school system. The largest single item of increased appropriations under my
administration appears in the educational group for the support of
common schools. Since 1919, when I first became Governor, this item
has grown from $9,000,000 to $82,500,000. My aim—and I may say
I have succeeded in achieving it—has been legislation for child welfare, the protection of working men, women, and children, the
modernization of the State's institutions for the care of helpless or
unfortunate wards, the preservation of freedom of speech and opinion
against the attack of war-time hysteria, and the complete reorganiza-
tion of the structure of the government of the State.

I did not struggle for these things for any single element, but
in the interest of all of the eleven million people who make up the
State. In all of this work I had the support of churches of all denominations. I probably know as many ecclesiastics of my Church as any
other layman. During my long and active public career I never received from any of them anything except cooperation and encouragement in the full and complete discharge of my duty to the State.
Moreover, I am unable to understand how anything that I was taught
to believe as a Catholic could possibly be in conflict with what is good
citizenship. The essence of my faith is built upon the Commandments
of God. The law of the land is built upon the Commandments of God.
There can be no conflict between them.

Instead of quarreling among ourselves over dogmatic principles,
it would be infinitely better if we joined together in inculcating
obedience to these Commandments in the hearts and minds of the
youth of the country as the surest and best road to happiness on this
earth and to peace in the world to come. This is the common ideal of
all religions. What we need is more religion for our young people,
not less; and the way to get more religion is to stop the bickering
among our sects which can only have for its effect the creation of

doubt in the minds of our youth as to whether or not it is necessary to pay attention to religion at all.

Then I know your imputations are false when I recall the long list of other public servants of my faith who have loyally served the State. You as a lawyer will probably agree that the office of Chief Justice of the United States is second not even to that of the President in its influence on the national development and policy. That court by its interpretation of the Federal Constitution is a check not only upon the President himself but upon Congress as well. During one-fourth of its history it has been presided over by two Catholics, Roger Brooke Taney and Edward Douglass White. No one has suggested that the official conduct of either of these men was affected by any unwarranted religious influence or that religion played with them any part other than it should play in the life of every God-fearing man.

And I know your imputations are false when I recall the tens of thousands of young Catholics who have risked and sacrificed their lives in defense of our country. These fundamentals of life could not be true unless your imputations were false.

But, wishing to meet you on your own ground, I address myself to your definite questions, against which I have thus far made only general statements. I must first call attention to the fact that you often divorce sentences from their context in such a way as to give them something other than their real meaning. I will specify. You refer to the Apostolic Letter of Pope Leo XIII as "declaring to the world that the orders of the Church of England were void, her priests not priests," and so forth. You say that this was the "strange fruit" of the toleration of England to the Catholics. You imply that the Pope gratuitously issued an affront to the Anglican Church. In fact, this Apostolic Letter was an answer to a request made at the instance of priests of the Anglican Church for recognition by the Roman Catholic Church of the validity of their priestly orders. The request was based on the ground that they had been ordained in succession from the Roman Catholic priests who became the first priests of the Anglican Church. The Apostolic Letter was a mere adverse answer to this request, ruling that Anglican priests were not Roman Catholic priests, and was in no sense the gratuitous insult which you suggest it to be. It was not directed against England or citizens of that Empire.

Again, you quote from the *Catholic Encyclopedia* that my Church "regards dogmatic intolerance, not alone as her incontestable right, but as her sacred duty." And you say that these words show that Catholics are taught to be politically, socially, and intellectually intolerant of all other people. If you had read the whole of that article in the *Catholic Encyclopedia*, you would know that the real meaning of these words is that for Catholics alone the Church recognizes no deviation from complete acceptance of its dogma. These words are used in a chapter dealing with that subject only. The very same article in another chapter dealing with toleration toward non-Catholics contains these words: "The intolerant man is avoided as much as possible by every high-minded person. . . . The man who is tolerant in every emergency is alone lovable." The phrase "dogmatic intolerance" does not mean that Catholics are to be dogmatically intolerant of other people, but merely that inside the Catholic Church they are to be intolerant of any variance from the dogma of the Church.

Similar criticism can be made of many of your quotations. But, beyond this, by what right do you ask me to assume responsibility for every statement that may be made in any encyclical letter? As you will find in the *Catholic Encyclopedia* (Vol. V, p. 414), these encyclicals are not articles of our faith. The Syllabus of Pope Pius IX, which you quote on the possible conflict between Church and State, is declared by Cardinal Newman to have "no dogmatic force." You seem to think that Catholics must be all alike in mind and in heart, as though they had been poured into and taken out of the same mold. You have no more right to ask me to defend as part of my faith every statement coming from a prelate than I should have to ask you to accept as an article of your religious faith every statement of an Episcopal bishop, or of your political faith every statement of a President of the United States. So little are these matters of the essence of my faith that I, a devout Catholic since childhood, never heard of them until I read your letter. Nor can you quote from the canons of our faith a syllable that would make us less good citizens than non-Catholics. In fact and in truth, I have been taught the spirit of tolerance, and when you, Mr. Marshall, as a Protestant Episcopalian, join with me in saying the Lord's Prayer, we both pray, not to "My Father," but to "Our Father."

But I go further to demonstrate that the true construction of your quotations by the leaders of Catholic thought is diametrically the opposite of what you suggest it to be.

I

Your first proposition is that Catholics believe that other religions should, in the United States, be tolerated only as a matter of favor and that there should be an established church. You may find some dream of an ideal of a Catholic State, having no relation whatever to actuality, somewhere described. But, voicing the best Catholic thought on this subject, Dr. John A. Ryan, Professor of Moral Theology at the Catholic University of America, writes in *The State and the Church* of the encyclical of Pope Leo XIII, quoted by you:

"In practice, however, the foregoing propositions have full application only to the completely Catholic State. . . . 'The propositions of Pope Pius IX condemning the toleration of non-Catholic sects do not now,' says Father Pohle, 'apply even to Spain or the South American republics, to say nothing of countries possessing a greatly mixed population.' He lays down the following general rule: 'When several religions have firmly established themselves and taken root in the same territory, nothing else remains for the State than to exercise tolerance towards them all, or, as conditions exist to-day, to make complete religious liberty for individual and religious bodies a principle of government.' "

That is good Americanism and good Catholicism. And Father Pohle, one of the great writers of the Catholic Church, says further:

"If religious freedom has been accepted and sworn to as a fundamental law in a constitution, the obligation to show this tolerance is binding in conscience."

The American prelates of our Church stoutly defend our constitutional declaration of equality of all religions before the law. Cardinal O'Connell has said: "Thus to every American citizen has come the blessed inheritance of civil, political, and religious liberty safeguarded by the American Constitution . . . the right to worship God according to the dictates of his conscience."

Archbishop Ireland has said: "The Constitution of the United States reads: 'Congress shall make no laws respecting an establishment of religion, or prohibiting the free exercise thereof.' It was a great leap forward on the part of the new nation towards personal liberty and the consecration of the rights of conscience."

Archbishop Dowling, referring to any conceivable union of Church and State, says: "So many conditions for its accomplishment are lacking in every government of the world that the thesis may well be relegated to the limbo of defunct controversies."

I think you have taken your thesis from this limbo of defunct controversies.

Archbishop Ireland again said: "Religious freedom is the basic life of America, the cement running through all its walls and battlements, the safeguard of its peace and prosperity. Violate religious freedom against Catholics, our swords are at once unsheathed. Violate it in favor of Catholics, against non-Catholics, no less readily do they leap from the scabbard."

Cardinal Gibbons has said: "American Catholics rejoice in our separation of Church and State, and I can conceive no combination of circumstances likely to arise which would make a union desirable to either Church or State. . . . For ourselves we thank God that we live in America, 'in this happy country of ours,' to quote Mr. Roosevelt, where 'religion and liberty are natural allies.' "

And referring particularly to your quotation from Pope Pius IX, Dr. Ryan, in *The State and the Church,* says: "Pope Pius IX did not intend to declare that separation is always unadvisable, for he had more than once expressed his satisfaction with the arrangement obtaining in the United States."

With these great Catholics I stand squarely in support of the provisions of the Constitution which guarantee religious freedom and equality.

II

I come now to the speculation with which theorists have played for generations as to the respective functions of Church and State. You claim that the Roman Catholic Church holds that, if conflict arises, the Church must prevail over the State. You write as though there were some Catholic authority or tribunal to decide with respect to such conflict. Of course there is no such thing. As Dr. Ryan writes: "The Catholic doctrine concedes, nay, maintains, that the State is coordinate with the Church and equally independent and supreme in its own distinct sphere."

What is the Protestant position? The Articles of Religion of your Protestant Episcopal Church (XXXVII) declare: "The Power of the Civil Magistrate extendeth to all men, as well Clergy as Laity, in all things temporal; but hath no authority in things purely spiritual."

Your Church, just as mine, is voicing the injunction of our common Saviour to render unto Caesar the things that are Caesar's and unto God the things that are God's.

What is this conflict about which you talk? It may exist in some lands which do not guarantee religious freedom. But in the wildest dreams of your imagination you cannot conjure up a possible conflict between religious principle and political duty in the United States, except on the unthinkable hypothesis that some law were to be passed which violated the common morality of all God-fearing men. And if you can conjure up such a conflict, how would a Protestant resolve it? Obviously by the dictates of his conscience. That is exactly what a Catholic would do. There is no ecclesiastical tribunal which would have the slightest claim upon the obedience of Catholic communicants in the resolution of such a conflict. As Cardinal Gibbons said of the supposition that "the Pope were to issue commands in purely civil matters":

"He would be offending not only against civil society, but against God, and violating an authority as truly from God as his own. Any Catholic who clearly recognized this would not be bound to obey the Pope; or rather his conscience would bind him absolutely to disobey, because with Catholics conscience is the supreme law which under no circumstances can we ever lawfully disobey."

Archbishop Ireland said: "To priest, to Bishop, or to Pope (I am willing to consider the hypothesis) who should attempt to rule in matters civil and political, to influence the citizen beyond the range of their own orbit of jurisdiction that are the things of God, the answer is quickly made: 'Back to your own sphere of rights and duties, back to the things of God.' "

Bishop England, referring to our Constitution, said: "Let the Pope and the Cardinals and all the powers of the Catholic world united make the least encroachment on that Constitution, we will protect it with our lives. Summon a General Council—let that Council interfere in the mode of our electing but an assistant to a turnkey of a prison—we deny the right, we reject the usurpation."

Our Supreme Court has marked out the spheres of influence of Church and State in a case from which you quote copiously, *Watson* v. *Jones*, 13 Wall. 729; but you refrain from quoting this statement:

"The right to organize voluntary religious associations, to assist in the expression and dissemination of any religious doctrine, and to create tribunals for the decision of controverted questions of faith within the association, and for the ecclesiastical government of all of the individual members, the congregation and officers within the general association, is unquestioned. . . . It is of the essence of these religious unions and of their right to establish tribunals for the decision of questions arising among themselves that those decisions could be binding in all cases of ecclesiastical cognizance, subject only to such appeal as the organism itself provides for."

That is the State's attitude toward the Church. Archbishop Ireland thus puts the Church's attitude toward the State:

"To the Catholic obedience to law is a religious obligation, binding in God's name the conscience of the citizen. . . . Both Americanism and Catholicism bow to the sway of personal conscience."

Under our system of government the electorate entrusts to its officers of every faith the solemn duty of action according to the dictates of conscience. I may fairly refer once more to my own record to support these truths. No man, cleric or lay, has ever directly or indirectly attempted to exercise Church influence on my administration of any office I have ever held, nor asked me to show special favor to Catholics or exercise discrimination against non-Catholics.

It is a well-known fact that I have made all of my appointments to public office on the basis of merit and have never asked any man about his religious belief. In the first month of this year there gathered in the Capitol at Albany the first Governor's cabinet that ever sat in this State. It was composed, under my appointment, of two Catholics, thirteen Protestants, and one Jew. The man closest to me in the administration of the government of the State of New York is he who bears the title of Assistant to the Governor. He had been connected with the Governor's office for thirty years, in subordinate capacities, until I promoted him to the position which makes him the sharer with me of my every thought and hope and ambition in the administration of the State. He is a Protestant, a Republican, and a thirty-second degree Mason. In my public life I have exemplified that complete separation of Church from State which is the faith of American Catholics to-day.

III

I next come to education. You admit that the Supreme Court guaranteed to Catholics the right to maintain their parochial schools; and you ask me whether they would have so ruled if it had been shown that children in parochial schools were taught that the State should show discrimination between religions, that Protestants should be recognized only as a matter of favor, that they should be intolerant to non-Catholics, and that the laws of the State could be flouted on the ground of the imaginary conflict. My summary answer is: I and all my children went to a parochial school. I never heard of any such stuff being taught or of anybody who claimed that it was. That any group of Catholics would teach it is unthinkable.

.   .   .   .   .

VI

I summarize my creed as an American Catholic. I believe in the worship of God according to the faith and practice of the Roman Catholic Church. I recognize no power in the institutions of my Church to interfere with the operations of the Constitution of the United States or the enforcement of the law of the land. I believe in absolute freedom of conscience for all men and in equality of all churches, all sects, and all beliefs before the law as a matter of right and not as a matter of favor. I believe in the absolute separation of Church and State and in the strict enforcement of the provisions of the Constitution that Congress shall make no law respecting an establishment of religion or prohibiting the free exercise thereof. I believe that no tribunal of any church has any power to make any decree of any force in the law of the land, other than to establish the status of its own communicants within its own church. I believe in the support of the public school as one of the corner stones of American liberty. I believe in the right of every parent to choose whether his child shall be educated in the public school or in a religious school supported by those of his own faith. I believe in the principle of non-interference by this country in the internal affairs of other nations and that we should stand steadfastly against any such interference by whomsoever it may be urged. And I believe in the common brotherhood of man under the common fatherhood of God.

In this spirit I join with fellow Americans of all creeds in a fervent prayer that never again in this land will any public servant be challenged because of the faith in which he has tried to walk humbly with his God.

Very truly yours,

Alfred E. Smith

The Days of Lost Tradition

GEORGE N. SHUSTER

"The return of civilization to religion is like the return of the energy stored in coal to the heat of the sun."

D. MEREJKOWSKI

The Catholic Spirit has been, and is, hard at work in modern English literature. By "Catholic" is meant here nothing sectarian or narrowly controversial, but instead the broad, traditionally Christian outlook upon life which through many centuries moulded European society into all but its ultra-modern forms. It antedated the agnostic and it superseded the pagan; it was both the enemy and the lover of Rome. Although inherently artistic, it condemned art for its own sake. We shall not try to account for it or to make an apology for what is so obvious that it has been ignored. Catholic art raised every structure worth looking at that has been built since the days of the Parthenon and the Capitol; wrote the "Divina Commedia," the "Morte D'Arthur," and, to some extent at least, the plays of William Shakespeare; and erected, finally, a social order in which the art of living was possible. There was nothing wooden or pedantic about it anywhere, but instead a surprising vitality, as of old Adam forgetting his age: yet it stood like a rock on two points—belief in God and in Man. Theology and politics were written into its poetics. No workman in whom the Catholic Spirit breathed would have admitted that religion can be excluded from life and art. Christianity sent thousands of its representatives to death for a Roman holiday; it carried armies

"The Days of Lost Tradition," from *The Catholic Spirit in Modern English Literature,* by George N. Shuster (New York: The Macmillan Company, 1928). Reprinted by permission of George N. Shuster.

over pestilential wastes to the conquest of a blighted town; it was everywhere alarmingly reckless of life: but it tried honestly to make that life worth the trouble. Woman believed and was honored; the slave was freed and the king became a slave. And from one end of Christendom to the other, the *Miserere* ended in a chorus of laughter.

Gradually that spirit died out of the world and its sacred temples were profaned. During nearly four hundred years of English history it was reviled and spit upon, and then it returned, disguised at first, cautiously showing its face to friends until it had once more the right to sit in the marketplace. It entered into the literature of England, wherever men lived again in the past of Christendom, wherever souls yearned for the faith and blessed peace that were symbolized by the spires of Lincoln and Canterbury, wherever the spell of modern pessimism was broken by sacramental mirth. Occasionally the hovels of the poor were shaken, and it got inside the gates of Oxford. Poets were thrilled with the rich music of mediaeval life, and thinkers battled with modern thought, clad in the armour of the schools. The world was shaken with memories and though many were heedless or distrustful or filled with rancour, those who loved them were given new courage and new vigour. They chanted songs that had long been forgotten and voiced hopes that had been changed into despair. While the world about them reeled in the din of its delusion, they stood serene; and when they wept their tears were pure. But they themselves shall tell the story of how they came to know the splendid continuity of Christendom, its interest in the fate of man, its trust in God.

That excellent knight, Sir Thomas More, who laid his head on the block during the first year of Henry's usurpation, had been saddened with the vision of evils which were to come over an England that had long been popular and merry and Christian. "Your shepe," he said, thinking of the growing tendency to oust the tenants from land that could be used for grazing, "that were wont to be so meke and tame, and so smal eaters, now, as I heare say, do become so great devowerers and so wylde, that they eate up and swallow downe the very men themselves." Sir Thomas did not live to witness the full rapacity of those sheep or of the wolves that went about in their clothing. He did not see the fiendish greed that would consume every bulwark in which the common man took refuge: the sacking of merciful monasteries, the bitter tyranny of kings and queens with lust in their bowels and blood in their eyes, the hunger and sickness of millions for whom there would be at length no refuge but the slavery of industrial towns, or the final darkness that would sit heavily on England's soul. He died in testimony to the past, and mindful of his serenity we shall hasten over the days of the democratic downfall, merely noting how every principle which the religious conscience had set up in defense of the poor was spurned; how the artistic impulse that had made of life a beautiful and holy thing was torn from the hearts of men; and how, at last, the very memory of the older Faith and the older Happiness was beaten into the dust by warriors' horses, the silken trains of courtesans, and all that musty paganism which is as brutal as it is proud. Verily, these were sheep that "swallowed downe the very men themselves" and they were remembered again and again, till even the gentle and goodly Tom Hood cursed them in his lyric verse. The middle years of the century into which that poet was born were indeed the days of the lost tradition, when England that had been gay was sad, and the throne of Edward a pedestal for gain.

The eighteenth century was sallow, stale. Over all of Europe walls began to crack, buttresses to sag. The humanistic solvent of the Great Revolt had steadily undermined the authority of the Church, but it was a long while at work before society began everywhere to decay. Clergy and nobility were, in the higher ranks at least, separated from the people by the new egoism of wealth; the sacred marks of consecration were not on their souls. France especially was restless. Under the thrusts of Voltaire, whose acrid pen was never at rest, tradition began to totter; and the false but fierce philosophy of the Encyclopedists stood out strong by comparison. Then, Rousseau, the watchmaker's son of Geneva, made the world believe that his drugged dreams of a perfect social order were capable of realization. Rousseau not only discovered a world by his writings, but conquered it also; and the already unstable structure of Bourbon society was doomed. In vain would his Lordship call for "Order" while he doubled the tithes; crass convention was at the death-grapple with radical vision. Add to this a new and widespread skepticism in matters of religion, and you will understand the eighteenth century soul. There were, at first, the French critics and dreamers; there was at the end the great Goethe, who is like a glass of Burgundy in a pint of Rhenish wine—both native and exotic. Everywhere the sufficiency of human reason was candidly assumed, and "Unknown" was subtly written over the name of God.

England, however, with much less to conserve was vastly more conservative. There was little demand for a change of political régime. What religion remained was firmly welded with the State, and the State was powerful, even though it would have to battle with revolutionary colonists in all its domains. Almost as if by design, the classes for whom reading was possible developed a code of genteel utilitarian morals slightly diluted with aristocratic sentiment. Aristotle came into his own and both the "Poetics" and the "Ethics" were consulted with some gusto. Except for the manly squirearchy of Fielding there is little in eighteenth century fiction which contains the substance of democratic thought. In general the novelists understood only one worth-while thing, laughter, and this the pre-modern Englishman seldom forgot. The representative thinkers followed the French lead to its ultimate conclusion and were either relentlessly Scotch or stubbornly British. The unstable epistemology of John Locke, the staid, cold skepticism of David Hume, the bitter and cruel politics of Hobbes, were adaptations of French thought to the more conservative attitude of an insular public; it seemed that men would gradually abandon, for the sake of a callous phrase, what remained of the decent philosophy of their fathers. History, which is philosophy in action, was courted by a brilliant pagan who appreciated fully the historic importance of the Gospel's success over the mandates of the Emperors. "It was at Rome, on the 15th of October, 1764," says Gibbon, "as I sat musing amid the ruins of the Capitol while the barefoot friars were singing Vespers in the temple of Jupiter, that the idea of writing the decline and fall of the city first started to my mind." His "Decline and Fall" was a gorgeous and stately tyrant who closed the doors to the mediaeval narrative for many years, and supported the impression, not yet dead, that the science of history must confine itself to ancient and modern times. What a mass of nonsense about "dark ages" and "mummery" and "ignorance" was used to blanket the fires of the most amazingly active and speculative era in human annals! Instead we got the private scandals of Medes and Parthians, Roman bankers and prehistoric fossils; "progress" and "evolution" and "freedom" and a hundred other perversions of common nouns, which the most prevaricating of mediaeval annalists would have been ashamed to use.

Again it was a man from the midst of the people who rallied all that was most charitable in the friendly world of letters; and Doctor Johnson, brusque of figure and mellow of heart, guided the Irish Goldsmith as well as any man could. Johnson made a thousand errors in judgment and taste, but he was the only person in the land who understood what the author of "The Deserted Village" and "The Vicar of Wakefield" was worth. For that delightful vagabond remembered the death-cry of the poor, despoiled of property as well as freedom, and faced the hard syllogisms of Adam Smith with simple fact. One of the truths which humanity can never part with is that *laissez-faire* will never do; and if in Goldsmith's songs of a dying peasantry there runs the wail of a dirge, it was something to have sung it in the teeth of commercial pride. Johnson's other good deeds were numerous and his heart was right; he was the Englishman at his level best.

In still another way Art made a final stand. Poetry, forever vibrant and untamed, forgot the taunts of Pope and the smooth controversy of Dryden and murmured some of the old hymns. Gray, Warton, Percy, Chatterton—all of them caught glimpses of ancient chivalry lost on haggard moors and set down something of what they had seen. A certain ploughman, whose name was Robert Burns, told more of human nature than the professors in his country had dreamed of. But through all of these and through the visions of Blake, the virulence of Byron, and even the nature-worship of Wordsworth, the face of Rousseau looked out, bathing in the smiles of Ceres, lost in the morning dew. They could not alter the fact that Europe had been built at the foot of the Cross and that its faith was dead. Old Triton and his horn were silent, indeed; chimney arose on chimney, loom next to loom, and around them were built the shambles of the new serfs. There was precious little religion left, just as there was no great freedom. The old stories of the Saints were derided; pilgrims no longer went to the rifled tomb at Canterbury, or clerks to Oxford. The former place was asleep and the latter was drinking port. A people that had been forbidden to utter the Virgin name of Mary was taught the monstrous fetish of the virgin-queen.

Meanwhile the peasant struck in France and the King went down. In his stead the minions of the new philosophy settled themselves in the judgment seat, the guillotine struck off heads with a kind of voluptuous cruelty, and men gathered in the temples to worship the goddess of reason. When the butchery had finally ceased and the standards of Napoleon had been furled forever, a new religious fervour was born out of the hearts of tired men. Chateaubriand in France, Görres and Chamisso in Germany, and Manzoni in Italy began to look back upon the bright days of Christendom and to hunger for the things of the soul. It seemed for a time that the powerful missionary spirit of Art had returned, but the destruction had been too complete. Wonderful things were accomplished in the face of odds; but the sadness of the romantics was only too prophetic, only too profoundly real.

England escaped political revolution and the people continued in their silence. Instead, the spirit of change, of Liberty, entered into literature and uprooted its conventions, despite the beautiful pathos of Edmund Burke. There was the atheistic rebellion of Shelley and Byron, Godwin and Mary Woolstonecraft: English Voltaires and Rousseaus respectively, lashed into fury by the cant of the prevailing civilization. And then, far greater and more influential than any of these, appeared the perennially virile Sir Walter, enchanted spectator of a thousand vanished tournaments, delightful magician of trysts and trappings, knights and fair ladies, of the whole picturesque life of the olden time. But though he sent all the world into a feverish study of heraldry, he was unconcerned with the soul of Christendom, the spirit which had created these thousand rapturous symbols for its inward joy. Bluntly, Scott was neither democratic nor spiritual, though his influence made in the end for both qualities throughout Europe. The people were best represented by a strange and violent journalist whose copy brought him eventually into Parliament, but never far away from his folk. In his "History of the Reformation" William Cobbett emphasized one tremendous matter which the student of the period had generally neglected—the spoliation of the poor. Through him was voiced, with a passion often boorish enough, their protest, which the philosophers and historians had apparently forgotten.

When Victoria came to the throne, the English had practically settled down to a smug admiration for trade. The girl-queen governed an Empire larger—and more cruel—than Caesar had dreamed of. This Empire had forgotten nearly all the traditions of Englishmen, being immensely more interested in the heathen. Commerce was god, and commerce implied a territorial policy, military force, and a continuous debate in Parliament over the subjugation of the Irish or the

Hindus. Such an enormous scheme had little to do with the public, although occasionally it would be pestered by a publicist. The mob stayed speechless, but it was a subject for conversation—a subject written in the miseries of a thousand industrial towns, in the crooked streets of London, in the quiet districts where men had kept their freedom. But for all of this the powers that ruled felt more or less contempt. That so good and great a man as Lord Macaulay could be utterly misled is significant of the times: he made his best speech against workingmen and his best poetry about Rome. It is not surprising either that Lord Monmouth, when talking of the established religion, should have felt the emotions of Caius Julius. These matters meant very simply that the popular institutions of the past had been swallowed up in a gigantic utilitarianism whose efficiency and refinement were utterly pagan. The most Christian thing economics could do was to use a French phrase; education confined itself to teaching wealthy boys how to quote Virgil and how to despise their neighbors; and the height of religious fervour was to sing a song for the Queen.

An hour had come, however, when this apparently fixed alignment would be violently assailed. First, England awoke to the giant protest of Charles Dickens. Here was a man, amazingly ignorant of ever so many historical details, who read history correctly; who was an optimist and yet a rebel; who walked the dirtiest streets of London and shook with laughter while his heart bled. Dickens' importance cannot be valued too highly, for, although he created no disturbance, he did create people—a mob of people whom nobody can put down and nobody ignore. They broke through the priggishness of the Victorian era as a hod-carrier might disturb an ethical society. Still, after this stupendous sermon on charity, the world went to dinner and to bed, a little more kindly, a little more restless, but essentially the same world.

Then there followed in quick succession a series of surprising outbursts against the "progress" which Macaulay had so highly complimented. John Ruskin, angry with the interminable smokestacks and their soot, inspected modernity by the light of Beauty and found it decidedly shabby; for a while he contented himself with praising the art of the older time, but finally he understood, nearly, that art cannot be dissociated from life, and he even tried to restore civilization. Ruskin's greatest hindrance was his education; somehow he never managed to look around it and see what lay beyond. Next, a dyspeptic Scotchman, who prided himself on "four walls" and some brains, discovered the amazing mediocrity of his environment, measured it by the rule of genius, and cursed it roundly. Carlyle was a good and worthy man but with all these prescriptions he did not even cure himself. The Positivists, from George Eliot to John Stuart Mill, consoled themselves with an altruistic version of the new gospel, advocated a thousand things which nobody would take, and died wondering at the folly of the world. It remained to suggest Culture pure and simple, and this Matthew Arnold did skillfully; but, though he has been quite largely complimented by the professors, Mrs. Grundy has lent a disdainful ear. George Meredith examined society by the gleam of nature's dawn, and Browning counseled vigour and exuberance. Thus one by one the thinkers railed at John Bull, but that stolid gentleman went on unperturbed.

The upshot of all this criticism was that the power of reason came at last to its goal. It scrutinized the bases of religious belief as matters quite independent of its own needs; and with the great catapult of Evolution set the entire structure of popular theistic opinion to tottering. Was it because man had become so like an ape that he was willing to concede that his ancestor was one? At least here was the paradox of reason equalling itself to Everything and consenting also to be Nothing. There came over England the final darkness: loneliness, the boredom of being alone. Solidarity of intellectual effort was destroyed; step by step idiosyncrasy usurped the seat of originality and society pursued unbelievable philosophic tangents. The powers of the State increased, as the meaning of man was lessened. Force was worshipped either with frank rejoicing or with bitter acquiescence. And even tears were idle things, "from the depths of some divine despair."

As not the least of the energies loosened against the complacency of the English mood, the Catholic Revival appeared. Wherever the religious spirit was strong, whether in poet or preacher, there developed a concern with the beautiful faith of the past, with its sacraments and saints, with its manifest confidence in the voice of God. Almost in the twinkling of an eye, the members of a creed that had long been despised as impotent and ridiculous stood with their loins girt for battle and recruited some of the most brilliant minds of Britain. Whereas there had been no great Catholic apostle in the country since the days of Campion and More, a dozen now moved the hearts of men; whereas the poetry of the old religion had been silent since Crashaw, singers took up the Catholic lyre with abounding and brilliant gifts; and even the press, grown more tolerant, carried the defenders' voices to the ends of the earth. The challenge of the modern mind was accepted and even forestalled: the missionary now coveted battle as he had once sought martyrdom. Christendom, as the Great Tradition that guarded the rights and guided the aspirations of common humanity, won crowds of men by its new expositions of the beauties of the faith and by the honesty of its literary effort. New voices stirred in shrouded Ireland, and the testimony of Britain lent confidence to the army of God that struggled in Europe. The issue between belief and denial has not become clear everywhere, and the modern philosophers, who scoffed at Christendom as something withered and outgrown, have discovered its branches over their heads. And even the critics shall have to reckon with the Cross.

The story of the Catholic Spirit working in modern English letters is at once the record of a movement and the biography of strong men. If literature be the expression of great personalities considering general truths, it is no less a series of flaming windows where the colour of Life is broken and reflected under the arches of towering minds. We shall deal here with many fascinating men; with books that have brought answers to numberless hearts; with the victories and failures of literary effort. Most of all, however, we shall deal with the Spirit which any of these men valued more highly than life or success, their insight into and love for the sanctity of their hope. We shall scarcely divine their purpose or their meaning unless we remember that, while facing the modern opponent wherever he appeared, they worshipped the beauty of the past. Behind them is the synthesis of mediaeval life, with the fervent symbolism of its cathedrals, the robust nobility of its moral code, and the success of its popular society. They kneel at shrines at which forgotten artisans laid down the glory of their buoyant lives and before which pilgrim and Crusader, saint and king, begged forgiveness of their sins. They go into battle gayly, but their voices tremble with the melody of dead songs. Only, they believe that the old realities can be again a reasonable ideal, and they have faith in God.

Cosmic Intimidation

BISHOP FULTON J. SHEEN

The modern man is humble, not with that old humility which made a man doubt his power, but with the new humility that makes a man doubt his humanity. The old humility was grounded on truth: man is what he really is. The new humility is grounded on insignificance: man is only a speck in the cosmos.

This new attitude towards humility is not due to the advance of religion, but to the advance of astronomy. Telescopes and science have revealed to us the immensity of the universe. Those who are in a position to know inform us that the earth is but a tiny detail of that universe. The planet Jupiter, for example, has eleven times the diameter of the earth; fourteen hundred bodies the size of the earth could be packed into it and still have room to stretch. But that is not all: the stars are larger than Jupiter. It is the distance that belies their bulk. Recent measurement shows that the nearest stars are at almost exactly a million times the distances of the nearest planets. Venus, for example, is twenty-six million miles distant from the earth, and the sun ninety-two million miles distant, while the nearest star, Proxima Centauri, is twenty-five million million miles away. Some of the stars, the Cepheids, are ten thousand times as luminous as the sun.

Because of the enormity of these distances, which cannot be understood in terms of miles, scientists have used a new measurement to make it intelligible, namely, the light-year. Light travels at the rate of 186,000 miles a second, and a light-year is therefore that number multiplied by 365 (days) by 24 (hours) by 60 (minutes) by 60 (seconds). In the language of a light-year, the nearest star is 4.27 light-years away from the earth. And yet this distance is trivial compared to the diameter of the galactic or starry system with its thirty thousand million stars, which is estimated to be two hundred and twenty thousand light-years. The radius of the entire universe is said to be two thousand million light-years; that is, it takes light traveling at the rate of 186,000 miles per second two thousand million years to pass from one end of the universe to the other.

These figures are positively staggering. In some minds they have awakened a greater understanding of the Majesty and the Power of God, or a humility which recognizes that God is the Creator and Lord of all. In other minds they have developed an awe of the immensity of the cosmos or a humility which insists that man is nothing. In this latter class are certain really learned astronomers who prove to the world that a man may know his stars without knowing his logic.

This group has developed a philosophy of cosmic intimidation, by which they attempt to browbeat man into acknowledging his nothingness, because the cosmos is bigger than he. Such statements as the following "taken from life" are typical of the philosophy of cosmic intimidation. "The growth of modern science has brought about a comparable transformation of our attitude towards mankind. . . . Man tends to shrink in terms of the new cosmic outlook. Far from being the lord of all creation, existing from the beginning of things, he now appears to be but a temporary chemical episode on a most tiny planet." In the same tone, but in a manner as typical of the new humility, another writes: "The thing that appalls me is not the bigness of the universe, but the smallness of us. We are in all ways small— little in foresight, shriveled in spirit, minute in material content, microscopic in the vastness of measured space, evanescent in the sweep of time—inconsequential in every respect except perhaps in the chemical complexities of our mental reactions. Man is an animal among many, precariously situated on the crust of a planetary fragment, that obeys the gravitational impulses of one of the millions of dwarf stars that wander in the remote parts of one of many galactic systems."

Not content with reducing man to a "jelly-like semi-solid substance pigeonhole" in the cosmos, another writer believes that even the greatness of Our Divine Lord Himself is dwarfed in the immensity of the cosmos: "In our present cosmic perspective it would seem more reasonable to suppose that our particular solar system has not even been noted and catalogued in the astronomical star-chart of the cosmic Deity. That the cosmic God, if there be one, has ever taken special cognizance of the nebulous personality and uncertain teachings of a historically vague and inconspicuous religious teacher who lived in Palestine some two thousand years ago, represents a conception which can be entertained only by a person seriously circumscribed by ignorance or limited in intellectual power."

It takes a great deal of crust to call man a "crustal phenomenon," but it takes but little logic to show that such cosmic intimidation is built upon, first, an ignorance of the imagery of greatness, and secondly, two false assumptions: namely, that greatness is value, and that man was considered great in the old cosmology because he lived presumably in the center of the universe.

There is ponderous imagery in the modern scientific description of the universe, compared to which man is less than a speck in size. But this imagery of contrast between greatness and littleness is nothing new; the newness consists only in the subjects contrasted. The modern mind contrasts man with the universe and makes man nothing; the perennial mind contrasts God with the universe and makes the universe nothing. The first concludes to the pettiness of men from the greatness of the cosmos; the other to the pettiness of the cosmos from the majesty of God. It is much easier to dwarf a little thing like man than to dwarf a big thing like the universe. Modern imagery does the first; abiding revealed imagery does the latter, and for that reason is far more impressive. The imagery which tells me that there are thirty thousand million stars peopling the heavens as so many "tapers lit about the day's dead sanctities" is thrilling, but when my reason tells me these stars did not make themselves, nor did they come from nothing, the imagery evoked by the mention of One Who made them and Who "telleth the number of the stars and calleth them by name," makes the first image pass into insignificance. My imagination is taxed when the scientists describe the brightness of the sun as having $3^{27} \times 10^{27}$ candle-power, but it is overwhelmed when I am told that a "woman is clothed with the sun," and "the moon is under her feet." The imagery of the heavens as being two thousand million light-years in diameter is awesome when compared to the tiny earth, but trivial when compared to the imagery of the "hand that measured the heavens."

A normal mind looking at the vast expanse of the heavens is naturally and almost imperceptibly led to the conception of an Omnipotent Being Who threw them into space and endowed them with a law so that orb could pass by orb, and planet by planet, without ever a hitch or halt. It is an abnormal mind that begins im-

mediately to think of pettiness when it sees power; it is not natural
for a man who looks at a sky-scraper to think of the littleness of a
flea, but rather of the greatness of the mind that conceived it. A
great mural painting that covers the side of a corridor does not make
a sane man think of a dwarf, but of an artist. When a modern mind
stands amazed at the size of the cosmos and argues that even on this
earth man is "far outdistanced by the cockroach," he is indulging in
the same kind of fallacious reasoning that would make him conclude
that L'Enfant, who designed the city of Washington, is only an infant,
because the city of Washington is bigger and bulkier and therefore
better than he is.

This brings us to the first false assumption underlying this type
of anaemic thinking, namely, that greatness is to be measured by
quantity rather than by quality.

The cult of magnitude is driving the modern mind mad; it has
so obscured its mental vision as to blind it to other dimensions than
those of length, breadth, and thickness. It is well to remember that
the contained is generally worth far more than the container, even
though the contained rattle around in the container like a diamond
in a cracker-box. The really great things of the world are not always
the immense things; great men are always little men in the sense that
they are humble, as Cardinal Mercier was. They are so big they can
always be seeming little, because it is only "seems." Sons of rich men
can dress poorly, because they are really rich; they need not the
panoply of the rich. Sons of poor men must dress richly to give the
impression of wealth, because they are really poor. Greatness is not
in size. Little things are much more impressive. Man never stumbles
over a cosmos, though he does stumble over a rug. Concerning the
confusion of greatness and value these few lines have been written:
"If God's lack of interest in us is because we are so little, then it
must follow that He would take interest in us if we were enlarged.
How large should we have to be before His interest began? If we
were a hundred miles tall should we attract His attention? We may
probably expect another negative. But if we towered up to a stature
equivalent to the orbit of Neptune, we might possibly enter upon
significance for Deity. And if we stood so high that our hair was
singed by Betelgeuse—might we be admitted to the honor of audience
with the Demiurge?

"Roaring nonsense? It is, indeed, but it is the roaring nonsense of very solemn and learned men who seem to shrink from thinking things out. They join together two incommensurable things—bulk, which has all the physical measurements, and meaning of value, which hasn't a single one. . . . But not only does the argument go thus far: it goes farther. I makes the higher of the two depend upon and be a function of the lower. It puts meaning or value as a secondary appendage to bulk. . . . Our learned friends, however, do not themselves adopt the valuation scheme which they attribute to God. If they did, they would judge a small child to be worthless, a man of normal size barely acceptable, and a mountain of fatness a paragon of the day."

One moment a modern prophet tells us that man is great because he has evolved from matter: then in the next moment he tells us that he is nothing because matter is bigger than he is. They forget that though it is true that astronomy has displaced the earth as the center of the universe, it is equally true that biology has replaced man as its crowning center. Why magnify the science of astronomy at the expense of biology? They cannot have evolution of man from matter and the domination of matter over man, at one and the same time. Either evolution of man from matter, or the supremacy of matter over man, must be given up. The two theories are contradictory. It is nonsense to sing Swinburne's hymn, "Glory to man in the highest, for man is the master of all," and then the next moment let the "all" master the man and immerse him in the very matter from whence he has risen. Such theorists cannot eat their cake and have it.

Magnify and extol the heavens as much as one pleases; multiply interstellar distances unto a mathematical infinity; the fact still remains that man understands the heavens and can interpret their movements in rational language. How could astronomers tell us about the bulk of the heavens unless in some way they got the bulk of the heavens into their heads—a task that, incidentally, is less important than the one of getting their heads into the heavens? To get the cosmos inside of a head and still have room on the inside of that head to look at it, think about it, search out its laws, is to sit, as it were, on the edge of still another great mental cosmos and let one's feet dangle into space, wishing all the while, like another Alexander, that there were more worlds to conquer.

This whole problem of the dignity of man was thought out years ago by Aristotle, who called man a microcosm or a little universe, because he contained the cosmos within himself. Man sums up the lower order of creation in a double way: first, physically, and secondly, mentally. Physically, he is made up of a combination of chemicals, vegetative processes, and animal activities; he is like matter, because he exists; like plants, because he lives; and like animals, because he feels. But he is above all these because he has his own peculiar perfection; namely, an intelligence, which enables him to know not only the phenomena of earth and the movements of the heavens, but the intelligibility of these phenomena in terms of causes and in particular, in terms of the First Cause, God.

The cockroach, which according to one's measurement has "remained unchanged for more than fifty million years," has seen many things evolve under his very eye. He has perhaps even seen bug-dynasties and flea-kingdoms rise and fall according to the Spenglerian formula, but the cockroach in all that fifty million years has never formulated even the simplest explanation of evolution that a man might formulate in an hour. It is that power to contain within his mind the infinitely great cosmos, and the infinitely little atom, and the infinite variety between the two, and to think of them all in the one thought—Order—that makes man the "beauty of the world and the paragon of animals." Science is but the reduction of multiplicity to the unity of thought, and just as there can never be science without a scientist, so neither can there be law and order in the cosmos unless it was made with law and order. The mind of man does not put law into the universe; it discovers it. If man discovers intelligibility there, some one must have put it there in making the cosmos intelligently. Thus the "very silence of the spheres" that frightened Pascal drove him on mentally until he found a Transcendent Source of Wisdom for that immanent order, which source is the Infinite God, to Whom be all honor and glory forever.

Those who refuse to unify the cosmos in terms of Pure Intelligence but content themselves with secondary causes may be likened to an all-wise mouse in a grand piano who laid the flattering unction to his soul that he had explained music by the play of hammers on the strings, the action of which he could see in his own narrow little world. "Scientists catch the tune but not the player."

The unification of the cosmos does not stop with man. Man has been met half-way on the upward progress by God, Who descended to earth and assumed his nature. In the circuits of the planets there are times when the heavens are under the earth, and in the ways of

God with men there was a time when Heaven was under the earth, and that was when Christ was born in the cave of Bethlehem. Just as in the world-order stars revolve about stars, planets and galactic systems around galactic systems, with a beautiful unity pervading all, so in the philosophical order, as all creation gravitates about man, either for his service, like the earth, or for his knowledge, like the cosmos, so does man gravitate towards creation's Creator. Man sums up the whole cosmos within himself. In assuming a human nature, then, Christ assumed in a certain sense the material world within His Immaculate Body, the whole spiritual world, intellectual and angelic, in His Pure Soul, and both of these touched the Divinity that was His by bonds of the Hypostatic Union—indissoluble bonds, stronger than love, stronger than life, stronger than time. Like a great and mighty pyramid the universe moves on to Unity under God. Man by his intellect masters the universe, subjugates it, rules over it, and possesses it within himself as knowledge; Christ, by assuming a human nature in the Unity of the Divine Person, brings all men to the Unity of His Law, His Peace, and His Life. He above all is fitted for the reconciliation of the finite in man to the Infinite in God, for He is both God and man, and to declare it to the world He died suspended between Heaven and earth, because He was the Pontiff, the *Pontifex,* the Bridge-Builder between the two. Such is the spiritual economy of a cosmic outlook that looks upon the cosmos not as a pluri-verse, but a uni-verse—things finding their unity in Christ, in accordance with that beautiful doctrine of Paul: "All are yours, you are Christ's and Christ is God's." What care we if Jupiter has more bulk than the earth? What matters it if Betelgeuse has more carbon than our tiny planet? Does that make dignity?

> Not a star of all
> The innumerable host of stars has heard
> How He administered this terrestrial ball.
> Our race have kept their Lord's enstrusted Word.
>
> Of His earth-visiting feat
> None knows the secret—cherished, perilous;
> The terrible, shame-faced, frightened, whispered,
> sweet
> Heart-shattering secret of His way with us.

We know too much about matter to be materialists; we know too much about stars to think we are but star-dust. The galaxy of suns and starry worlds may boast of bulk and size and speed, but we too have our boast: Christ walked *our* earth.

The "New" Liturgy: Its Function and Its Challenge

GERALD ELLARD, S. J.

It used to be said that the Church was the one unchanging thing in a changing world. Now we know that the Church herself is changing, if not her doctrine or her mission, at least her appearance to the world. It has gradually become clear that the cooperation of the laity with the hierarchy in the work called Catholic Action is not a new Papal name for our familiar organizational activity, but something new, something that has for its foundation a new concept of the Church. Thus, when writing the classic description of Catholic Action to the great Cardinal Patriarch of Lisbon, so recently a guest in America, Pope Pius XI spoke of Catholic Action as a duty inherent in Christian life:

> If one considers well it will be seen that the very sacraments of Baptism and Confirmation impose—among other obligations—this Apostolate of Catholic Action. . . . Through Confirmation we become soldiers of Christ. A soldier must labor and fight not so much for himself as for others. Baptism . . . imposes the duty of the apostolate since through it we become members of the Church or of the Mystic Body of Christ; and among the members of this Body, as of any organism, there must be solidarity of interests and reciprocal communication of life. One member must, therefore, help the other; no one may remain inactive, and as each receives he must also give. Now, as every Christian receives the supernatural life which circulates in the veins of the Mystic Body of Christ, that abundant life that Christ Himself said He came to bring on earth, so he must transfuse it into others who either do not possess it, or who possess it too scarcely and only in appearance. (*Catholic Mind,* April 8, 1934.)

Now would not such language have puzzled a member of an altar society, say ten years ago? Did she feel in joining the altar

"The 'New' Liturgy: Its Function and Its Challenge," by Gerald Ellard, reprinted from *The Catholic Mind,* January, 1937, by permission of The America Press.

society that she was carrying out a duty imposed by Baptism or Confirmation? Did she envisage her work therein as an apostolic transfusion of supernatural life to others? Would she not have asked in some bewilderment: "What *is* this Mystic Body of Christ of which the Holy Father speaks?"

Again, in the Encyclical "On the Reconstruction of the Social Order" the same Vicar of Christ, mouthpiece of the Holy Spirit, teaches clearly that the spirit of unity necessary for the new social order is impossible until all sections of society are intimately convinced that they are members of the Mystic Body, It is clearly something new that the Holy Father has in mind:

> Then only will it be possible to unite all in a harmonious striving for the common good, when all sections of society have an intimate conviction that they are members of a single family, and children of the same Heavenly Father, further, that they are "one body in Christ, and members one of another." (*Catholic Mind,* June 8, 1931.)

Catholic Action is the inevitable inescapable action of the Mystic Body; the Christian Social Order must necessarily be built on an intimate conviction of belonging to this Mystic Body. This language, I admit, does sound strange to us. But the whole Papal program remains vague and nebulous until we penetrate this language; should we shirk the task the entire Papal remedy runs grave risk of remaining untried and inoperative. The Holy Father *is* teaching us a new way of thinking about the Church and our functions therein; and until we possess that way of thinking, we lack a prerequisite to Catholic Action as he understands it.

Now it happens that an active liturgical life is the ideal working model of the New Christianity.

Everyone knows that there has been an enormous increase of interest in the liturgy of the Church in recent years. Literally there are hundreds of Study Clubs in individual dioceses, as that of Great Falls, and Wichita, the members of which are studying the liturgy. Not nearly so well known, however, is the fact that what is permeating the Church to the ends of the earth is not merely *new interest* in liturgy, but actually a new concept of liturgy. It is an interest in the "new" liturgy that really matters. The "old" liturgy, so to speak, was the ceremonial externals of public worship. Everything that pertained to the correct appointment of the church building, the altars, the vestments, the music, and in a word everything an expert master of ceremonies should know for the correct arrangement of Divine Worship. This is in brief what the lexicographers give for the meaning of the word *liturgy*. The "new" liturgy is something quite different. Let us define it as clearly as we can.

New Socialized Liturgy Different

The "new" liturgy may well be defined as: "Public worship socialized by the cooperation of the laity with the hierarchy." That definition has manifest advantages. By stressing lay cooperation with the hierarchy, it integrates the so-called liturgical movement with other phases of Catholic Action. Again, such a definition clearly indicates the program of the "new" liturgy, the socialization of public worship. But still that definition would *not* be the clearest for our present purpose; it would lead one to think that the "new" liturgy was being fostered only as an end in itself. When Pius XI speaks of it, as he often does, it is usually as a step towards something beyond. That something beyond, and for us an equally important purpose of the "new" liturgy, is what we were speaking of a moment ago, the realization of our membership in the Mystic Body of Christ. We, therefore, define the "new" liturgy from this function: The "new" liturgy is conscious and active public worship through Christ, with Christ, and in Christ, in the common membership of the Mystic Body.

It will be seen that there are two steps in the progress of inculcating in Catholics this *new* concept of liturgy. First, there is an induction into conscious and active cooperation while worshiping; secondly, there is a resultant sense of Mystic Body solidarity, which will carry over into the good and peaceful fight of Christ in all other spheres of Catholic Action.

Briefly then, the "new" liturgy is socialized worship as a teacher of Mystic Body consciousness. The "new" liturgy is, therefore, largely a key, and the value of a key is understood fully only in terms of what it can unlock. Thus a happy necessity lies on us of saying something about the Mystic Body of Christ into which we were incorporated as members by the laver of baptismal regeneration. But by the designs of a benevolent Providence, the realization of this mystic membership has only in our day come to the forefront of the popular consciousness.

The Mystical Body of Christ

The doctrine here referred to has come to the fore *so* rapidly that we can all sympathize with the good old lady who was wearying her friends not long ago with her sudden enthusiasm for the "mythical body" of Christ. Suppose we dwell briefly on the doctrine, so that if in any of our minds it is still a "mythical body," it may at least become real, even if it remains mystic or mysterious.

It is a question, after all, of how far God can go, even on this earth, in uniting Himself with man. That man, whom God had created out of love, had been raised at creation to a state in which he partook in a certain measure of the Divine Life. Man threw away that highest of all possible endowments, that sharing in the Divine Life-principle, and cast himself down. Then God had the problem of raising him up once more. This time the august councils of the Trinity determined, that at one given point in world history the Divine Nature and the human nature should meet in inseparable personal union in the Person of the Word, the Son. The union here was so intimate that the human nature lost even its personality, in the technical sense of the term. The second Person of the Holy Trinity, had the divine nature and had our human nature. In Him it pleased the Father that all supernatural life should dwell and of His fulness of the Supernatural life we have all received. The doctrine of the Mystic Body affirms that Christ is for us not merely Lord and Saviour, not merely King and Model, but becomes a living bond of supernatural life with us, nay, more, that Christ forms a living Bridge by which the Holy Trinity joins us to Itself in a real, but mysterious unity not unlike the unity of the Three-in-One. This is how Pius XI described this doctrine in his Encyclical on the Priesthood last year:

> There is no need, my Venerable Brethren, to enlarge upon the beautiful doctrine of the Mystical Body of Christ, a doctrine so dear to St. Paul; this beautiful doctrine that shows us the Person of the Word made Flesh in union with all His brethren. FOR FROM HIM TO THEM COMES A SUPERNATURAL INFLUENCE, so that they, with Him as Head, form a single body of which they are the members. (*Catholic Mind,* February 8, 1936.)

The ineffable words which Christ addressed to us the night before He died speak of a living union that must be maintained between Himself, the Vine, and ourselves, the branches, if we are to bear fruit. Again in addressing newly converted Christians at Rome, who were vaunting their Christianity over the rejected Jews, St. Paul reproves them sharply and bids them remember that they were shoots of the wild olive only recently engrafted into Christ, from whom comes their life, their fruitfulness, and worth (Rom. xi.). St. Paul goes on to add that the cast-off Jews could be again engrafted into Christ even as the Christians could be cast off; "It is not thou that upholdest the stem, but the stem thee." Speaking to the Ephesians, St. Paul could find no better way to illustrate Christian marriage than to point out that it resembles the living union between Christ and the Christians (Eph. v.). But, as the Holy Father says, this doctrine so dear to St. Paul is taught by him again and again under the analogy of the human head and members. Christ is the head of His Body the Church; we are together the Body of Christ. In this comparison St. Paul brings out the primacy of the head, the diversity of organs, the diversity of functions, mutual dependence, and the indwelling in head and members of the Holy Spirit of God. How are we to understand these various figurative expressions of Holy Writ? The Council of Trent answers our questions, with all the solemnity of a doctrinal definition, when speaking of the nature of sanctifying grace: ". . . Jesus Christ Himself, as the Head (acting) on the members, and as the Vine (vivifying) the branches, ceaselessly communicates a life-force (virtus) to the justified, and this life-force always precedes, accompanies, and follows their every good action, and without it these could in no way be pleasing or meritorious before God . . ." [DBU 809.]

Clearly then, between Christ and Christians there is a ceaseless communication of life and this life-force "makes us live," as St. John says, "with the life that is of God." We are all one living person in Christ in Christ Jesus, as St. Paul says so graphically (Gal. iii. 28). This union is not indeed a union unto singleness of personality; we each retain our full personality and responsibility, while intimately united to Christ through the mutual sharing of the same supernatural life. This is not Pantheism, of course, as though we became God, but it may be and is, called *Panentheism*—all in God—because in a manner that remains mysterious, we are made partakers, as St. Peter says (2 Pet. i. 4), of the Divine Nature. This living bond of union is not perceptible by any of the senses; is not classifiable in any known category; it remains unique and mysterious. When we say mystic or mystical body, then, we merely mean what Maritain calls: "One single mysterious body with a supernatural life which it receives from Christ" (*Things That Are Not Caesar's,* p. 4).

Perhaps it would help us to visualize this if I recalled a singular instance of horticulture which could have been seen in California some years ago. A certain gardener there had succeeded in grafting on to some ordinary fruit tree, let us say a pear tree, because I have forgotten just what tree it actually was, slips of all the fruit trees we have in our climate, the citrous alone excepted. Apples, peaches, plums, prunes, apricots, cherries, and the like, all modified by the stalk into which they were engrafted but all preserving much of their characteristic flavor and appearance, were there seen maturing on one parent stem. That is a good illustration of the diverse fruitfulness of the mystic body: it is not we who uphold the Stem but the Stem us.

Such then is this doctrine of the Mystic Body of Christ, the un-wearied theme of all the recent Popes from Leo to Pius, and, naturally, of course, the Apostolic Delegate, His Excellency Arch-bishop Cicognani. Nothing has contributed more to the spread of this doctrine in the English-speaking world than the translations and original writings of the late Monsignor John J. Burke, C.S.P. This theme has come to us over the air through the broadcasts of Mon-signor Fulton Sheen, has illuminated the writings of Father Daniel Lord, S.J., and a host of modern authors. It is an intimate conviction of this doctrine that socialized worship is to impart.

I enter a church on Sunday morning. If I am not mystic-body conscious, I may enumerate one priest at the altar, one server in the sanctuary, I fancy I can distinguish the voices of about eighteen singers in the choir above, and I can count, if I try, nine hundred and seventy-nine separate worshipers. Adding myself to the total, I have a sum of one thousand individual worshipers. If all of them similarly lack the concept of the Mystic Body, as engaged in worship, there are a thousand separate acts of homage, and allowing for a few prayers that may be said in common for a person recently deceased, and for the short vocal prayers at the end of Mass, it may well be that there is no conscious unity of mind and heart of the people and priest, one with another, and all with Christ, in this repetition of His Sacrifice of Calvary.

In a neighboring parish, where the corporate character of worship as a function of the Mystical Body has been well inculcated, what do I find? The priest at the altar, the server, the choir, and the multitude of the Faithful are all vividly conscious that Christ, the great High Priest, is engaged in reenacting His deathless Act and all know well that in this great Act each one has his own share, his own place, his own function; because each is conscious of a personal sharing in the priesthood of Christ. I see the vision of St. Paul in Hebrews fulfilled before my eyes:

> "Such (is) the High Priest fitted for our needs—
>   holy, guileless, undefiled,
> set apart from sinners,
> and made higher than the heavens . . .
> One who is Son, forever perfect—(Heb. vii. 26–28)

> Now to crown what we have said:
> Such a High Priest we have,
> Who hath His seat at the right hand
> of the throne of Majesty in heaven
> as Liturgist of the sanctuary,
> and of the true 'tabernacle, which the Lord'
> and not man, hath set up—(Heb. viii. 1, 2)

> He hath attained to a liturgy
> so much the more excellent,
> as the testament is better,
> whereof He is Mediator."—(Heb. viii. 6).

Conscious Socialized Worship

The "new" liturgy we defined as "conscious, active worship through Christ, with Christ, in Christ, together with all other Christians." Suppose that we focus our attention for a moment on this *consciousness* of worshiping as a member of the Body of Him whom St. Paul calls our Liturgist. I go to Mass on Sunday morning to dedicate myself to God in the form of a material gift, for I recall that the basic idea of sacrifice is the service of God by a gift which stands for self. Just as I am about to enter a pew, I see a person who offended me a few days ago, so I give her a meaning look and go on to another pew. But as I kneel down I am ashamed of myself, for did not Christ say something about leaving one's gift at the altar and going first to be reconciled to an offended brother and only then coming to offer the sacrifice? In my present endeavor, then, to "present my body a sacrifice, living, holy, well pleasing to God," (Rom. xii. 1), I propose that the oblation of my service will be the fulfilment of God's will in the matter of Christian patience and charity. So at the

Offertory I present my penny's worth of bread and wine in gifts that stand not only for myself and my present good resolution, but for the priest at the altar, for every soul in the church building, for every soul in the world-wide Church itself. Next to me is the landlord, and he is putting his gift on the altar in token of conformity to God's will in the matter of decent housing. Behind me is a laborer, a labor leader in fact, and he is offering himself for the perfect observance of the law of Christ in the relationships of master and man. I note nearby a banker, whose bread and wine signify his willingness to fulfil the mind of Christ as to the stewardship of our goods. By ourselves we are weak and shrink from sacrifice, but the Stem supports us, and so the altar is heaped with our poor crooked selves in the form of common bread and wine. By these offerings we express our willingness to practice self-control, to shoulder the cost of a Christian education, to assume the full responsibilities of citizenship, to extend the hand of fellowship to those of other races and other nationalities, and, in a word, to dedicate to God a union of minds and hearts, which we call in the Canon "the oblation of our service." As our gifts are put on the altar we pray that in a contrite heart and humble spirit we may be received by God, and be made partakers of His divinity, who vouchsafed to share our humanity. Then, in the process of our giving, the bread and wine, that stand for all of us, are caught up with Christ's great Gift and become the Body and Blood. The Body that was broken for us and the Blood that was shed for the remission of our sins, so uniquely precious in the sight of Majesty on High, that is what God sees in what had before been our poor self in token. The Body that was broken for us and the Blood that was shed for us, even they are enriched by this oblation of our service, just on the other hand, as our Holy Father has reminded us in the Encyclical "Miserentissimus Redemptor," they may be deprived of something of their requisite sanctity if our own self-oblation do not support them. And so, with our little gifts become the great Gift, we offer through Christ, and with Christ, and in Christ, all honor and glory to the Father.

We go one step farther in our peerless Act of homage along with Christ and fellow Christians. I refer to our participation in a Communion Breakfast at the Table of the Father. Mankind regards sharing in a common meal the acme of social union. To invite others to break bread with us is to extend them the right and position of members in the family. The fellowship of all artificial societies is both symbolized and fostered by eating common rations, just as no convention is thinkable, as we know, without the final banquet. Now, all that is preserved of the Eucharistic practice in New Testament times we have on the word of St. Paul, and speaking of the effect of Holy Communion, he mentions only this, that it is the bond of union among the recipients. "The cup of blessing which we bless, is it not fellowship in the Blood of Christ? The bread which we break, is it not fellowship in the Body of Christ? We many are one, for we all partake of the one Bread" (1 Cor. x. 15–17).

And so at Mass we press forward to the Banquet Table, sacramentally, if possible, or at least spiritually, to eat of the one Bread that makes us all one Body. Banker and laborer and landlord, educator and politician and industrialist, the proud, the self-centered, the unforgiving, all partake together of the good things that God had prepared for us. And it chances that I find next to me at the railing the very person I snubbed on entering the church. Arising from Communion I follow and kneel beside her and praise God present in her, as well as in myself, for I know now what St. Thomas meant when he said that the effect of this Sacrament is union with the Mystic Body. We leave the church together, thankful that the Light which is the life of men, hath made us understand that we are members of Christ and members one of another. . . .

Active Socialized Worship

But we said that the "new" liturgy is not only conscious, but *active* worship through Christ, with Christ, and in Christ in the Mystic Body. Let us draw out some of the implications of this activity. "The faithful gather at sacred shrines," our Holy Father tells us, "that they may draw piety thence, from its chief source, as it were, by *actively participating* in the venerated mysteries of the Church and in her public and solemn prayers . . . It is quite necessary that the Faithful, not as visitors or silent onlookers, . . . should mingle their voices with the priests' and the singers." ("Divini Cultus" December, 1928) This is in obedience to that basic law of our corporeal nature, which requires, as St. Thomas says, an external expression of interior homage, and which in its turn vastly increases that inner worship of the heart. (S.T.2,2,84 a.2.) In the Mass which we considered above, there was merely the union of minds and hearts, joined in silent

homage. Now to that sublime picture add the additional circumstance
of a thousand voices exultantly affirming their corporate homage,
whether by making the responses now made in our stead by the server
or joining in the ideal method of congregational plain-song. And that
matter of congregational song is so very important that one must
dwell on it for a moment. We shall never understand the Church's
mind, or our own singular opportunity to share most intimately in
her worship until we divest ourselves of the idea that congregational
singing has of necessity to be *good music*. No, its primary function
is to be *good worship* in song, and only secondarily is it to be judged
as music. Why does any gathering of people enjoying one another's
company eventually break into song? The very expression "break
into song" reflects the psychological necessity of song to express
exalted emotion. Why are there marching songs, boating songs, college songs, drinking songs, why light opera, why grand opera, if not
because song is a psychological necessity of man, be the actual singing musically good or ever so wretched? Why does man use song in
worship, if not because his very nature tells him it is the noblest
expression of common prayer? When the *Gloria in Excelsis* is sung
at the Mass, or the threefold *Sanctus, Sanctus, Sanctus* is intoned
along with all the angels of Heaven, why do I throttle my impulse to
sing, and stand by a mute spectator? "Must I wait until I get to
Heaven," inquired one lay worshipper some time ago, "before I can
sing my *Credo* along with the world-wide Church?" One of the most
sharply worded documents I have seen issue from the Holy See is
the Apostolic Constitution "Divini Cultus" mentioned a moment ago.
It was drawn up in 1928 to reaffirm and reenact the plain-song regu-
lations of Pope Pius X, and as the paternal voice of the Pontiff
lamented that these had not been observed in many places, he *did*
point out that where they were being observed the Christian spirit
was flourishing widely, "because the people imbued with the meaning
of the liturgy, had become accustomed to participate more zealously
in the service of the Holy Eucharist, in sacred psalmody, and in public prayers."

.   .   .   .   .

When we the Catholic workers, and we the Catholic financiers,
the Catholic clergy and the Catholic laity, the Catholic teachers and
the Catholic students, the Catholic white and the Catholic yellow or

red or black, the Catholic governed and the Catholic governing, when all of us shall have consciously and actively worshipped God, our common Father, as fellow members of the body whose head is Christ, His Son, then there will be solidarity on what we may call the liturgical front. Then shall we be ready "to play our part in this good and peaceful fight of Christ . . . In the Christian renewal of society," you will recognize your rallying cry from the "Quadregesimo Anno."

. . . . .

When we shall have socialized worship everywhere in America, then we shall have 20,000,000 persons intimately convinced of their membership in the Mystic Body, and of membership in one another. Twenty million Americans, knowing that they are Christ-ed at Baptism, made Christ-strong at Confirmation, charged Christ-ful day by day at the Eucharist, will be an irresistible army of Christocrats, from Maine to California, from Duluth to Galveston, fighting the peaceful fight in home and school and factory and shop and bank and legislature to make Christ King of American living and the crown of American culture.

New Life

DOROTHY DAY

My child was born in March at the end of a harsh winter. In December I had to come in from the country and take a little apartment in town. It was good to be there, close to friends, close to a church where I could stop and pray. I read the *Imitation of Christ* a great deal. I knew that I was going to have my child baptized a Catholic, cost what it may. I knew that I was not going to have her floundering through many years as I had done, doubting and hesitating, undisciplined and amoral. I felt it was the greatest thing I could do for

"New Life," reprinted from *From Union Square to Rome,* by Dorothy Day. Published by the Preservation Press, Missionary Servants of the Most Holy Trinity, Silver Springs, Maryland, 1940. Reprinted by permission of the publisher.

a child. For myself, I prayed for the gift of faith. I was sure, yet not sure. I postponed the day of decision.

A woman does not want to be alone at such a time. Even the most hardened, the most irreverent, is awed by the stupendous fact of creation. No matter how cynically or casually the worldly may treat the birth of a child, it remains spiritually and physically a tremendous event. God pity the woman who does not feel the fear, the awe, and the joy of bringing a child into the world.

Becoming a Catholic would mean facing life alone, and I clung to family life. It was hard to contemplate giving up a mate in order that my child and I could become members of the Church. Fred would have nothing to do with religion or with me if I embraced it. So I waited.

Those last months of waiting I was too happy to know the unrest of indecision. I was waiting. The days were slow in passing, but week by week the time came nearer. I spent some time in writing, but in general I felt inactive, incapable of going to meetings, of seeing many people, of taking up the threads of my past life.

And then the little one was born, and with her birth the spring was upon us. My joy was so great that I sat up in bed in the hospital and wrote an article for the *New Masses* about my child, wanting to share my joy with the world. I was glad to write it for a workers' magazine because it was a joy all women know, no matter what their grief at poverty, unemployment, and class war.

The article so appealed to my Marxist friends that the account was reprinted all over the world in workers' papers. Diego Rivera, when I met him some four years afterward in Mexico, greeted me as the author of it. And Walt Carmen, who was at that time editor of the *New Masses,* said that it had been printed in Russian newspapers and that I had rubles awaiting me in Moscow.

There was a Catholic girl in the bed next to me in the ward. She was a young Italian, not more than twenty-two, and she had just had her third child. She had a very serious and very obscure heart condition which led every physician who examined her to declare that she should not have children, that death was certain if she did. But she had had three, and, day by day, doctors gathered around her bed to examine her and exclaim over the novelty of her heart disease and expostulate with her for bringing children into the world. Several times they stood there giving her information on birth control and she listened with her eyes cast down, not answering them. They assumed she was stupid and repeated in the simplest phrases their directions, speaking in phrases as they spoke to foreigners who cannot understand English. Then when they looked on her chart and saw she was a Catholic they expressed their impatience and went away.

"I just don't pay any attention," she told me. "God will take care of me. I know I have to be careful. We live on the first floor and I never walk up and down stairs, and my mother-in-law helps me all the time, so I'm all right."

She did not care much for reading, and lay there watching with interested eyes what went on in the ward, that small world in which we were so contentedly confined for ten days.

"What you going to name your baby?" she asked me. "Teresa? I have a medal of the Little Flower here—you can have it if you want it."

I told her I didn't believe in such things, and she didn't take it amiss. "If you like someone, you like to have something to remind you of them," she said, and I was ashamed and took the medal.

Due to an attack of grippe after I left the hospital, Teresa's baptism was postponed for a time. Not being a Catholic myself, and not having been baptized myself until I was twelve, I didn't know the anxiety of Catholic mothers, that feeling almost that the baby had not yet been born until it had been baptized.

When Teresa was six weeks old and I was still very weak, we went down to the country. It was April and though it was still cold, it was definitely spring.

Every morning while Teresa napped on the sunny porch, well swathed in soft woolen blankets, I went down to the beach and with the help of Smiddy brought up driftwood, enough to last until the next morning. My husband was home only week-ends and then he chopped enough wood to last a few days. But when the wind was high and piercing it penetrated the house so that much wood was needed, and it was a pleasure to tramp up and down the beach in the bright sun and collect wood which smelled of seaweed, brine, and tar. It was warmer outside than it was in the house, and on the porch Teresa was nicely sheltered. Sometimes in the afternoon I put her in her carriage and went out along the woods, watching, almost feeling the buds bursting through their warm coats. Song sparrows, woodpeckers, hawks, crows, robins, nuthatches, and of course laughing gulls made the air gay with their clamor. Starlings chattered all day in the branches of the old pine in front of the porch. We collected azalea buds, dogwood, sassafras, and apple tree branches to decorate the room. Best of all there were still skunk cabbages small enough to make a most decorative center piece, propped up with stones, gleaming mottled-green, dark red and yellow. They were never so colorful as they were that year, and spring after spring since I have watched for them bursting up vigorously in marshy places. Skunk cabbages and the spring peeper mean that the winter is over and gone, and the voice of the swallow is heard in the land.

There was arbutus still buried under the leaves so that you had to look carefully for it like buried treasure. There were spring beauties and adder's tongue and dandelion greens. The year before I had been planting radishes on March first but this year gardening gave way to more delightful tasks.

Supper always was early and the baby comfortably tucked away before it was dark. Then, tired with all the activities that so rejoiced and filled my days, I sat in the dusk in a stupor of contentment. Outside, dozens of fleecy pink clouds were caught in the top of the hickory trees at the head of the bank and below them were whole fleets of lavender gondolas, then the deeper purple shadows of the Jersey shore. The three lighthouses stood out black against the silver water and there was not a wave, only a rippling, a scalloping along the yellow beach.

Soon the pink and rose clouds faded to a dingy smoke color, and those nearer the horizon changed to a purplish gray. The water remained silver with a peculiar surface glow which the sky did not have though they were the same color. Away off, miles away, through the bare trees on the point, the lights of a roadway flickered like candles.

The meadow before the house became a yellow deeper than the beach with a peculiar afterglow, and at the edge of the meadow, before the bank swept down to the sands, some dead weeds gallantly stood, goldenrod with the tufts still on it, sturdier sumac, and the tangle of wild grape and bayberry bushes. No life was showing on the bare branches of the honey locust trees, those trees so late in budding, but life was there, and life was there too in the room with me, throbbing silently.

And always, those deep moments of happiness gave way to a

feeling of struggle, of a long silent fight to be gone through with. There had been the physical struggle, the mortal combat almost of giving birth to a child, and now there was coming the struggle for my own soul. I knew Teresa would be baptized, and I knew also the rending it would cause in human relations around me. I was to be torn and agonized again, I knew, and I was all for putting off the hard day.

Then one afternoon as I wheeled her in her little carriage along the road which led down to St. Joseph's Home, a former estate of Charles Schwab, which had been given to the Sisters of Charity, I met a Sister who was on her way to visit a neighbor of mine.

That estate had been one of my stumbling blocks. I could never pass it without thinking of Schwab's career as head of the Bethlehem Steel Corporation, of his work in breaking the Homestead strike, of how he, to this day, refuses to recognize unions of workers in his Bethlehem Steel Corporation.

I could not but feel that his was tainted money which the Sisters had accepted. It was, I felt, money which belonged to the workers. He had defrauded the worker of a just wage. His sins cried to heaven for venegeance. He had ground the faces of the poor. "Let not the oil of the sinner fatten my head" (Psalms 140:5), I thought with the Psalmist. "He that offereth sacrifice of the goods of the poor, is as one that sacrificeth the son in the presence of his father." "He that sheddeth blood, and he that defraudeth the labourer of his hire, are brothers" (Ecclesiasticus 34:24–27). The words of the son of Sirach went through my brain, wearying me. Yet strangely enough, in bitterness of soul these thoughts led me inevitably to the problem: how to have Teresa baptized.

That bitterness felt by so many in the radical labor movement towards what they call "organized religion" was mixed with the knowledge of the divinity of the Catholic Church. It was ever in my mind that human frailties and the sins and ignorance of those in high places throughout history only proved that the Church *must* be divine to have persisted through the centuries. I would not blame the Church for what I felt were the mistakes of churchmen.

I could only always console myself with Christ's words that the greatest enemies would be those of the "household."

I felt, too, that there were going to be many obstacles put in my path, and that this in a strange way was one of them.

That afternoon I was emboldened by a sense of compulsion to speak to the Sister who was hurrying by me, to ask her how to go about having a baby baptized. I had a warm feeling as I approached her, a feeling that whatever the errors of Charlie Schwab, Sister Aloysia had no part in them in her simplicity and poverty.

She was very matter-of-fact. She seemed to take things for granted, and was not surprised that a mother of a new baby would stop her in this casual fashion and ask her so stupendous a question. Of course a mother, no matter how heathen she might be, would want her baby to be sure of eternal life! She knew of me by reputation—indeed all the neighborhood knew that we and our friends were either Communist or Anarchist in sympathies. But those same dear Catholic neighbors who heard sermons excoriating "the fiendish and foul machinations of the Communists" (I have heard just such expressions used), were kindly people who came to use our telephone and bring us a pie now and then, who played with us on the beach and offered us lifts to the village in their cars. Sister Aloysia, too, had no fear, only a neighborly interest in us all. Perhaps she had been praying for us these past two years as she swept past down the lane on a visit to some of the Catholics at the end of the road. Perhaps her work-worn hand was clutching that rosary which jingled at her side just a little more fervently and comfortingly.

She felt my liking and I was warmed by her interest. She took me under her protection immediately. She did not make little of my difficulties, nor did she think for a minute that they were insurmountable. There was a hard row to hoe in front of us, was her attitude, but we could get through it. She would hang on to that long, formidable-looking rosary of hers, hang on to it like an anchor, and together we would ride out the gale of opposition and controversy. All we had to do was depend on prayer.

And as for practical details, we would just go ahead as though it were very simple. Did I have any Catholic relatives?

Yes, there was cousin Grace. She was married and she and her husband could be reached, though I had not seen them nor any relatives for years.

All right then, she herself, Sister Aloysia, would get in touch with the parish priest in Tottenville, a young man, very obliging. He had been coming down to offer up Mass at the Home and she could see him after breakfast the next morning.

Somehow or other, with the irregularities of her parents not being Catholic, Teresa's baptism did not take place until late June. Sister Aloysia in her anxiety that all should go well dropped in every day to see if I were persisting in my determination. She also was quite frank in her anxiety for the baby's welfare. One morning she came rushing up on the porch—"She's not dead yet?" she wanted to know, and then praised God that the baby was living and also struggling towards her baptism. Sister was sure that the powers of darkness were struggling hard for my little one—"He's greedy for souls," she said, meaning the devil, and in this case I had more confidence and hope than she because I assured her Christ must be even more so. Anyway, Teresa thrived lustily and was beginning to throw back her head and crow and gurgle, competing with the birds to make the morning joyful.

"Don't be afraid of this old black crow," Sister used to tell her as she bent over her crib. And Teresa used to open her mouth in a toothless smile, embellished by a delightful dimple which she has since lost.

But Sister Aloysia did not neglect me in her anxiety for the baby. "You must be a Catholic yourself," she kept telling me. She had no reticences. She speculated rather volubly at times on the various reasons why she thought I was holding back. She brought me pious literature to read, saccharine stories of the saints, emasculated lives of saints young and old, back numbers of pious magazines.

William James, agnostic as he was, was more help. He introduced me to St. Teresa of Avila and St. John of the Cross. And I already had St. Augustine and the *Imitation* and the Bible from which I derived strength and comfort. But isolated as I was in the country, knowing no Catholics except my neighbors who seldom read anything except newspapers and secular magazines, there was not much chance of being introduced to the good literature of the present day. Chesterton's paradoxes wearied me. Belloc's histories I enjoyed but they did not inspire me. I was in a state of dull content—I was not in a state to be mentally stimulated. I was too happy with my child. What faith I had I held on to stubbornly. The need of patience emphasized in the writings of the saints consoled me on the slow road I was traveling. I would put all my affairs in the hands of God and wait.

Three times a week Sister Aloysia came to give me a catechism lesson which I dutifully tried to learn. But she insisted that I recite word for word, with the repetition of the question that was in the book. If I had not learned my lesson she rebuked me. "And you think you are intelligent!" she would say witheringly. "What is the definition of grace,—actual grace and sanctifying grace? My fourth-grade pupils know more than you do."

I hadn't a doubt but that they did. I struggled on day by day, learning without question. I was in that agreeable and lethargic and almost bovine state of mind, filled with an animal content, not wishing to inquire into or question the dogmas I was learning. I made up my mind to accept what I did not understand, trusting light to come, as it sometimes did, in a blinding flash of exultation and realization.

She criticized my housekeeping. "Here you sit at your typewriter at ten o'clock and none of your dishes done yet. Supper and breakfast dishes besides . . . And why don't you calcimine your ceiling? It's all dirty from woodsmoke."

She used to bring me vegetables from the garden of the Home, and I used to give her fish and clams. Once I gave her stamps and a dollar to send a present to a little niece and she was touchingly grateful. It made me suddenly realize that in spite of Charlie Schwab and his estate, the Sisters lived in complete poverty, owning nothing, holding all things in common.

She never came into the house directly but used to peer in the window or back door with a sepulchral whisper, "Is he here?" as though it were the devil himself she were inquiring after. And if Fred were there, he used to slam out of the other door to show his displeasure, greeting her through clenched teeth. I didn't blame him, nor did I blame her. She would probably have regarded any husband so, no matter how Catholic, how exemplary. She knew little of the world of men.

Finally the great day arrived and was a thing of the past. Teresa was baptized, she had become a member of the Mystical Body of Christ. I didn't know anything of the Mystical Body or I might have felt disturbed at being separated from her.

But I clutched her close to me and all that summer as I nursed her and bent over that tiny round face at my breast, I was filled with a deep happiness that nothing could spoil. But the obstacles to my becoming a Catholic were there, shadows in the background of my life.

I had become convinced that I would become a Catholic, and yet I felt I was betraying the class to which I belonged, you my brothers, the workers, the poor of the world, the class which Christ most loved and spent His life with. I wrote a few articles that summer for the *New Masses* but did no other work. My life was crowded because friends came and stayed with me, and some of them left their children. Two little boys, four and eight years old, joined the family for the summer and my days were full, caring for three children and cooking meals for from six to ten people three times a day.

Some few times I could get up to the village to Mass on Sunday, when I could leave the baby in trusted hands. But usually the gloom that descended on the household, the scarcely-voiced opposition, kept me from it. There were some feast days when I could slip off in the middle of the week and go to the little chapel on Charlie Schwab's grounds. There were "visits" I could make, unknown to others. I was committed, by the advice of a priest I consulted, to the plan of waiting, and trying to hold together the family. But I felt all along that when I took the irrevocable step it would mean that Teresa and I would be alone, and I did not want to be alone. I did not want to give up human love when it was dearest and tenderest.

During the month of August many of my friends, including my sister, went to Boston to picket in protest against the execution of Sacco and Vanzetti, which was drawing near. They were all arrested again and again.

Throughout the nation and the world, the papers featured the struggle for the lives of these two men. Radicals from all over the country gathered in Boston and articles describing those last days were published, poems were written. It was an epic struggle, a grand tragedy. One felt a sense of impending doom. These men were Catholics, inasmuch as they were Italians. Catholics by tradition, but they had rejected the Church.

While enjoying the fresh breeze, the feel of salt water against the flesh, the keen delight of living, the knowledge that these men were soon to pass from this physical earth, were soon to become dust, without consciousness, struck me like a physical blow. They were here now; in a few days they would be no more. They had become figures beloved by the workers. Their letters, the warm moving story of their lives, had been told. Everyone knew Dante, Sacco's young son. Everyone suffered with the young wife who clung with bitter passion to her husband. And Vanzetti with his large view, his sense of peace at his fate, was even closer to us all.

The day they died, the papers had headlines as large as those which proclaimed the outbreak of war. All the nation mourned. All the nation, that is, that is made up of the poor, the worker, the trade unionist,—those who felt most keenly the sense of solidarity,—that very sense of solidarity which made be gradually understand the doctrine of the Mystical Body of Christ whereby we are the members one of another.

Teresa's father was stricken over the tragedy. He had always been more an Anarchist than anything else in his philosophy. He did not eat for days. He sat around the house in a stupor of misery, sickened by the cruelty of life and of men. He had always taken refuge in nature as being more kindly, more beautiful and peaceful than the world of men. Now he could not even escape through nature, as he tried to escape so many problems in life.

During the time he was home he spent days and even nights out on the water fishing, so that for weeks I saw little of him. He stupefied himself in his passion for the water, sitting out on the bay in his boat. When he began to recover he submerged himself in maritime biology, collecting, reading only scientific books, and paying no attention to what went on around him. Only the baby interested him. She was his delight. Which made it, of course, the harder to contemplate the cruel blow I was going to strike him when I became a Catholic.

These pages are hard to write. The struggle was too personal. It was exceedingly difficult. The year passed and it was not until the following winter that the tension reached the breaking point. My health was bad, but a thorough examination at the Cornell clinic showed only nervous strain.

Finally with precipitation, with doubts on my part at my own unseemly haste, I made the resolution to bring an end to my hesitation and be baptized.

It was in December, 1927, a most miserable day, and the trip was long from the city down to Tottenville, Staten Island. All the way on the ferry through the foggy bay I felt grimly that I was being too precipitate. I had no sense of peace, no joy, no conviction even that what I was doing was right. It was just something that I had to do, a task to be gotten through. I doubted myself when I allowed myself to think. I hated myself for being weak and vacillating. A most consuming restlessness was upon me so that I walked around and around the deck of the ferry, almost groaning in anguish of spirit. Perhaps the devil was on the boat.

Sister Aloysia was there waiting for me, to be my godmother. I do not know whether I had any other godparent. Father Hyland, gently, with reserve, with matter-of-factness, heard my confession and baptized me.

I was a Catholic at last though at that moment I never felt less the joy and peace and consolation which I know from my own later experiences religion can bring.

A year later my confirmation was indeed joyful and Pentecost never passes without a renewed sense of happiness and thanksgiving. It was only then that the feeling of uncertainty finally left me, never again to return, praise God!

Primitive Christianity Once Again

JAMES M. GILLIS, C.S.P.

Many writers and speakers in the Catholic camp have made the point that we can learn much from the Communists. Our ideological enemies are devoted to their cause, determined, resolute, confident, indefatigable. One cannot say that they are conscientious, for they repudiate conscience as a superstition. But whatever it is that they have in place of conscience, they certainly are faithful to it. In one word, they have a religion and every man-jack of them is an apostle. Their zeal makes our Catholicity seem apathetic or even lethargic by contrast. They are what we used to be when we were in our pristine vigor.

It seems inconceivable that twelve men should have been sent out to revolutionize the world. Indeed it seemed incredible and impossible even to them. When our Saviour had been gone several years

"Primitive Christianity Once Again," taken from Chapter 2 of *This Our Day,* by James M. Gillis. Published 1949 by the Paulist Press, New York, N.Y. Reprinted by permission of the publisher.

the Apostles were—so to speak—still hanging around Jerusalem. But they finally got the idea into their heads that when He had said they should go into the whole world and make all men His disciples, He was not talking poetry or rhetoric. He meant that they should do just that and nothing less. So (as our colored brethren would say) they up and went and did it. It took time; it required sacrifice, but the fact is that those twelve peasants turned the world upside down.

It sometimes seems that the inheritors of the zeal of the early Christians are not Catholics but Communists. They have done what the poet says cannot be done—recaptured the "first fine careless rapture" of a new religion. They have stolen our stuff, our confidence, our courage. Two of them, Lenin and Trotsky took over the vast Russian Empire. The successors of those two coryphaei have gone their conquering way and have absorbed a territory 5,000 miles wide and 3,000 miles across, with a population of some 400 million. As if that were not enough they now keep the rest of the world on tenterhooks. They have us hypnotized, paralyzed, waiting for their next move, and without the slightest idea of what we shall do when they make it.

I do not exaggerate. The head of the only power on earth that can—perhaps—halt the onward march of Communism doesn't know what he will say or do or recommend if Stalin doesn't stop. Nor do we the American people know what we shall be expected to do, or what we shall be willing to do. All we know is that whatever is to be done must be done by us. No other power on earth can do it. Britain is sunk.

One might say of England what the Roman said of Troy, *Fuit Ilium, Fuit Britannia*. The British Empire was, but is no more. France is out of the running. She doesn't know which way her own electorate will move in the next election. Italy squeezed through, but eight million Italians tried to vote themselves into subjugation to Moscow. There remain Belgium, Holland and—don't laugh—Luxembourg. As for the United Nations, what can they do but sit on the side lines and watch the game hoping that it may not end in a rout? As a specimen of diplomatic and moral impotence the U.N. is pitiable and tragic. So there we are. No one remains in all the world to challenge the present enemy but Uncle Sam, and he doesn't know what to do or whether or not to do anything.

One of our candidates for the presidency, Mr. Dewey, seemed to be about to say something when he uttered the epigram, "You can't kill an idea with a gun." But having ventured that first step in the right direction, he didn't dare take a second. Rather he took two steps backward, suggesting Universal Military Training and a bigger and better system of American spies in Europe and Asia. By way of completing his first and second idea with a third, he said, "we must not permit Russia to steal elections." What we are to do if Russia does steal other elections he failed to say.

Candidates for political office should take lessons in golf. "Follow through," says the instructor. But your Trumans and Deweys and Stassens and Wallaces never follow through. So they slice or hook and foozle their shots. It's especially unfortunate that Mr. Dewey didn't follow through—or follow up—his epigram, "You can't kill an idea with a gun." The only thing that can kill an idea is a better idea. It may be not another idea, but the same idea doing service for a better cause.

In two recent books, *France Alive* and *Priest-Workman in Germany* we have a fine illustration of that fact. The first principle of Communist strategy is to be found, strange to say, in a papal encyclical: "*Go to the workingman, go to the poor.*" That strategy was stolen from us. Stolen while the good man of the house was asleep, in spite of the Gospel warning.

The Christian religion started in a dwelling house, in a room at a supper table. Not a supper table converted into an altar and never again used as a supper table, but a supper table that had been and was to continue to be a supper table. A church was not necessary, still less a basilica, a cathedral, an ecclesiastical monument. The little room sufficed. The "cell" idea, stolen by the Communists was primarily Christian. You find it in the Acts of the Apostles.

We started very humbly and we should never have ceased to proceed humbly. But as time went on the disciples became numerous and some of them were rich. As soon as the rich came in the priests commenced to discriminate between rich and poor. Read the scathing rebuke of the rich and the pamperers of the rich in the Catholic Epistle of St. James.

Persecution came, and we went underground. We taught the Communists that device also. As we had taken refuge in the catacombs, they took refuge from the czars in cellars and caves and

dens. But when the days of persecution were over, we went "high hat."
Kings, emperors, aristocrats came to us. They heaped gifts upon us.
Perhaps in the beginning they did so out of gratitude to God, but
later the privileges, favors, immunities, exemptions they bestowed
upon us were meant to be and were a *quid pro quo*.

When a poor man gives something to the Church he does not
take it back. When a rich man does the Church a favor (that's the way
he puts it) he demands compensation. Royalty, nobility, aristocracy
beguiled us and made us forget that we were, that we are, and must
forever be the Church of the poor. We became like the man in that
same Epistle of St. James who "beholding his own countenance in a
glass, went his way, and presently forgot what manner of man he was."

Finally, by an incredible reversal of its primary position, the
Church became identified in the mind of the poor as the rich man's
possession. In France, for example, as far back as the Revolution of
1798 the poor held the clergy and the hierarchy in equal abhorrence
with the king and his entourage. In the days of the Terror priests were
killed, not simply because they were priests but because being priests
they ran with the wrong people. Of course there were simply, saintly
Curés de campagne quite as poor and humble as the villagers to whom
they ministered. But in a revolution men go berserk; they are not
judicious; they make no distinctions.

In the court of the Capets and in all other courts before them for
1,300 years there was an ecclesiastical aristocracy, as pompous and
as haughty as the political aristocracy. They had, as the saying goes,
"risen in the world" since the days when Peter was a fisherman and
Paul earned his living making and mending tents. The ecclesiastical
aristocrats seem not to have caught the scorn in the statement of
Jesus, "They that are clothed in soft garments, are in the houses of
kings." The only time our Saviour was in the house of a king or even
in a king's courtyard, He was standing trial for His life.

Every one of those churchly nabobs had read, unless he skipped
his breviary, St. Fulgentius' biting contrast between Jesus in the stable
and Archelaus in the palace, and some of the court preachers had
doubtless preached upon the theme, "Christ on the Cross, Herod on
the throne." But when churchmen forget to be humble, the most
eloquent expression of truth makes no more impression upon them
than the most banal platitude.

At any rate they didn't learn. Even the Reign of Terror couldn't teach them. They came out of the courts of kings—not that they wouldn't have remained if the kings and the courts had remained—but they couldn't find their way back to the poor people. They remained a class—perhaps even a caste—apart from the people. They took the separation as a matter of course and as unavoidable. The people wouldn't come to them and they wouldn't go to the people.

Finally such a deep rift occurred that the Cardinal Archbishop of Paris has found it advisable to declare France a "mission country" (as if the "eldest daughter of the Church" were as heathen as Siam or Senegambia or the Solomon Islands). So, the clergy in France must start all over again as the Apostles had started in Judaea and Pontus and Pamphylia and Libya and Phrygia. With the approbation of their bishops and of the superiors of religious orders, numbers of priests have removed the Roman collar and the soutane (which had come to be, like the phylacteries and fringes of the Pharisees, the badge of a caste apart from the people). They work all day in mines and factories, coming back to the stinking verminous tenements at night, saying Mass on a kitchen table—presently used again as a kitchen table—sitting down with the proletariat, eating and drinking with them, walking and talking with them, precisely after the manner of our Lord Himself.

In a word the clergy in France, under the direction of the hierarchy, are trying to obliterate the aristocratic tradition that had grown indurate after 1,500 years.

So we see Communist tactic stolen from us now restored to its original practitioners. We have something practical in place of barren epigram, "you can't kill an idea with a gun." To be quite accurate, you cannot kill an idea even with an idea. If Mr. Dewey had read Plato he would have known that an idea is invulnerable and immortal. But you can pursue an idea that has got away from you, bring it back, convert it to good use if it has been used for bad. That's what we must do with the pope's idea (which of course was the first pope's as well as the last), "Go to the workingman, go to the poor." And that, in turn, is only a variant upon the original "Go into the highways and byways."

In spite of the fact that the movement back to primitive Christianity is sponsored by Cardinal Suhard and that Jesuits, Dominicans, Benedictines and diocesan priests are engaged in it, a certain type of Catholics in America—and I dare say also in France—will affect

to be scandalized. Such "scandal" would be nothing new. There were
potential Christians in Jerusalem who would have gone along with
Jesus if He had done His work in what they would have called a
more dignified way, and had made His appeal primarily to important
people. Our Lord's critics spoke of "this accursed multitude who
know not the law," and asked, "Have any of the leaders believed
in Him?" In their view He should have taken possession of the great
golden temple as His own and enthroned Himself in it. They couldn't
stomach His preference for open air preaching, with a rock by the
wayside or a boat on the bank of the lake as a pulpit, and a field for
a church. As for the rag-tag and bobnail mob that traipsed after Him,
they were enough to frighten off all "self-respecting persons."

In our own day there are millions of half-convinced, would-be
converts to Catholicism who would come over to us if Catholics were
all "nice" people. The Yankees in New England used to complain
that the Catholic Church was the Church of the Paddies and the
Biddies, of stablemen and servant girls, of uncouth, smelly people
with an Irish brogue. More recently in certain sections it isn't the
brogue but the garlic that keeps interested but fastidious observers
out of our pews and away from our altar rails.

We can understand that sort of snobbery on the part of non-
Catholics, but the more distressing fact is that persons within the
Church turn up their nose at, for example, a woman who goes into
slums and lives with poor people, especially if the poor people are
blacks. In general the accusation is that those devoted women who
inaugurated in this country the kind of work that clergy and laity
are now taking up in France, lack judgment, mental and emotional
balance, discretion, prudence—all varieties of the neutral virtue of
caution—in a word that they are extremists or even fanatics.

Granting for the sake of avoiding argument that the critics are
partly right, the reply is obvious: every human being has the defects of
his qualities. St. John the Baptist lacked the poise, the courtliness, the
politesse of St. Francis de Sales; St. Paul didn't accept or couldn't
practice the *ne quid nimis* of the stoic philosophers; at Athens they
called him a madman. Savonarola hadn't the sweet patience of St.
Philip Neri. Henry Suso and St. Peter of Alcantara had no such sense
of humor as St. Teresa. You can't have all qualities in one person.
In the history of mankind there is no absolute paragon except Jesus
Christ.

So how can we demand perfect poise of a woman possessed of such zeal as to live by choice with the proletariat and endure all the discomforts of cheap tenements, crawling vermin and foul odors seeping in from neighboring flats? I wouldn't expect such a woman, especially if she had the nerve to brave the scorn of being called a "nigger-lover," to exhibit at the same time the nonchalance and complacence of those who don't care what happens so long as it doesn't happen to them. When comfortable Catholics complain about those of their fellows who, for the love of God and man have foresworn comfort, my invariable suggestion is, "If you don't like the way they do it, go in and do it better; if they make mistakes, how about your doing the same work without the mistakes?" The discussion usually comes to a conclusion at that point.

As of heroes and heroines in the slums of American cities, so of those priests, laymen and laywomen who have plunged into the hell's kitchens of Paris with the same holy abandon as missionaries who plunge into the jungles of the Congo, or who choose for life companions ex-cannibals or head hunters or some different but equally offensive brand of savages.

We clerics, when reminded of our unlikeness to the saints, sometimes reply—with a rather sickly sense of humor—that the more extreme characteristics of the saints are to be admired, not imitated. But we know in our souls that the reason we take refuge behind that convenient adage is that we haven't the courage to live our faith or practice our vocation to the full. We read in books of ascetical and mystical theology that we all have the divine grace to be saints, but our meditations on that theme, like the discussion mentioned above, come to their conclusion as soon as they commence. George Eliot says of the Englishman that he doesn't know just how far he should go in religion; all he knows is that he should not go too far. Most of us are like that Englishman.

Sanity Is the Point

FRANK J. SHEED

Our treatment of *anything* must depend, in the last resort, on what we think it is: for instance, we treat people one way and cats another, because of our idea of what a man is and what a cat is. All our institutions—family, school, trade union, government, laws, customs, anything you please—grew out of what those who made them thought a man was. If you want to understand them profoundly, you must get at the idea of man that they express. There are periods of human history when it is not immediately and obviously necessary to make this sort of profound enquiry. When institutions are long-established, functioning healthily, serving happiness, the mass of men may very well decide simply to live by them and ask no questions. But when anything goes wrong with an institution—so that we have to decide whether to mend it (and if so, how) or to scrap it (and if so, what to put in its place)—then the question what man is immediately becomes not only practical, but of the first practicality.

This is so for two reasons, one of them vital but in our day widely denied, the other vital and not in any day deniable. The first reason is that all social orders are made for men and must be tested by their aptitude to men. There are those who would smile at this, and for the moment I shall not argue with them, but go on to the second reason, which nobody can deny, that all social orders are made *of* men. People making engines study steel, people making statues study marble, people making social systems should study man, for man is as much the raw material of social systems as steel is of engines, or marble of statues. And whereas we are not all making engines or statues, we are all involved in the making of social systems, from small ones like the family, up to the largest, the State to which we belong.

Our whole life consists in getting along with other human beings. In our personal relations, therefore, the question is, how should men be treated; in the political order, the question is exactly the same.

Now you cannot intelligently decide how anything should be treated until you are quite clear what the thing is. You cannot know how men should be treated until you are quite clear what a man is.

That is why the word Sanity is in the title of this book. Sanity means seeing what *is,* living in the reality of things. If a man sees what is not—snakes crawling out of his wallpaper, for instance, or himself as Napoleon—he is not sane. The trouble is that we do not always know when people are seeing what is not or failing to see what is, it can happen less spectacularly than in the instances quoted; but the principle abides, mistaking what is not for what is means that sanity is defective. Wishful thinking, for example, taking one's wishes for reality, is mental defect; so is taking one's fears for reality; so is taking anything but what is for reality. Wishful thinking is the commonest, in Sociology and Politics it is almost universal. It is horribly easy. We concentrate upon the thing we want—a particular arrangement of Society, say—so that it grows larger and larger in our mind; we regard obstacles, naturally, with impatience, get no pleasure out of looking at them, look at them less and less, finally stop seeing them: the obstacles are still there, of course, but they are no longer there for us: only the wish is real. We may still allude to the obstacles, but only to assure our hearers, and reassure ourselves, of the firmness of our hold on reality. Wishful thinkers love the slogans of realism—when you hear a speaker say "Facts, gentlemen, are stubborn things," prepare for a ramble through Utopia.

In every field the test of sanity is *what is;* in the field of human relations, the special test is *what man is.* This is the point at which Sociology must be rooted in reality. If it is not, no amount of accurate investigation and scientific weighing of evidence at subsequent stages will heal the defect at its roots.

I

But in the whole of our social life Man is overlooked. Man is taken simply as a word, the label for a particular kind of being (the kind to which we belong ourselves), and nobody stops for any serious consideration of what the word means. We proceed immediately to consider how to make the creature happier without ever asking what the creature is. It should be just the other way round. When some new proposal is made which affects the way men live, our immediate reaction is always to ask, Will it make men happier?

But this should be the second question, not the first. The first question should be, Does it fit the nature of man?

The total ignoring of this question runs all through modern life. Education provides an illustration perfect enough to be almost farcical. Throughout most of the Western World, the State is regarded as the normal educator. Schools not conducted by it are regarded as eccentric and in most countries they exist only precariously. This situation, I say, is taken as normal, whereas in fact it is grotesque. There are hundreds of definitions of education. But one may take as a minimum definition, one which would be accepted by practically everybody, that education is to fit men for living. Supposing you were to write to the Education Department of your State something to this effect: "I note that you are in the business of fitting men for living. Would you mind telling me what a man is?" The only possible answer would be that we live in a liberal democracy: every man is entitled to accept any religion or philosophy he pleases, and according to its teaching hold his own view—that man is matter, or spirit, or both, or neither: the State does not decide among them, it is wholly neutral, it does not know what a man is. If you were then to write further and say: "I note that as the State you do not know what a man is. Do you know what living is for?" the answer could only be the same— that it is a matter for each citizen to decide for himself, the State is neutral, the State does not know. I have called this grotesque, and that is to flatter it. To be fitting men for living, not only without knowing what man is or what life is for, but without even thinking the questions relevant, indeed without ever having asked them—it is odd beyond all words. Yet it does not strike people as odd. And the depth of their unawareness of its oddness is the measure of the decay of thinking about fundamentals.

Not only do they not see for themselves that it is odd, they cannot even be shown how odd it is. If one presses the point, they simply change the definition of education. The schools, they say, give their pupils a mass of valuable information, and train them in certain techniques so that they can earn a living, integrate with their fellows, and do the things the State requires of its citizens. But this is merely to take the oddness out of the school system by showing the same oddness firmly rooted in the life of society as a whole.

For what makes information valuable? How can we integrate with our fellows unless they are integrated themselves, and how do we know? And, given the strange things that some States *do* require of their citizens, how do we know that our own State's requirements are not harmful to us as men? None of these questions can be answered till we know what man is. Information is valuable if it helps man to be more fully and richly human: a man is integrated when all the elements of his nature are rightly related to one another and to the goal of life: the State must not require anything of its citizens which, with whatever increase of efficiency or material well-being, will diminish them as men. At every turn not only in education, but in the whole life of Society, the treatment of human beings by one another and of the citizens by the State needs testing by the question, What is man. And it is never asked. The State does not know what man is, and is taking more and more control of man's life.

In Karl Marx you see this ignoring of man in the pure form. The Western democracies do not know, or care, what man is, but they have some notion of what men want and how they are likely to react. Marx had not. Those who agree with him and those who disagree are at one in calling him a sociologist. But he was not a sociologist at all. He was a mathematician. Consider a problem in arithmetic: If one boy can mow a lawn in two hours, how long will it take two boys to mow it? The answer, of course, is one hour—two boys would take half the time that one boy would take. But this is mathematics. In fact, the two boys would start talking, arguing, wrestling: they would get their lawnmowers hopelessly entangled, go off for a swim and never come back. That is sociology. This is the sense in which I say that Marx was a mathematician and not a sociologist. He solved all social problems without reference to the human element. He had only to look at the first man he met to see that the Classless Society would not work with human beings. But he never looked: he had his own theory as to what man is and did not need to look! His most notable follower, Lenin, did at least look: he saw that the Classless Society would not fit man, but he did not let that worry him: "The great socialists in foreseeing the arrival [of the Classless Society] presupposed a person not like the present man in the street." In other words, by that time men will be different. Man, of course, is the sociologist's nightmare. It would be pleasant to be able to dismiss him so cavalierly. But it was left to Bernard Shaw, in this as in so many things, to go the whole way. He, too, saw what Lenin saw and Marx did not. His solution had its own charm: "If the human race will not

serve, nature must try another experiment." In other words, the
Classless Society is an end in itself: if man is not adequate for it, then
nature must find some creature that is. But for us, the problem is to
construct social institutions *for ourselves,* not for some unknown race
not yet on the horizon, and *of the material available,* namely, men
as they are—which includes their real possibilities of improvement,
though the sensible sociologist will not exaggerate the possibilities.
This precisely is sanity, a steady refusal to lose contact with what is.

II

The ignored question arises every day, in relation to a man's
handling of himself and his treatment of other people, in the smallest
personal and the largest national issues.

To take a question on which there is difference of opinion, Is
divorce or free love right? Swallows do not take one wife for life,
alley cats are promiscuous; and the most rigid priest thinks no worse
either of swallows or alley cats. Obviously we are back at the question
of what man is. We must settle that, before we can give an intelligent
answer to these or any other questions of personal morality. It would
be a strange coincidence if the answers were the same whether man
is a being akin to the angels, or an animal which has made better use
of its opportunities than the other animals, or a mere collection of
electrons and protons, a chemical formula, a thing for which a
doctor might write a prescription.

Matters like divorce and free love, you might say if you knew
very little of the world, are personal and can safely be left to the
individual to settle as he pleases. Take some more general question
which cannot be written off like that. Is it right to handle men solely
for our convenience? We put animals to work for us, thinking only of
our needs, wholly ignoring their preferences. Our medical men use
animals for their experiments, infecting them with appalling diseases,
vivisecting them. Is it wrong to make slaves or laboratory guinea-pigs
of men, to vivisect men? "Certainly it is wrong," you reply. "You
cannot treat men like animals." Personally I agree that you cannot:
but only because, knowing what man is, I know how he differs from
the lower animals, and what difference the differences make. Which
only means that to answer the question intelligently, you have to
settle what a man is. It is not enough to say that men would suffer from
being enslaved or infected with disease or sliced up. Animals do not

enjoy any of these things. Why should we consider a man's feelings and not a pit pony's or a dog's? Obviously it depends on our view of what man is. You think my examples are fantastic, that it will be sufficient to answer that sort of question when it arises. Who wants to treat men like that? If you can ask that, then you have forgotten about the forced-labour camps of Russia today, the scientific experiments on living men in German concentration camps a few years ago. You may never personally meet a man, although our whole civilization is threatened by a system, that argues in favour of these things. But if you do meet such a man, you will not be able to refute his arguments unless you can state, *and support,* a view of what man is that renders them untenable.

I do not want to go on multiplying examples every one of which will seem more obvious than the one before it. Once we are aware of this line of thought, it is clear that all intelligent sociology is bound up with it. We attach, for example, immense value to human equality. All men, we say, are equal. But equal in what? There is not a single quality in which all men are equal, or in which any two men are equal. Is the phrase meaningless? It has meaning only on one condition, a condition which most of those who use it do not fulfil. All men are equal only in the sense that all men are equally men, just as all triangles are triangles, or all elephants, elephants. So that men are equal to one another in all that is involved in being a man. But we do not know what is involved in being a man, till we know what a man is.

Indeed something even more obviously practical than human equality is at stake, namely human rights. The phrase "rights of man" too often means what it is good, or humane, or socially useful to concede him. But concessions, however liberal, are not rights. Rights are what man is entitled to, not what society is willing to let him have. They belong to man because he is man, and are valid even against society. Unless they are this, they are not rights at all, but only a more or less hopeful expectation of society's kindness. But *has* man rights? Obviously the answer depends on what man is.

I repeat that in quiet times where customs long established go their untroubled way, questions like this might be left to the philosopher. But in our own day there is not a single human institution that is not under fire. Every question under discussion, every revolutionary idea and every conservative reaction—all boil down to the question *how should man be treated,* and we can only answer this in the light of our view of *what man is.* No society can be united, if it is not united about this fundamental question. The United Kingdom is not thus united, nor the United States, nor the United Nations. The case is not so bad with the first two, because both our nations inherit certain ways of living and acting together, established by ancestors who did agree as to what man is. The United Nations has no such common past. There is neither present agreement in principle as to how man should be treated, nor any agreement in practice flowing out of a long past, for the United Nations has no past, and its constituent members inherit no common attitude to man. But we of the United States or the United Kingdom are in only slightly better case. We will not forever go on agreeing in practical action when all agreement about the reality involved has vanished.

Are Catholics Thought-Controlled?
(*October, 1951*)
JOHN LAFARGE, S. J.

This August past a million or so German youth marched the streets of the Russian sector of Berlin. Every mother's son and daughter from tots to adults was drilled to sing one same theme: to praise the great Stalin, to shout the same slogans of hate against Americans, to swallow the same Leninist-Marxian, made-to-order ideas. If any one dared to think or speak differently he or she was on the way to the cattle cars or to the concentration camps. And when a free mind falls into the clutches of the commissars behind the Iron Curtain bodies are tortured, brains are washed.

Every American is determined, cost what it may, never to permit that such a system be imposed on this country. The most telling accusation we can make against an American citizen is to suggest that he is in any way sympathetic to such procedures.

"Are Catholics Thought-Controlled?" by John LaFarge, from *A John LaFarge Reader* (New York: The American Press, 1956). By permission of The American Press.

Yet against some twenty-five million American citizens just such an accusation is leveled. Along with the vast majority of their Protestant and Jewish brethren, who worship the Creator and honor the Ten Commandments, these twenty-five million American Catholics abhor the Stalinist-Marxian slavery as they abhor everything that destroys the very image of God in man. To anyone who has even a passing acquaintance with Catholics such an imputation seems absurd. To one who like myself is a Catholic it seems not only absurd but criminal.

Last winter a Catholic priest and professor, a profound student of social and economic problems in questions of population growth, attended the annual meeting of a national learned society at one of our major universities. One of the scientists who took part in the discussion used the opportunity to denounce the Catholic belief shared by countless non-Catholics that pre-marital intercourse was sinful. The professor had gone out of his way and out of his specialty to make this un-called-for attack. When the priest ventured a quiet and reasoned reply the scientist shut off the discussion with the remark that of course the Reverend Father had to talk that way since he belonged to a Church that permitted no free thought or free discussion among its members. Again, one of our most widely advertised 1951 books on religious questions warned the American public that Catholics are thought-controlled.

If I drop into a rear pew of St. Patrick's Cathedral Sunday morning and take a look at that congregation, I find it hard to figure out they are of the thought-control type. Without being a mind-reader or using a dowsing rod I can state two things confidently of all these people who are quietly reading their book or saying their beads. First, they all do accept and hold as more precious than life itself that body of teaching which in their belief is given by the Creator to mankind by His Scriptures, His prophets and most of all by His own Son Jesus Christ. It has been passed on for near two thousand years by the Church that Christ founded. Lots of their fellow citizens don't hold this belief. But the Catholics do hold it for reasons that seem to them to be good and sound. They have no intention of giving it up on anyone's say-so. In this they are like all other sincere religious believers. Some people assume that Catholics are the type of people who are easily impressed, for instance, by claims of absolute authority; that they are psychologically or temperamentally different from other human beings. But do the facts bear this out?

Nothing but their conscience forces Catholics to stay in the Church. Priests and bishops make a very eloquent appeal to that conscience but no priest or bishop or Pope can stop anyone in that whole congregation—or all of them for that matter—from walking out of the Church at any time that they felt like doing so. The final reckoning for such conduct would be with God and not with man. As I said, this is a free country and Catholics to a man are determined it shall remain so. If you *accept* that body of teaching you accept it as a whole because it hangs together logically. If it didn't hang together it wouldn't be worth the attention of a logical mind. No alien is obliged to become a citizen of the United States, but if he does take out his American citizenship papers he is expected to subscribe to our Constitution, our laws, our Government, our entire Federal system as a whole. He cannot pick and choose for the simple reason that he undertakes to be an American. So if you accept the Catholic teaching you accept the standards, the safeguards, the institutions which that teaching has set up. You deeply deplore any sins and the weaknesses of the Church's members, high and low, but if you believe in the Church you take the Church in its essentials. You do not, however, need to accept or approve of its accidental shortcomings.

The second item I would notice about these people in St. Patrick's to whom the usher is now passing the church collection basket is a simple matter of ordinary observation. Outside of that common bond of religious faith and belief in a relatively small number of doctrines, they are as disputatious as any body of people in the world. The idea that Catholics are thought-regimented, that they all think and talk alike—outside of trifling disputes—is so far from being the truth that it is laughable. My own experience is that Catholics by and large make up for their unity in the matter of essential religious belief by differing vigorously about everything else. Let us look at some of these differences in detail.

1. *The political scene.* In every national election for the past hundred years the political dopesters have tried to figure out the Catholic vote. Yet Catholics were fiercely divided about Franklin D. Roosevelt through every one of his four terms. Some of his most intense and persistent opponents before as well as after his death

were found in Catholic ranks. So, too, among Catholics were found some of his staunchest friends and most ardent admirers. The same rule applies to the political situation today. Whoever may be the future candidates, however violently they may differ, Catholics will infallibly be on both sides of the political fence.

Yes, some prejudiced members of the Church, journalists or professional campaigners or just ordinary Joes may try to insinuate that the Pope has taken sides either with the Democrats or with the Republicans. Outside the Church there will always be people who speculate or accuse along the same line. They will be definitely and positively wrong. In order to clear up any misunderstandings on that line Pope Pius XII told the 1,300 delegates from seventy-four countries who attended the World Congress on the Lay Apostolate held in Rome October 7–15, 1951 that it was of course the duty of Catholics to assume political responsibility. As citizens of the State they should shoulder the citizens' burdens in the State. This means it is a matter of sound Catholic conscience for them to unite with all decent citizens in fighting abuses and advocating sound legislation. It does not mean they should as Catholics become "entangled in party politics." The Church wants its members to be politically responsible and politically active. It doesn't want them to be dodging elementary duties of the citizen of a democracy. It doesn't want them to write "count me out" on the walls as young people were doing in Germany shortly after the war. At the same time it doesn't want its own members or any of its friends or foes to be trying to use her authority on behalf of their own pet candidates.

2. *The atom bomb.* Among Catholics as among religious people of other beliefs there are wide differences of opinion as to our right to use so terrible an instrument of human destruction as the atom bomb. Should the A-bomb be used at all even in self-defense? Few Catholics at least in this country go so far in their thinking as to hold that it would not be necessary for us to use the A-bomb in defense were our country to be attacked by the same weapon. Yet some do hold even this radically pacificist view and they are Catholics in good standing who voice their views without let or hindrance from the Church. Some who would indignantly reject such an attitude seriously doubt whether it would be right to use the A-bomb even a moment in advance of others, even if they were reasonably sure the enemy was about to explode his deadly weapon. On the other hand, one of the

country's most distinguished Catholic educators holds tenaciously to the view that we should be amply justified in using the A-bomb if we were reasonably certain that the bomb was immediately to be launched against us.

3. *American representation at the Vatican.* So loud and so numerous have been the protests against President Truman's nomination of General Mark Clark as Ambassador to the State of Vatican City that many might believe the Catholics are just as thoroughly in favor of the idea as Protestants are opposed to it. In point of fact, this is far from being the case. The majority of Catholics in this country have never given ten minutes thought to the idea of U.S. diplomatic representation to the Holy See. Among those who have done a little thinking along this line I don't know of any who object to the idea of diplomatic representation in principle. I know Catholics who think the step would be unwise and a mistake in view of all the commotion it seems to cause among our non-Catholic brethren; others who believe that regardless how people feel about the matter our country is losing a valuable contact with the great center of moral world leadership as long as we have no way to deal with the Holy See directly. Personally, I share this latter view and I think that in time a calmer attitude will prevail among my fellow citizens. However, I am completely free to judge differently. If and when the U.S. Senate debates the matter, after reconvening in 1952, I shall expect the Catholic members of the Senate to debate the Mark Clark appointment simply and solely from the standpoint of what is good for the country here and now. Any other attitude would be untrue not only to their duty as legislators but as Catholics themselves.

4. *Schools and education.* The proposal of the Federal Government of the United States to provide for national assistance to the schools has met all along with varied reactions from Catholics. Some feel it is only fair that Catholic schools and colleges built and supported by American citizens should not be excluded from any aid given to tax-supported schools by the Government. Others would be unwilling to receive such help even if it were offered since they fear it would lead to complete Government control of non-tax-supported as well as public schools, and whatever benefits the aid might confer would be bought at the price of educational freedom. Today I do not know that Catholics oppose the idea as such of Federal aid to the country's schools. The needs of the country are too obvious, problems

are too grave and too many backward regions are handicapped. Catholics, however, do stand firm in their insistence that Catholics who attend free schools should not be stigmatized as second-class citizens. For this reason they consider they are entirely fair in asking for some form of *indirect* aid in case the Federal legislation is ever enacted.

5. *Literary criticism.* The last thing you will find is a uniform judgment on current productions, even from a strictly religious or Catholic point of view. There is the greatest width of individual judgment. All Catholic critics without exception, like other decent Americans, are completely opposed to pornographic literature. They show, however, varying degrees of sensitiveness in putting up with degrees of realism. Some of our critics are impressed first and last by the amount of artistic humbug that is palmed off on the public under "realism's" hallowed title. They see clean and young minds being introduced by a spate of popular writers to plain smut in the guise of a factual presentation of life. Hence they feel fairly cool even to very famous Catholic authors such as Evelyn Waugh, François Mauriac, Georges Bernanos or Graham Greene who make free use of what to them is always a dangerous, sometimes a suspect medium. Others, however, hold Christian art itself is stultified by what seems to them to be a too fastidious attitude towards realism. They quote Shakespeare, Chaucer, the Bible itself as their justification. Such Catholic critics have naturally no respect for a writer who abuses his brilliant talents merely to tell of man's foulness, vileness with no clear moral principle behind the story. But they do see genuine merit in an author who sets down in print the grim story of man's weaknesses and sins not because he is sympathetic to sin but because he loathes it.

Every week brings new books, new plays which in one way or another try to wrestle with man's big spiritual problems. The biggest drama today, as it always has been, is that played between man's soul, his passions, his conscience and his God. The story that grips a Frenchman or German may confuse an American, and vice versa. None of us think alike in any particular instance, and so help us we never will.

Someone will ask: "How can a church that tolerates any differences still maintain an Index of Forbidden Books?" The Index is concerned with writings that clearly contradict certain of the Church's

limited list of express teachings as to doctrine or as to morals, or else
—in certain instances—encourage the reader to serious sin. I think
that most people would agree that any responsible teacher who is
aware that a certain book can do serious harm to his pupils would
feel justified in keeping it out of their hands, especially where it is
likely to be confusing and contains errors that are not apt to be
detected by the ordinary reader. The existence of the Index is a
witness to the Church's conviction that it is passing on to mankind,
through its teaching, certain unchanging and necessary truths entrusted to it by its Founder, Jesus Christ. On the same principle, the
Church forbids certain books as seductive and subversive of morals
precisely because the Church, in a demoralized age, holds to the
absolute validity of certain primary moral truths. The "Index" is an
index of the Church's deep concern for the souls of its members; and
most Catholics, I would say, consider that abiding by it is a very small
item in the cost of belonging to the true Church.

In point of fact, the number of works designated by the Index
is small, and most of these are of interest only to clergymen and
theologians.

6. *Films.* In regard to realism in films Catholic critics of literary
realism are more cautious and sensitive, for the motion pictures are
mass media. Any group of children can drop into the motion picture
theatre at any time and the stuff is handed to them in visual form.
As to the worth of the individual screen plays, Catholic theatre-
goers and critics differ very widely like everybody else.

7. *Modern art.* Catholics disagree and constructively disagree on
the subject of "Modern Art." The Catholic Church is the home of
beauty, the greatest of all patrons of the arts, painting, music, sculpture, architecture, the crafts, etc. I think most Catholics who think
or talk about such things agree that art when placed at the service
of the Church's worship should not be hidebound by too rigid an
adherence to forms which derive from the past. We don't always
have to be building pseudo-Gothic churches; we don't always have
to imitate the stained-glass windows of Chartres. There is ample
difference as to what form and how far this adaptation in the modern
spirit should take place. Many Catholics are disgusted with much
that is palmed off as religious art in this country and abroad and sold
as commercial venture by certain church-goods dealers. There is
discussion in turn among Catholic artists and art lovers as to what

form a genuine non-commercial religious art should take. How far should we use for our churches the techniques and trends developed by modern types of artistic workmen, the so-called "abstract" or non-objective art?

What place has modern music in the service of the Church? Do we train our congregations to learn and appreciate the ancient ritual chants of the Church, some three thousand in number, or should we develop modern religious church music which people can sing and like?

8. *Franco.* On no topic can you start more arguments in Catholic circles than on the rights and wrongs of Spain. The only point is that they are arguments. The Church has no prescription for Americans or anyone else on the matter of Franco or any other Government for that matter, except as of course when in the case of Russia and its satellites it is openly and avowedly atheistic and persecutory of all religion. There are thousands of practicing Catholics of the Basque Republic in exile. Yet they are bitter opponents of General Franco. Even among those who live in friendly relations with the government there is criticism. Spain's own Archbishop of Valencia did not hesitate recently to point out frankly certain patent faults of the regime. American Catholic views on Franco range over a wide sector. Some very articulate persons are one hundred percent admirers of Franco and all that he is or will be. Others admire him for his past achievements and believe he was supremely necessary when Spain had the grim alternative of going Communist or staging the Nationalist revolt, and yet they are dubious as to his continued value at the present time. Many Catholics feel intensely that whether we like Franco or not at any time the only practical thing for the U.S. to do is to extend to his Government sincere cooperation in the face of the acute economic and strategic needs of Europe and the world today. There are dozens of anti- and pro-Franco opinions but there is no Catholic Franco party line.

9. *Attitude on non-Catholics.* Catholics differ, too, as to how to deal with their friends and neighbors who are not members of the Catholic Church. There is no sense just crying narrow-mindedness in this respect. No American likes to be considered a second-class citizen whether it be for his creed or his national descent or for his race and color. But there are plenty of places in this country where to be a Catholic means just that. In some country sections you are nobody

if not an Odd Fellow or a Mason. In New England until very recent years there was a stigma attached to the fact that your progenitors had entered the country later than 1800. Catholics, rightly or wrongly, feel a good many sore grievances on the school question. All Catholics who know their Faith agree that religious differences are not to be watered down or submerged. But they are in continual disagreement as to the emphasis that is to be placed upon these differences once we are outside the respective houses of worship. Some Catholics find it hard to put much credence in the good faith of Protestants and Jews. They are skeptical and suspicious of them even in ordinary affairs of daily living. Others, however, believe the soundest policy is to take good faith for granted wherever and whenever possible. They share the viewpoint of the Knights of Columbus of Plainfield, N.J., who every year get together with the Masons in the same town for a friendly social gathering, and work with them wholeheartedly throughout the rest of the year.

From coast to coast in 1943 Americans of all three major faiths, Protestants, Catholics and Jews, united in publicizing "The Pattern for Peace" issued by the Federal (now National) Council of Churches of Christ, the Synagogue Council of America, and the National Catholic Welfare Conference of Catholic Bishops. The effect of this document was stronger than perhaps any religious utterance that has been known in recent times in the history of this country. It profoundly influenced the thinking of the founders of the United Nations and of our Government officials. Since that time the same course has been followed in numerous other instances in this country and abroad. Today an increasing number of intelligent and educated Catholics believe in "the policy of presence," that it is their duty *as Catholics* just as it is their duty as American citizens to take their full share in the active organized life of the community, to be "involved" in the cares and joys of their fellowmen.

Roughly speaking, we can say that there are three main policies among Catholics with regard to the relation of Catholics and non-Catholics. One attitude is that of habitual criticism of the non-Catholic which, however, I do not think is the prevailing view. Secondly, simply to ignore those who are not of our Faith, forget about them and devote ourselves to leading an integrally Catholic life, carrying out our Faith in all its details. The third point of view is the policy of "presence."

10. *Nationalists and internationalists.* At once the deepest and the most surprising difference among U.S. Catholics has to do with international organization. There is a sharp division between nationalists and internationalists. In view of the centuries of official teaching on the necessity of some sort of world organization, no other example of dissent so clearly gives the lie to the charge that Catholics are intellectually regimented.

For many seemingly compelling reasons, American Catholics should be more international-minded than any of their fellow-citizens. They belong to a universal Church, they worship in Latin, a universal language, they send their sons and daughters as missionaries to all parts of the world, they read in their diocesan weeklies of the activities of the Church in every country on the face of the globe. The greatest Catholic thinkers have taught that the whole world must someday be organized into some sort of political unit, as the smaller groups of society have been progressively organized. In our day, the Holy Father, Pope Pius XII has taken for granted the need for an international organization, as did the American Bishops in their annual Statement of 1944, when they said, "The international community already exists; now it is necessary to organize it." The Catholic Association for International Peace, affiliated with the Social Action Department of the National Catholic Welfare Conference, has for twenty-five years published pamphlets and held conferences on various phases of world organization.

Despite this weight of practice and theory, it must be admitted that some American Catholics are belligerently nationalist-isolationist. It is likely that most of this group would take the same stand even if Soviet Russia were not anomalously numbered among the "peace-loving" United Nations. A complete analysis of their attitude is not in place here. Suffice it to say that they seem to be trying to prove their "100 per cent Americanism" to those who they imagine question it. Having heard their loyalty to America so often questioned, they are led by a certain sense of inferiority to the opposite extreme of per-fervent protestations of loyalty. In this frame of mind, they are easy victims of professional isolationist agitators, and are willing accomplices of reactionary groups in opposing anything that smacks of internationalism, down to and including liberalization of immigration quotas.

Even among Catholic internationalists, there is a wide variety of opinion on organization of the world for peace. The dominant part played by the Soviet Union in the United Nations is so repugnant to most Catholics, that they see little future for the organization unless the Soviet influence is reduced or removed. Others, equally detesting being linked in any way with the empire of politically organized atheism, are inclined to go along in every way humanly possible with the UN, in the hope of staving off the final and irrevocable cleavage of the world. And they wish that their co-religionists would not use Russia as an excuse for opposing such UN agencies as the dozen or so specialized agencies, in which the Soviets do not participate.

11. *Society and government.* On the domestic scene Catholics show a startling variety of opinions as to the merits or demerits of the New Deal, the Fair Deal, the right of labor to organize and campaign for organization, or the right of the individual workingman to refuse organization. At the time the New Deal came into being many outstanding Catholics hailed it as something profoundly Catholic in spirit if not in letter. One of the strongest supporters of the New Deal's social and economic principles was the late Monsignor John D. Ryan, a professor of moral theology at the Catholic University of America, Washington, D.C. Monsignor Ryan held that it was entirely a Catholic idea to hold that the Government should exercise certain controls over business and industry. A large and influential group of Catholic writers and teachers, and clergy and laymen think today along the same line. The Department of Social Action of the National Catholic Welfare Conference in Washington, D.C. is a center and clearing house for Catholic thought on social questions. It believes in a relentless battle of defense against Communism, since we are facing a vastly subtle and malicious conspiracy. But it also believes that a purely negative and defensive action gets us nowhere unless it is united with sharp constructive action and courageous social reform as well.

Many social-minded Catholics believe that the most effective way to get the Communists out of the unions is to encourage sound unionism from the inside, and they appeal to experience in support of their view. They take very literally the language of the great utterances that priests and popes have made on the subject of social and economic justice. They quote the encyclical "On the Condition of the Workingman," *Rerum Novarum,* of Pope Leo XIII issued in

1891 and "On the Reconstruction of the Social Order," *Quadragesimo Anno*, of Pope Pius XI issued in 1941, and the many discourses and pronouncements of Pope Pius XII and the American Bishops collectively and individually.

On the other hand, many Catholics are uneasy about anything that seems to them to savor even remotely of the New Deal or of the Fair Deal. They are disturbed at what they see as the growing power of unionism. The Hearst press, in general, is widely read and enjoyed among Catholics, and Westbrook Pegler can count on a fair body of Catholic adherents.

James Carey, militant secretary of the CIO and James Farley, conservative-minded head of the Coca Cola Corporation are pretty hard to list under one common denominator in their public life, yet Mr. Carey and Mr. Farley are both practicing Catholics. Different as are their social viewpoints, each of them is striving might and main to interpret the Church's teachings about the love of their fellowman according to what he judges is the most thoroughly Catholic course. Even persons so radically conflicting as Walter Trohan of the *Chicago Tribune* and Ed Marciniak, editor of the labor-minded monthly *Work*, are bound by a common basic faith.

12. *Free enterprise.* You do not need to search far to find a sharp cleavage of Catholic thought upon the subject of Free Enterprise, as you can suspect from what has just been said about social policies and the unions. On the one side you find those who place a practically unlimited faith in the American system of free enterprise. They look upon it as the salvation of the country and, through our nation's influence, as the economic salvation of the world. They have great confidence in the essential integrity of American business at all levels. They fear any restrictions placed upon it as tending to Socialism, and do not consider that their religion should have any part in such restrictions. Other Catholic teachers and publicists, however, are deeply concerned with what they consider to be dangerous tendencies in Big Business itself. They fear that without certain necessary governmental restrictions and without the careful development of a network of voluntary self-help and cooperative organizations to protect the individual, huge business monopolies will develop their own planned economy, and in that way pave the way for socialism to take over.

This cleavage in Catholic social thought was brought to a focus during 1951 by the publication of a book strongly favoring the Free Enterprise point of view, "Key to Peace," by Dr. Clarence E. Manion, Dean of Notre Dame University's Law School. Dr. Manion's book was sharply condemned and warmly praised by Catholic critics, and the controversy it created will doubtless continue. William F. Buckely's *God, Man and Yale,* which espoused a view on economic matters in many ways similar to that of Dr. Manion, has likewise met with a varied Catholic reception.

13. *Racial questions.* When Governor James F. Byrnes of South Carolina declared on January 14 and March 16, 1951, his undying opposition to any change in the South's segregated school system, plenty of Southern Catholics were ready to go along with him. They believe that the Church would have got nowhere in the South in the last fifty years if it had not conformed to the South's social structure. Furthermore, they believe that the Church's mission work for the Southern Negroes would have been hopelessly frustrated if the Negroes had not been cared for in separate churches and separate schools. Under existing circumstances, therefore, they are opposed to any move to change the segregation policy in public life or in the life of the Church.

However, a steadily growing body of Southern Catholics are taking a definitely different attitude. Whatever need there may have been for compulsory segregation in the past, they look upon it as a wasteful and unworkable policy if continued indefinitely in the future. They believe a start should be made now to prepare people's minds, by a carefully planned education of the public as to the Christian concept of human rights, for a change that is bound to come in the fairly near future. Catholics need to learn more of the teaching of their own religion as to sinfulness of racialism, the equality of all souls before God, and the world scope of the Redemption.

They are backed up in this position by the strong stand taken on racial justice by Southern church authorities in recent times, as well as by recognized Catholic organizations like the dynamic Catholic Committee of the South.

In other parts of the country, we find a somewhat similar cleavage among Catholics on the racial question. The vast migration in recent decades of Negroes from the South to the cities of the North and West has changed the population in countless Catholic parishes. Immigrants from the West Indies, from Puerto Rico and from Mexico have raised still further problems. In many a locality these newcomers have met with firm resistance on the part of the older Catholic parishioners: the parishioners have set up restrictive measures, such as neighborhood "improvement" associations born out of a very serious concern for real-estate values and the morale of the local community.

Yet a rising tide of Catholic opinion wants to deal with the alleged danger in quite a different way. They are afraid that the lid-sitting process will result in more and more race-conflict explosions such as have already occurred in some of our larger cities. So they have embarked on a policy of systematic enlightenment of the public on the main ideas of interracial justice. They are active in working out plans whereby the different racial and religious or national-origin groups in the community can learn to cooperate with one another.

Catholics not only differ in their views on racial matters, but they also find ways and means to discuss these differences. Among the most interesting experiences of my life have been the interracial forums which I have personally conducted at which the proponents of the opposing points of view talk the matter out in friendly fashion, but perfectly frankly. Catholics can argue and do argue with one another bluntly and plainly, because we have certain definitely agreed-upon premises to start from. We like clear definitions and well-defined question matter, and we like, too, to reach clear-cut and definite working conclusions. One of the most interesting of these experiences has been in the form of a courtroom scene, where the public itself is supposed to be on trial for prejudice and unfair racial discrimination. The "law" is declared by a competent theologian, who quotes the Church's teachings on human unity and social justice. The "public" is indicted by an official of one of the various Catholic Interracial Councils, and members of the minority group testify as to the factual truth of his indictments, while the opposing defense is made by questions from the floor. The "judges" hand down a decision and some practical resolutions or declarations are drawn up. In this way contested issues are clarified, and lasting policies are projected.

Why they differ. After all, there is nothing particularly surprising that Catholics differ. True, they all hold to a common faith. These differences will crop up most readily when people who hold the same basic belief take, as we have already seen, very varying views of its application to questions of social, political or international morality.

The Church, too, is a *universal church* in which no two peoples feel alike. Missionaries have told me how their congregations in the Arctic or in Tropical Africa learn and sing the ancient chants of the Church with the greatest of ease and joy. Yet you will struggle a long time before you will induce an educated congregation in one of our big American cities to sing the same ancient music. Young Americans squirm under the Church's strict teaching on the obedience due to parents by the young, yet Oriental youth would take these teachings for granted. People think that all Catholic nuns are the same the world over. Yes, they are the same in their consecration to a great ideal of love and service. They have a like dress and like customs and rules with only slight variations. Yet an American nun humorously confided to me how many good old Anglo-Saxon prejudices she had to lay aside when living with her genuinely loved and immensely respected native fellow nuns in faraway China.

People with a common faith will also clash in their very attitude toward life itself. In my boyhood I knew two old Irish ladies, by name Miss Ann Hogan and Miss Ann Ward, who lived in the same household for some fifty years. Ann Hogan believed that the best way to prepare for the future life was to get the feel of death while she was still in this world, so she ordered her coffin ahead of time and kept it in her bedroom and lay in it each night for a little meditation. Ann Ward, equally pious, was cheerfully convinced that there was no use anticipating trouble and she was not interested in her companion's penitential practices. Yet both of these were good loving souls. To my young mind they stood for two approaches to the one unshaken belief. The Church has had her optimists and her pessimists, her stricter and her broader interpreters since the beginning. There will always be discussion as to how much part is to be allotted to sorrow over evil and how much to rejoicing in the good, how much is to be accomplished by the use of our native reason and how much is to be trusted to the grace of God. Someone may ask why the Church permits such differences to exist. If she is so definite on some things, why not definite on everything? The simple reason is that the Church sticks to her God-given character and function. Her task is not to lay down a party line but to preserve and transmit to all ages and countries a certain body of teaching that was entrusted to her by the Divine Founder, and she depends upon the Holy Spirit of God

As for the new in poetry, the less said the better. There is no need for anyone to be ill-tempered about this. Poetry, new or old, is strenuous reading. One is pleased and perhaps even a little surprised to come upon people who do read it. One is pleased to find even a novelist who reads it, or a scholar; even a scholar in English literature, if it is new poetry that he is reading. I mean if it is poetry that has not been explained. It is nobody's *business* to read it; not even the English scholar's. Naturally I would like a lot of people to read it—for their sake and for the sake of my fellow poets. And I think that a few more people would enjoy reading it if they tried. But because poetry, at the most typical, is always making an idiom where hitherto there was no idiom, I know what the difficulties are; and I do not think that the Good Society depends on everybody's reading poetry.

For literature from its more popular to its less popular forms, the situation then is one of general resistance, with such progress as we can hopefully and perhaps too eagerly detect. In all this the American Catholic will share as he shares in American culture generally. Up to this point we see him only as part of the statistics in the common problem of the "general reader" in America.

It is here that we can begin to see the peculiar complication he brings to this problem. I would say that it is a three-fold complication, and I see it best in terms of two vices and one virtue.

One vice might well be called the Double Standard. There is literature and then, *miserere*, there is "Catholic" literature. Literature has to be good; Catholic literature has to be "Catholic." It is as if one read each of these literatures with a separate sensibility; or, where "Catholic" literature is concerned, with *in*sensibility. In its best practice, this tendency causes even a good Catholic writer to be praised in grotesque disproportion to his true merit, and at the same time it denies him the professional standards, which, as a matter of both pride and honesty, he would want to be measured by. In its worst practice this vice would lead one to think that the sacrament of baptism, even when received fairly late in life, forgave not only mortal and venial sins but also faults of style.

How stubborn this habit of judgment is, I do not have to tell the conscientious teacher in the Catholic universities or the conscientious critic in the few literate Catholic magazines. They and their small audience find themselves in the ungrateful role of dissenters, scolds, or prophets of culture, constantly having to repeat what is as boring for them as it is annoying to others, all in the simple business of trying to be honest.

I have put it this way—in terms of honesty—because I do not think that any movement needs to be started, any battle fought, or any reform made in the name of culture. I am not urging the importance of esthetic values; I am only urging honesty in judging them when one sets about judging them at all. There is no question of a choice between art and piety—the choice for a Christian is quite clearly decided—although I do not think that the choice arises, in authentic terms, as frequently as we are led to think when we read "Catholic" criticism. Even when the choice is made, we should be doubly careful not to confuse piety with art by praising the vulgar for the sake of piety but in the name of art: that is no choice at all but an attempt to have it both ways.

Ideally the choice need not be made. Piety is free of the demands of art not by cheating those demands but by transcending them. Surely there are the special purposes of devotional reading; and those purposes are quite apart from and quite superior to esthetic pleasure. But if the purpose is high, so much the greater insult to it if the writer or the reader cheats to attain it. Saint Augustine does not cheat. Saint John of the Cross does not cheat. Distortion, exaggeration, sentimentality, these are distractions from contemplation, not helps to it. In them a man only flatters himself or does something far worse, for I think there is a sense in which one can speak of flattering God. Flattery is not praise but the *use* of praise. These are contraries: for praise gives, and flattery solicits; praise rejoices in truth, and flattery makes its own truth; praise comes from faith, flattery from the lack of it.

In the light of this the Double Standard begins to show itself as Multiple. There is the tendency to divide literature into two parts, the shabbier part being "Catholic," and within that section to divide it again in order to get a separate esthetic standard—or no esthetic standard at all—for devotional reading. Even further divisions might be possible and in fact are implicitly made, for the notion of a Catholic literature is at best ambiguous.

Is it literature *by* Catholics? On any subject at all, including some of the obiter dicta I have seen appearing in the same advertisement with patristics and hagiography? Apparently some special

standard canonizes even the most casual scribblings of the Guaranteed
Catholic Author. Is it literature *for* Catholics but not necessarily *by*
Catholics? I think I have seen such literature given even more special
treatment, usually in some form whereby the reader manages to con-
gratulate both the author and himself. The Holy Spirit breathes where
It will, but there is an ever vigilant cheering section capable of following these manifestations and even attempting to direct them. The
Scripture tells us to rejoice for the lost sheep brought home; but when
the cheers express a wish for the slick triumph in argument, the hit
with the newspapers, the proprietorship over the truth rather than
the humble living in the faith of it, I rather suspect that what we have
is not a lost sheep but a golden calf.

Or is Catholic literature (if one must use the term at all) any
work in which there is some implication of the Christian concept of
man? If this is so, we can leave our discussion of the Double Standard,
now Multiple, and turn to the second vice, not unrelated to it. Let
us call it Xenophobia.

Literature is many countries and many ages and many beliefs,
clear or clouded. It has its own legitimacy and its own goodness; it
is its own world and an extraordinary one, for merely to enter is to
be enfranchised. It asks us to make no excuses for our coming to it,
except the wonder and delight it promises. The entrance can be made
only in the same spirit. Its full skies and its full landscape will not open
to those who do not *wish* to enter; or to those who enter without the
wish—I mean to say, by force. Those who would take it over in the
name of politics, or psychology, or anthropology, or even religion
are using force. Oddly enough, they will not even get what they are
looking for.

Religious values, in their full depth and complexity, cannot be
wrenched from literature without some feeling for the art and some
sense of its tradition in the full scope. The point (again) is not
whether literature is important or unimportant; if anything, I would
argue that literature is relatively unimportant. This is a way of saying
that it is not religion nor even the confirmation of religion.

The point here is the tendency among American Catholics, and
not only the uninstructed, to refuse the exploration of literature on
these terms. I leave it to others to discuss the basic sociology of which
this is only one manifestation. The tendency as it concerns us here
is puritanical, negativistic, defensive, and rather nervous. Obviously,

these characteristics go a long way toward explaining the Double Standard as well as Xenophobia. And I can wonder sometimes whether they are the result of one's having faith or the result of one's *not* having quite as much faith as one would like to think one has.

Recently a colleague at the university where I teach told me that he had met one of my friends, a priest, at a meeting of a philosophical association. My colleague was greatly impressed to meet a priest so thoroughly inside the problems of contemporary philosophy and so open to their consideration in the terms they demand. I understood my colleague's surprise, but in my own feelings there was no surprise at all. A man of genuine faith and genuine charity does not need cheap assurances, nor does he need to strain for intellectual generosity. Such a man is free, and the center of his freedom is not a philosophy; it is not even a theology; it is faith, which is infinitely beyond both. Paradoxically this faith can make philosophy most truly itself: the love of wisdom. Love is the opposite of fear.

As with philosophy, so, surely, with literature. Although literature has its own subtle relations to truth, its claims on truth are more humble than those of philosophy. If philosophy begins with wonder, literature is content to end where philosophy begins; for literature asks us not to judge a possibility but only to delight in it, not to believe but to wonder.

I mention the "subtle relations to truth" without analyzing them; they would require a complete disquisition on a problem that has exercised most of the critics of our time. I give the problem no treatment rather than an unjust and distorted simplification. It is enough to say here that "truth" does not guarantee literary merit, nor does literary merit guarantee "truth." I am afraid that literature simply has to be read before it can be judged, even before it can be judged for "truth."

I intended, after talking about two vices, to talk of one virtue. That virtue should now be obvious; we have been assuming it all through this discussion, and it has been making itself clearer and clearer as the center of the entire problem. The virtue is Christian faith. We have already seen it in its distortions. But we have been seeing also that in its purity it is the very poise and the very freedom of the free mind. It comes to literature, as it comes to everything, with complete largesse; it can afford literature as it can afford everything; it is the acceptance of all that is.

The Christian will find deeper reason than Terence had for saying that nothing human is alien to him. By the central mystery of the Incarnation, he has commitments everywhere and in everything; he will refuse nothing, as the Logos, which is his life, refuses no history. If he suffers amid the divisions of the secular movements of his time, it is in the division itself that his suffering is most profound; it is in what these movements *refuse*. He will not bargain with literature or with anything else in the world to give him what only his faith can give him completely, and he will love literature more, for loving it freely.

This is the ideal. In the incomparably humble problem of reading literature, it manifests itself where it manifests itself. For most of us, it is best described as a virtuality rather than as a virtue. One mentions it not as a fact of history but as a hope.

Meanwhile, by and large, the hope is not lived up to. The best critics in America are, most of them, not Catholic. The most pure-minded reading of literature is done, generally speaking, at the non-Catholic universities. And the best way to see so nebulous a matter as the place of the Catholic among the more literate "general readers" is to reflect that the serious Catholic writer in America writes "for" an audience that is chiefly non-Catholic. I am not adept at statistics but even in these broad statements I am trying to take into account the fact that Catholics are a minority in this country.

Nor can I soften these remarks by agreement with those who speak of a Catholic literary revival. I do not think it exists in America. We can say that there is a handful of good writers who are Catholics, only a handful, and since we are concerned with reading rather than writing, the most we can say is that the best of them refuse an easy reading, so that in reading them at all the Catholic must become aware of literary values in their own right. This may be a circumstance that was not present in the typical Catholic predilections of, say, twenty or thirty years ago. The circumstance is reinforced by the demands which a handful of English and French Catholic writers also make on their readers. But this is a circumstance, not necessarily a sign of anything greater to come; and even as a circumstance it has only to be placed in the long history of literature to indicate an epoch somewhat less than luminous. The French contribution would seem greatest. But I would say that the "revival" in France is much more intellectual than artistic. Among the creative writers I see only one artist of the magnitude of Valéry, Proust, and Gide; that is Paul Claudel.

But it should be clear that the question of a Catholic literary revival is largely irrelevant, except as it would induce more Catholics to read. The dangers of so special an inducement also ought to be clear. (I cannot help noticing that the inducement itself is somewhat questionable, even on its own grounds: if it is a question of reading literature for a Christian view of life, I would spend very little time with some of the writers who are frequently mentioned in connection with a Catholic literary revival, and I would find much more completeness and compassion in the work of writers who happen not to be Catholic.)

The inducement to literature should be literature. The *interference* with it can be left to the rationalists, the short-term optimists, the partisans of political slogans, and the "socio-psychological" critics impetuous to decide what is "healthy" and what is "unhealthy." All these have been active in their operations on modern literature. Each is a dogmatist not because he has a dogma he believes but because he has a dogma he wishes to *institutionalize,* and he would like to take literature over for the purpose. But literature is not to be possessed; it is to be enjoyed. In the Epilogue to *The Tempest* it is the pure delight of the audience—the applause of their "good hands"—that sets Prospero free and enables the play to be complete. Here wisdom defers to joy, and perhaps this pure joy is its own kind of wisdom.

Poetry and Contemplation

THOMAS MERTON, O. C. S. O.

It would be difficult to say why many who could be contemplatives in the strict sense of the word, never actually reach the end of their vocation on earth. The answer lies hidden in the mystery of each individual vocation. Contemplation is a gift of God, which He some-

"Poetry and Contemplation," by Thomas Merton, reprinted from *The Commonweal,* October, 1958, with the permission of the author. © 1958 by The Commonweal Publishing Co.

times gives to those who have done less to prepare themselves, and refuses to some who have suffered and prayed and labored much to obtain it. Normally, we might think that a desire for contemplative union with God, and a certain aptitude for the contemplative life, a taste for silence and prayer, a love for the Cross, would be a good indication of a contemplative vocation. And indeed these factors are important. But they do not, of themselves, give us a strict right to expect this great gift. Indeed, the more one feels that he has "deserved" the gift, the less likely he is to receive it in any fullness. It is, in fact, those who seem to think that the gift of contemplation can be earned by their own efforts, who sometimes end by becoming false mystics, unless God, in His mercy, teaches them the wisdom and the humility of the Cross!

The contemplative life is a life entirely occupied with God—with love and knowledge of God. It can be considered from three points of view, as it were in three degrees. There is first of all possible a kind of natural contemplation of God—that of the artist, the philosopher, and of the primitive or non-Christian religions. Then there is the contemplative life in the usual sense of the word: a life in which a baptized Christian, making full use of all the means which the Church puts at his disposal—Sacraments, Liturgy, penance, prayer, meditation, spiritual reading and so on—strives to conform his will with God's will and to see and love God in all things and thus to dispose himself for union with Him. This is active contemplation, in which grace indeed is the principle of all the supernatural value and ordination of our acts, but in which much of the initiative belongs to our own powers, prompted and sustained by grace. This form of the contemplative life prepares us for contemplation properly so called: the life of *infused* or *passive* or *mystical* contemplation.

Contemplation is the fullness of the Christian vocation—the full flowering of baptismal grace and of the Christ-life in our souls.

Christian contemplation is not something esoteric and dangerous. It is simply the experience of God that is given to a soul purified by humility and faith. It is the "knowledge" of God in the darkness of infused love. "This is eternal life, that they should know Thee, the One True God, and Jesus Christ Whom Thou hast sent" (John 17:3) or "But we all, beholding the glory of the Lord with open face, are transformed into the same image from glory to glory, as by the Spirit of the Lord." (2 Corinthians 3:18). St. Paul, in his Epistle to the

Hebrews, rebuked those who clung to the "first elements of the words of God" when they should have been "Masters," and he urged them to relinquish the "milk" of beginners and to desire the "strong meat" of the perfect, which is the contemplation of Christ in the great Mystery in which He renews on earth the redemptive sacrifice of the Cross. "For every one that is a partaker of milk is unskillful in the word of justice: for he is a little child. But strong meat is for the perfect: for them who by custom have their senses exercised to the discerning of good and evil" (Hebrews 5:13–14). *Omnis qui ad Dominum convertitur contemplativam vitam desiderat,* said St. Gregory the Great, and he was using contemplation in our sense: to live on the desire of God alone; to have one's mind divested of all earthly things and united, insofar as human weakness permits, with Christ. And he adds that the comtemplative life begins on earth in order to continue, more perfectly, in heaven. St. Thomas echoed him with his famous phrase: *quaedam inchoatio beatitudinis* (Contemplation is a beginning of eternal blessedness). St. Bonaventure goes further than any of the other Doctors of the Church in his insistence that all Christians should desire union with God in loving contemplation. And in his second conference on the Hexaemeron, applying Christ's words in Matthew 12:42, he says that the Queen of the South who left her own land and traveled far to hear the wisdom of Solomon will rise up in judgment against our generation which refuses the treasures of divine wisdom, preferring the far lesser riches of worldly wisdom and philosophy.

Infused contemplation is a quasi-experimental knowledge of God's goodness "tasted" and "possessed" by a vital contact in the depths of the soul. By infused love, we are given an immediate grasp of God's own substance, and rest in the obscure and profound sense of His presence and transcendent actions within our inmost selves, yielding ourselves altogether to the work of His transforming Spirit.

By the light of infused wisdom we enter deeply into the Mystery of Christ Who is Himself the light of men. We participate, as it were, in the glory that is radiated mystically by His risen and transfigured Humanity. Our eyes are opened to understand the Scriptures and the mystery of God's intervention in man's history. We become aware of the way in which the infinite mercy and wisdom of God are revealed to men and angels in the Mystery of the Church, which is the Body of Christ. The contemplative life is the lot of those who have entered most fully into the life and spirit of the Church, so that the contemplatives are at the very heart of the Mystery which they have begun really to understand and to "see" with the eyes of their soul. To desire the contemplative life and its gifts is therefore to desire to become in the highest sense a fruitful and strong member of Christ. But it means also, by that very fact, to desire and accept a share in His sufferings and death, that we may rise with Him in the participation of His glory.

Now whether we speak of contemplation as active or passive, one thing is evident: it brings us into the closest contact with the one subject that is truly worthy of a Christian poet: the great Mystery of God, revealing His mercy to us in Christ. The Christian poet should be one who has been granted a deep understanding of the ways of God and of the Mystery of Christ. Deeply rooted in the spiritual consciousness of the whole Church, steeped in the Liturgy and the Scriptures, fully possessed by the "mind of the Church," he becomes as it were a voice of the Church and of the Holy Spirit, and sings again the *magnalia Dei,* praising God and pointing out the wonder of His ways. The Christian poet is therefore the successor to David and the Prophets, he contemplates what was announced by the poets of the Old Testament: he should be, as they were, a mystic, full of divine fire. He should be one who, like the prophet Isaias, has seen the living God and has lamented the fact that he was a man of impure lips, until God Himself sent Seraph, with a live coal from the altar of the heavenly temple, to burn his lips with prophetic inspiration.

In the true Christian poet—in Dante, St. John of the Cross, St. Francis, Jacopone da Todi, Hopkins, Paul Claudel—we find it hard to distinguish between the inspiration of the prophet and mystic, and the purely poetic enthusiasm of great artistic genius.

Consider also what a tremendous mine of literary inspiration is in the Liturgical life. The Liturgy itself contains the greatest literature, not only from Scripture, but from the genius of the Patristic and Middle Ages. The Liturgy stands at the crossroads of the natural and supernatural lives, and exploits all the possibilities of both in order to bring out every possible meaning and implication that is in them with respect to our salvation and the praise of God. It surrounds those founts of all supernatural vitality, the Sacraments, with a music that is perfect in its integrity and dignity, and with ceremonies that are most meaningful by reason of their tremendous, dramatic simplicity,

not to mention all the resources of pictorial and plastic art still unknown in this land which has never yet possessed a Chartres or an
Assisi.

The Liturgy is, then, not only a school of literary taste and a
mine of marvelous subjects, but it is infinitely more: it is a Sacramental system built around the greatest Sacrament, the Blessed
Eucharist, in which Christ Himself is enthroned, in mystery, in the
very heart of His wonderful creation.

Christ on the Cross is the fount of all art because He is the Word,
the fount of all grace and wisdom. He is the center of everything, of
the whole economy of the natural and the supernatural orders. Everything that is made subsists in Him and reflects His beauty. Everything
points to this anointed King of Creation Who is the splendor of the
eternal light and the mirror of the Godhead without stain. He is the
"image of the invisible God, the firstborn of every creature . . . in
Him were all things created, by Him and in Him . . . He is before
all and by Him all things consist . . . in Whom it hath pleased the
Father that all things should dwell . . . for in Him dwelleth all the
fullness of the Godhead corporeally," that in all things He may hold
the primacy. (Colossians, 1 and 2.)

The Christian's vision of the world ought, by its very nature,
to have in it something of poetic inspiration. Our faith ought to be
capable of filling our hearts with a wonder and a wisdom which see
beyond the surface of things and events, and grasp something of the
inner and "sacred" meaning of the cosmos which, in all its movements and all its aspects, sings the praises of its Creator and Redeemer.

No Christian poetry worthy of the name has been written by
anyone who was not in some degree a contemplative. I say "in some
degree" because obviously not all Christian poets are mystics. But
the true poet is always akin to the mystic because of the "prophetic"
intuition by which he sees the spiritual reality, the inner meaning of
the object he contemplates, which makes that concrete reality not
only a thing worthy of admiration in itself, but also and above all
makes it a *sign of God*. All good Christian poets are then contemplatives in the sense that they see God everywhere in His creation
and in His mysteries, and behold the created world as filled with
signs and symbols of God. To the true Christian poet, the whole world
and all the incidents of life tend to be sacraments—signs of God,
signs of His love working in the world.

However, the mere fact of having this contemplative vision of God in the world around us does not necessarily make a man a great poet. One must be not a "seer" but also and especially a "creator"— a "maker." Poetry is an art, a natural skill, a virtue of the practical intellect, and no matter how great a subject we may have in the experience of contemplation, we will not be able to put it into words if we do not have the proper command of our medium. That is true. But let us assume that a man already has this natural gift. If the inspiration is helpless without a correspondingly effective technique, technique is barren without inspiration.

Christ is the inspiration of Christian poetry, and Christ is at the center of the contemplative life. Therefore, it would seem fairly evident that the one thing that will most contribute to the perfection of Catholic literature in general and poetry in particular will be for our writers and poets to live more as "contemplatives" than as citizens of a materialistic world. This means first of all leading the full Christian sacramental and liturgical life insofar as they can in their state. Obviously, the poet does not have to enter a monastery to be a better poet. On the contrary, what we need are "contemplatives" outside the cloister and outside the rigidly fixed patterns of religious life —contemplatives in the world of art, letters, education, and even politics. This means a solid integration of one's work, thought, religion, and family life and recreations in one vital harmonious unity with Christ at its center. The liturgical life is the most obvious example of "active contemplation," but it is hard enough to find a parish where the liturgical life is anything more than a bare skeleton. And even then, the liturgist is sometimes liable to be a "faddist" with narrow and obsessional views, striving to subject everyone else to certain esoteric tastes of his own. Such deviations should not prejudice us against the immense vitality and permanent value of the liturgical revival. It is quite certain that the most valid achievements in the realm of Christian art in our time are to the credit of the Monks of Solesmes, with their revival of Gregorian chant.

A sincere and efficacious desire to enter more deeply into the beauty of the Christian mystery implies a willingness to sacrifice the things which are called "beautiful" by the decadent standards of a materialistic world. Yet the Christian contemplative need not confine himself to religious, still less to professionally "pious" models. He will, of course, read Scripture and above all the contemplative saints:

John of the Cross, Teresa of Avila, John Ruysbroek, Bonaventure, Bernard. But no one can be a poet without reading the good poets of his own time—T. S. Eliot, Auden, Spender, Rilke, Garcia-Lorca. One might add that a fully integrated vision of our time and of its spirit presupposes some contact with the genius of Baudelaire and Rimbaud, who are Christians turned inside out.

Contemplation has much to offer poetry. And poetry, in its turn, has something to offer contemplation. How is this so? In understanding the relation of poetry to contemplation the first thing that needs to be stressed is the essential dignity of esthetic experience. It is, in itself, a very high gift, though only in the natural order. It is a gift which very many people have never received, and which others, having received, have allowed to spoil or become atrophied within them through neglect and misuse.

To many people, the enjoyment of art is nothing more than a sensible and emotional thrill. They look at a picture, and if it stimulates one or another of their sense-appetites they are pleased. On a hot day they like to look at a picture of mountains or the sea because it makes them feel cool. They like paintings of dogs that you could almost pat. But naturally they soon tire of art, under those circumstances. They turn aside to pat a real dog, or they go down the street to an airconditioned movie, to give their senses another series of jolts. This is not what one can legitimately call the "enjoyment of Art."

A genuine esthetic experience is something which transcends not only the sensible order (in which, however, it has its beginning) but also that of reason itself. It is a supra-rational intuition of the latent perfection of things. Its immediacy outruns the speed of reasoning and leaves all analysis far behind. In the natural order, as Jacques Maritain has often insisted, it is an analogue of the mystical experience which it resembles and imitates from afar. Its mode of apprehension is that of "connaturality"—it reaches out to grasp the inner reality, the vital substance of its object, by a kind of affective identification of itself with it. It rests in the perfection of things by a kind of union which sometimes resembles the quiescence of the soul in its immediate affective contact with God in the obscurity of mystical prayer. A true artist can contemplate a picture for hours, and it is a real contemplation, too. So close is the resemblance between these two experiences that a poet like Blake could almost confuse the two and make them merge into one another as if they belonged to the same order of things. And yet there is an abyss between them.

This resemblance between the experiences of the artist and of the mystic has been extensively discussed in the long and important article on "Art and Spirituality," by Fr. M. Leonard, S.J., in the *Dictionnaire de Spiritualite.*

This theologian pushes the dignity of the esthetic institution practically to its limit. He gives it everything that it is ontologically able to stand. He insists that the highest experience of the artist penetrates not only beyond the sensible surface of things into their inmost reality, but even beyond that to God Himself. More than that, the analogy with mystical experience is deeper and closer still because, he says, the intuition of the artist sets in motion the very same psychological processes which accompany infused contemplation. This would seem to be too much: but no, it is not. It fits in with the psychology of St. Augustine and St. Bonaventure and the latter's notion of contemplation *per speculum,* passing through the mirror of created things to God even if that mirror may happen to be our own soul. It also fits in with the ideas of the Greek Fathers about *theoria physica* of "natural contemplation" which arrives at God through the inner spiritual reality (the logos) of the created thing.

The Augustinian psychology, which forms the traditional substratum of Christian mystical theology in the Western Church, distinguishes between an inferior and superior soul. Of course, this is only a manner of speaking. There is only one soul, a simple spiritual substance, undivided and indivisible. And yet the soul insofar as it acts through its faculties, making decisions and practical judgments concerning temporal external things, is called "inferior." The "superior" soul is the same soul, but now considered as the principle or *actus primus* of these other diverse and multiple acts of the faculties which as it were flow from this inner principle. Only the superior soul is strictly the image of God within us. And if we are to contemplate God at all, this internal image must be re-formed by grace, and then we must enter into this inner sanctuary which is the substance of the soul itself. This passage from the exterior to the interior has nothing to do with concentration or introspection. It is a transit from objectivization to knowledge by intuition and connaturality. The majority of people never enter into this inward self, which is an abode of silence and peace and where the diversified activities of the intellect and will are collected, so to speak, into one intense and smooth and spiritualized activity which far exceeds in its fruitfulness the plodding efforts of reason working on external reality with its analyses and syllogisms.

It is here that mystical contemplation begins. It is into this substance or "center" of the soul, when it has transcended its dependence on sensations and images and concepts, that the obscure light of infused contemplation will be poured by God, giving us experimental contact with Himself without the medium of sense species. And in this contact, we are no longer facing God as an "object" of experience or as a concept which we apprehend. We are united to Him in the mystery of love and its transcendent subjectivity, and see Him in ourselves by losing ourselves in Him.

Yet even in the natural order, without attaining to God in us, and without perceiving this "inner spiritual light," the esthetic experience introduces us into the interior sanctuary of the soul and to its inexpressible simplicity. For the esthetic intuition is also beyond objectivity—it "sees" by identifying itself spiritually with what it contemplates.

Obviously, then, when the natural contemplation of the artist or the metaphysician has already given a man a taste of the peaceful intoxication which is experienced in the supra-rational intuitions of this interior self, the way is already well prepared for infused contemplation. And if God should grant that grace, the person so favored will be much better prepared to recognize it, and to cooperate with God's action within him. And this, as a matter of fact, is a tremendous advantage. The artist, the poet, the metaphysician is, then, in some sense already naturally prepared and disposed to remove some of the principal obstacles to the light of infused contemplation. He will be less tempted than the ordinary man to reach out for vulgar satisfactions and imaginable thrills. He will be more ready to keep himself detached from the level of crude feeling and emotionalism which so easily corrupt the integrity both of the artist and of the man of prayer. The mere fact of the artist's or poet's good taste, which should belong to him by virtue of his art, will help him to avoid some of the evils that tend to corrupt religious experience before it has a chance to take root and grow in the soul.

Mystical contemplation is absolutely beyond the reach of man's natural activity. There is nothing he can do to obtain it by himself.

It is a pure gift of God. God gives it to whom He wills, and in the way and degree in which He wills. By cooperating with the work of ordinary grace we can—and, if we really mean to love God, we must —seek Him and even find Him obscurely by a love that gropes humbly in the darkness of this life. But no amount of generosity on our part, no amount of effort, no amount of sacrifice will make us into mystics. That is a work that must be done by God acting as the "principal agent" (the term is that of St. John of the Cross). If He is the principal agent, there is another agent: ourselves. But our part is simply to consent, to listen and to follow without knowing where we are going. All the rest that we can do amounts to the more or less negative task of avoiding obstacles and keeping our own prejudiced judgments and self-will out of His way. St. Bonaventure tells us in many places that prayer and ardent desire can persuade God to give us this gift, and that *industria* on our part can open the way for His action. The term *industria* stands for active purification, and St. Bonaventure means, by that, precisely the same thing that St. John of the Cross talks about all through the "Ascent of Mount Carmel," namely the active emptying of the soul, clearing it of all images, all likenesses of and attachments to created things so that it may be clean and pure to receive the obscure light of God's own presence. The soul must be stripped of all its selfish desires for natural satisfactions, no matter how high, how noble or how excellent in themselves. As long as it rests in things for their own sake, seen and possessed as "objects" to gratify our own self-love, it cannot possess God and be possessed by Him, for the love of the soul for objectivized beings is darkness in the sight of God.

It is the common doctrine of Christian mystical theologians that a great obstacle to "unitive" or "connatural" or "affective" knowledge of God by infused contemplation (the terms are those of St. Thomas and his followers) is attachment to human reasoning and analysis and discourse that proceeds by abstraction from sense images, and by syllogizing, to conclusions. In other words, a man cannot at the same time fly in an airplane and walk along the ground. He must do one or the other. And if he insists on walking along the ground—all right, it is no sin. But it will take him much longer and cost him much more effort to get to his destination, and he will have a much more limited view of things along his way. What the Holy Spirit demands of the mystic is peaceful consent, and a blind trust in Him: for all this time,

since the soul does not act of itself, it remains blind and in darkness,
having no idea where it is going or what is being done, and tasting
satisfaction that is, at first, extremely tenuous and ineffable and
obscure. The reason is, of course, that the soul is not yet sufficiently
spiritualized to be able to grasp and appreciate what is going on
within it. It remains with nothing but the vaguest and most general
sense that God is really and truly present and working there—a sense
which is fraught with a greater certitude than anything it has ever
experienced before. And yet if one stops to analyze the experience,
or if one makes a move to increase its intensity by a natural act, the
whole thing will evade his grasp and he will lose it altogether.

Now it is precisely here that the esthetic instinct changes its
colors and, from being a precious gift, becomes a real danger. If the
intuition of the poet naturally leads him into the inner sanctuary of
his soul, it is for a special purpose in the natural order: when the
poet enters into himself, it is in order to reflect upon his inspiration
and to clothe it with a special and splendid form and then return to
display it to those outside. And here the radical difference between the
artist and the mystic begins to be seen. The artist enters into himself
in order to work. For him, the "superior" soul is a forge where inspiration kindles a fire of white heat, a crucible for the transformation of natural images into new, created forms. But the mystic enters
into himself, not in order to work but to pass through the center of
his own soul and lose himself in the mystery and secrecy and infinite,
transcendent reality of God living and working within him.

Consequently, if the mystic happens to be, at the same time, an
artist, when prayer calls him within himself to the secrecy of God's
presence, his art will be tempted to start working and producing and
studying the "creative" possibilities of this experience. And therefore
immediately the whole thing runs the risk of being frustrated and
destroyed. The artist will run the risk of losing a gift of tremendous
supernatural worth, in order to perform a work of far less value. He
will let go of the deep, spiritual grace which has been granted him,
in order to return to the reflection of that grace within his own soul.
He will withdraw from the mystery of identification with Reality
beyond forms and objectivized concepts, and will return to the realm
of subject and object. He will objectivize his own experience and seek
to exploit and employ it for its own sake. He will leave God and return
to himself, and in so doing, though he follows his natural instinct to

"create" he will, in fact, be less creative. For the creative work done directly in the soul and on the soul by God Himself, the infinite *Creator Spiritus,* is beyond all comparison with the work which the soul of man itself accomplishes in imitation of the divine Creator. Unable fully to lose himself in God, doomed by the restlessness of talent to seek himself in the highest natural gift that God has given him, the artist falls from contemplation and returns to himself as artist. Instead of passing through his own soul into the abyss of the infinite actuality of God Himself, he will remain there a moment, only to emerge again into the exterior world of multiple created things whose variety once more dissipates his energies until they are lost in perplexity and dissatisfaction.

There is, therefore, a likelihood that one who has the natural gift of artistic intuition and creation may be unable to pass on to the superior and most spiritual kind of contemplation, in which the soul rests in God without images, without concepts, without any intermediary. The artist may be like the hare in the fable, who far outstrips the tortoise without talent in the beginnings of the contemplative life, but who, in the end, is left behind. In a word, natural gifts and talents may be of great value in the beginning, but contemplation can never depend on them. They may, indeed, prove to be obstacles, unless by some special grace we are completely detached from them. And so the artist may well receive the first taste of infused prayer, for, as St. John of the Cross says, that is granted to relatively many souls, and often quite soon in their spiritual life, especially where conditions are favorable: but, because of this tragic promethean tendency to exploit every experience as material for "creation" the artist may remain there all his life on the threshold, never entering into the banquet, but always running back into the street to tell the passersby of the wonderful music he has heard coming from inside the palace of the King!

What, then, is the conclusion? That poetry can, indeed, help to bring us rapidly through that early part of the journey to contemplation that is called active: but when we are entering the realm of true contemplation, where eternal happiness is tasted in anticipation, poetic intuition may ruin our rest in God "beyond all images."

In such an event, one might at first be tempted to say that there is only one course for the poet to take, if he wants to be a mystic or a saint: he must consent to the ruthless and complete sacrifice of his

art. Such a conclusion would seem to be dictated by logic. If there
is an infinite distance between the gifts of nature and those of grace,
between the natural and the supernatural order, man and God, then
should not one always reject the natural for the supernatural, the
temporal for the eternal, the human for the divine? It seems to be so
simple as to defy contradiction. And yet, when one has experience in
the strange vicissitudes of the inner life, and when one has seen something of the ways of God, one remembers that there is a vast difference between the logic of men and the logic of God. There is indeed
no human logic in the ways of interior prayer, only Divine paradox.
Our God is not a Platonist. Our Christian spirituality is not the in-
tellectualism of Plotinus or the asceticism of the stoics. We must
therefore be very careful of oversimplifications. The Christian is
sanctified not merely by always making the choice of "the most perfect thing." Indeed, experience teaches us that the most perfect choice
is not always that which is most perfect in itself. The most perfect
choice is *the choice of what God has willed for us,* even though it
may be, in itself, less perfect, and indeed less "spiritual."

It is quite true that esthetic experience is only a temporal thing,
and like all other temporal things it passes away. It is true that
mystical prayer enriches man a hundredfold in time and in eternity.
It purifies the soul and loads it with supernatural merits, enlarging
man's powers and capacities to absorb the infinite rivers of divine
light which will one day be his beatitude. The sacrifice of art would
seem to be a small enough price to lay down for this "pearl of great
price."

But let us consider for a moment whether the Christian contemplative poet is necessarily confronted with an absolute clean-cut
"either/or" choice between "art" and "mystical prayer."

It can of course happen that a contemplative and artist finds
himself in a situation in which he is morally certain that God demands of him the sacrifice of his art, in order that he may enter more
deeply into the contemplative life. In such a case, the sacrifice must
be made, not because this is a general law binding all artist-con-
templatives, but because it is the will of God in this particular,
concrete case.

But it may equally well happen that an artist who imagines himself to be called to the higher reaches of mystical prayer is not called
to them at all. It becomes evident, to him, that the simplest and most

obvious thing for him is to be an artist, and that he should sacrifice his aspirations for a deep mystical life and be content with the lesser gifts with which he has been endowed by God. For such a one, to insist on spending long hours in prayer frustrating his creative instinct would, in fact, lead to illusion. His efforts to be a contemplative would be fruitless. Indeed, he would find that by being an artist—and at the same time living fully all the implications of art for a Christian and for a contemplative in the broad sense of the word—he would enjoy a far deeper and more vital interior life, with a much richer appreciation of the mysteries of God, than if he just tried to bury his artistic talent and be a professional "saint." If he is called to be an artist, then his art will lead him to sanctity, if he uses it as a Christian should.

To take yet another case: it might conceivably be the will of God —as it certainly was in the case of the Old Testament Prophets and in that of St. John of the Cross—that a man should remain *at the same time a mystic and a poet* and ascend to the greatest heights of poetic creation and of mystical prayer without any evident contradiction between them. Here again, the problem is solved not by the application of some abstract, *a priori* principle, but purely by a practically practical appeal to the will of God in this particular case. We are dealing with gifts of God, which God can give as He pleases, when He pleases, to whom He pleases. It is futile for us to lay down laws which say when or how God's gifts must be given, to whom they can be given, to whom they must be refused. It remains true that at a certain point in the interior life, the instinct to create and communicate enters into conflict with the call to mystical union with God. But God Himself can resolve the conflict. And He does. Nor does He need any advice from us in order to do so.

The Christian life is the life of Christ in the soul. Christian wisdom is the wisdom of God's only-begotten Son, Who is begotten Wisdom—*sapientia genita.* To be wise with the wisdom of Christ, we must let Christ be born and live within us in His own way. He does not come to all in the same way, because we all have different functions in His Mystical Body. "There are diversities of graces, but the same Spirit, and there are diversities of ministries but the same Lord: and there are diversities of operations, but the same God Who worketh all in all. And the manifestation of the Spirit is given to every man unto profit." (I Corinthians 12:4–7).

We may apply the last words of this text to our present case. If the Christian poet is truly a Christian poet, if he has a vocation to make known to other men the unsearchable mystery of the love of Christ, then he must do so in the Spirit of Christ. And his "manifestation of the Spirit" not only springs from a kind of contemplative intuition of the mystery of Christ, but is "given to him for his profit" and will therefore deepen and perfect his union with Christ. The Christian poet and artist is one who grows not only by his contemplation but also by his open declaration of the mercy of God. If it is clear that he is called to give this witness to God, then he can say with St. Paul: "Woe to me I preach not the Gospel." At the same time, he should always remember that the hidden and more spiritual gifts are infinitely greater than his art, and if he is called upon to make an exclusive choice of one or the other, he must know how to sacrifice his art.

SEVEN

Reassessments and New Directions

American Catholics and the Intellectual Life
MONSIGNOR JOHN TRACY ELLIS

.   .   .   .   .

Fourteen years ago (1941) one of the most perceptive of living foreign observers of American life and institutions, Denis W. Brogan, professor of political science in the University of Cambridge, stated in a book on the United States: ". . . in no Western society is the intellectual prestige of Catholicism lower than in the country where, in such respects as wealth, numbers, and strength of organization, it is so powerful." No well-informed American Catholic will attempt to challenge that statement. Admittedly, the weakest aspect of the Church in this country lies in its failure to produce national leaders and to exercise commanding influence in intellectual circles, and this at a time when the number of Catholics in the United States is exceeded only by those of Brazil and Italy, and their material resources are incomparably superior to those of any other branch of the universal Church. What, one may ask, is the explanation of this striking discrepancy? The remainder of this paper will be devoted to an attempt to answer that question by a development of certain major points based, for the most part, on the history of the American Church.

The first point, namely, the implanting in this soil of a deep anti-Catholic prejudice by the original English settlers in the early seventeenth century, requires no elaborate proof for any educated American. One has but to read the exhaustive monograph of Sister Mary

From *American Catholics and the Intellectual Life,* by John Tracy Ellis (Chicago: The Heritage Foundation, Inc., 1956). Reprinted by permission of the publisher.

Augustina Ray, B.V.M., on eighteenth-century America, or the general work of Gustavus Myers, to understand how thoroughly hostile to all things Catholic great numbers of Americans have always been, and the pains that they have taken to perpetuate that bias since it first entered the stream of American history at Jamestown and Plymouth Rock. In the spring of 1942 I had the fact brought home to me in a forceful way when Professor Arthur M. Schlesinger, Sr., of Harvard University, one of the outstanding authorities in American social history, remarked to me during a friendly chat in Cambridge, "I regard the bias against your Church as the most persistent prejudice in the history of the American people." Any notion that this sentiment was only a part of our past has been thoroughly dispelled by the substantial support afforded to groups like the Protestants and Other Americans United for Separation of Church and State since World War II.

Historically speaking, the American intellectual climate has been aloof and unfriendly to Catholic thought and ideas, when it has not been openly hostile, and it places no burden upon the imagination to appreciate how this factor has militated against a strong and vibrant intellectual life among the Catholics of this country. All but the most sanguine of men feel discouragement in circumstances of this kind and the majority usually give way to the natural tendency to slacken their efforts. What is more serious, the presence of so widespread a prejudice among the great majority of the population prompts the minority to withdraw into itself and to assume the attitude of defenders of a besieged fortress. That this situation has such an effect on many Catholics, there is no doubt. Even so brave and talented a man as John Carroll, the first American Catholic bishop, revealed the timidity engendered among the Catholics of his day by hatred of their Church when he was compelled to go into print in 1784 to refute a subtle attack on Catholic doctrine from the first American apostate priest. As Carroll remarked, "I could not forget, in the beginning, progress, and conclusion of it, that the habits of thinking, the prejudices, perhaps even the passions of many of my readers, would be set against all the arguments I could offer. . . ." How many Catholics since Carroll's day could attest to the same reluctance when they sought to exercise their talents in behalf of Catholic truth? And yet anti-Catholic bias should not be advanced as the prime factor in this situation. More damaging than its direct effect on the intellectual shortcomings of American Catholics, has probably been the fostering by this historic bias of an overeagerness in Catholic circles for apologetics rather than pure scholarship.

A second major consideration which helps to account for the failure of American Catholics to make a notable mark upon the intellectual life of their country is the character and background of the major portion of the people who, until a relatively recent date, made up the Church in the United States. From the 1820's, when the Irish began immigrating to the new world in large numbers, to the 1920's, when Congress locked the doors upon all but a small proportion of the immigrants who sought these shores, the Catholic Church was faced with the staggering task of absorbing an estimated 9,317,000 immigrants of its faith. We do not need to be told what the immigrant status implied by way of poverty, hardship, yes, and even illiteracy. Most of us learned it from tales told by our grandparents within the intimacy of the family circle. And since we have had the advantage of a finished education and know what that requires, we can easily understand how impossible it was for our ancestors to produce anything approaching a thriving intellectual life. Moreover, the grave responsibility that these unceasing waves of immigrants imposed upon the leaders of the Church to see that they had the rudiments of religious instruction and the facilities for Mass and the sacraments, left little time, funds, or leisure for a more highly cultivated training. . . .

But even if the energies of the American Catholic body down to a generation ago had not been so completely absorbed in the primary duty of assimilating the millions of immigrants, any true intellectual distinction—had it been there—would have met with very slight appreciation in the United States. Historically Americans have been wary of their scholars, and it is doubtful if there is a major nation in the world whose history reveals more suspicion of its academicians than our own. . . .

In this respect, I regret to say, I can see no appreciable difference between the attitudes assumed by American Catholics and those commonly held among their fellow countrymen of other religious faiths. The historian looks in vain—always excepting the lonely few— for a higher evaluation and a more understanding attitude toward the pursuits of the mind among those who are Catholics in this country. In that—as in so many other ways—the Catholics are, and have been, thoroughly American, and they have shown no more marked disposition to foster scholarship and to honor intellectual achievement than have any other group. . . .

One of the principal reasons for the lack of such an exception is, I think, the absence of an intellectual tradition among American Catholics. Obviously the establishment of such a tradition was impossible amid the stifling persecution and discrimination which Catholics experienced in colonial America. With the dawn of religious liberty after the American Revolution there was a brief span of years when it seemed that a tradition of this kind was slowly taking root among the families of the Maryland Catholic gentry. For the personal wealth of some of these families like the Carrolls, the Neales, and the Brookes, along with their deep and ardent Catholic faith, had enabled them to send their children to Europe where they acquired an education that was second to none among Americans of their generation. Moreover, when the French Revolution had turned violently anticlerical in the 1790's there came to this country a large number of highly cultivated French priests who exercised a strong and uplifting influence upon the intellectual life of the small and beleaguered Catholic body. One has but to recall the names of Francois Matignon, Jean Cheverus, Simon Brute, Benedict Flaget, and Gabriel Richard—all men of a finished education, fine personal libraries, and a deep love of learning—to know what is meant. But before this high promise of the early nineteenth century had time to attain fulfillment the arrival of the great mass of immigrants dissipated the early hope for intellectual distinction which faded away before the all-important task of saving souls.

.   .   .   .   .

One of the main reasons why the American Church after a century of organized existence in the United States found itself with no intellectual tradition was, I am convinced again, due to the character and background of its adherents. Had there been a sufficiently large number of American Catholic families with several generations of a solid tradition and love of learning in their midst, the appeals of men like Brownson and Spalding might, indeed, have borne more fruit. The LaFarge family is a case in point. In the correspondence of John LaFarge, the artist, during his school days at Mount St. Mary's College in Emmitsburg one finds, for example, that before LaFarge had reached his sixteenth birthday he had in the course of two and a half months requested his father to send him works of Herodotus, Plautus, Catullus, Theocritus, Dryden, Goldsmith, Michelet, Moliere, Corneille, and Victor Hugo. And that the love of books acquired by the great artist was passed on to his children, was recently witnessed when his Jesuit son published his interesting memoirs and described how seriously reading was taken in the LaFarge household. There his uncle, Thomas Sergeant Perry, professor of English at Harvard, his father, and his mother read regularly to the children from the best books. Out of habits such as these there developed a taste for good literature and Father LaFarge tells us:

> One day in August when I was about thirteen, I finished devouring Boswell's *Life of Johnson* and a feeling of desolation came over me as I turned the last page. . . . Then the bright idea occurred to me, why not read the two fat volumes through again? It was a wise choice and I shall never regret it.

That is the kind of background from which true intellectuals are born, but how many American Catholic families are there of whom that could be said? This is what John J. Wynne, S.J., had in mind when he discussed with Monsignor Edward A. Pace in the letters they exchanged early in this century the need for stimulating Catholics to read. As Wynne remarked on one occasion, the habit of reading must be started in the home. "We must, therefore, devise some means," he said, "of inculcating this habit in the homes of our people; otherwise we shall be providing books for our own bookshelves or for the libraries of a small number of priests and a few seminaries."

It is a sad fact but, I think, a true one that on the whole American Catholic families have largely failed in this regard, just as the families of Americans generally have failed. The tradition that established itself in the LaFarge family circle has never enjoyed wide acceptance in Catholic households, and when an attempt to foster such a tradition is sometimes made in Catholic institutions of higher education it is often found that the effort has come too late.

But the lack of serious reading habits is not the only national characteristic which the Catholics of the United States have thoroughly imbibed. From the time when the Duc de Liancourt traveled through the states along the eastern seaboard in the 1790's and wrote

one of the earliest books by a foreigner on the new Republic to the
essays of recent observers like Evelyn Waugh, few visitors from
abroad have neglected to comment on the American attachment to
material goods and the desire to make a fortune as dominant characteristics of our society. One is reminded of the emphasis that Plato
gave to this point when he said that " 'in proportion as riches and
rich men are honoured in the State, virtue and the virtuous are dis-
honoured. And what is honoured is cultivated, and that which has
no honour is neglected." That this has been true from the beginning
of our national life was the burden of some of the finest chapters of
Henry Adams' famous *History*. Speaking of New England, where one
might expect to find the best that the young Republic had to offer,
Adams said:

> The intellectual wants of the community grew with the growing pros-
> perity; but the names of half-a-dozen persons could hardly be mentioned
> whose memories survived by intellectual work made public in Massa-
> chusetts between 1783 and 1800.

If that was true of the green wood of New England Protestantism after a century or more of Harvard and Yale, what was one to
say of the dry in the small and despised community of American
Catholicism? Moreover, time saw no improvement for, as Adams
noted, the more the seemingly inexhaustible riches of this vast land
were unearthed, the more fixed did the American ideal of wealth
become in the national mind. The fact lent plausibility to Brownson's
indictment at the mid-century when he deplored the dethroning of
every vestige of true aristocracy and distinction as a result of the
French revolutions of 1789, 1830, and 1848, to which he added:

> Such are rapidly becoming our own American nobility, or aristocracy.
> Our gentlemen are bankers, sharpers, brokers, stock-jobbers, traders,
> speculators, attorneys, pettifoggers, and in general worshippers of mam-
> mon.

As far as I can see, it would be difficult to maintain that the picture
has changed essentially since Brownson wrote his trenchant lines in
1853.

Here, too, the prevailing American ethos took captive the Catholics as well as those affiliated with other churches. In no single phase
of national life have Catholics made the contribution to leadership
which might be expected of them, but if there be any exception to

this general statement, it almost certainly lies in the field of business. For example, six years ago William Miller of Harvard made a study of 187 business leaders and 163 political leaders for the first ten years of the twentieth century. In neither category were the Catholics distinguished, but it is worthy of note that they comprised almost double (7 per cent) the number of leaders in business that they did in politics (4 per cent) during the years 1900–1910. A similar investigation by Liston Pope, professor of social ethics in Yale University, which centered around the years 1939–1946 tended to bear out the same conclusion. In this case a scrutiny of the relation between the religious affiliation and economic status of Protestants and Catholics at the opening of the 1940's led to the equally interesting observation that "Protestantism had a larger representation from the lower class and Catholicism had more middle-class members than popular generalizations have assumed." In other words, Catholics have moved up the economic ladder beyond the rung where popular impression had placed them.

.   .   .   .   .

But has the arrival of a fairly large number of American Catholic businessmen at the status of millionaires—many of whom are college graduates—occasioned any notable change in their attitude toward or increase in their support of the intellectual pursuits of their coreligionists? First, to return to the question of the laity, the answer is not, I believe, a clear Yes or an unqualified No. About the only norm of judgment that one can apply to their attitude, unless one knows them personally, is their outward action in the form of endowments of the things of the mind. In that respect one can say that the situation at present reveals a higher appreciation of intellectual values on the part of Catholics of wealth than it did two generations ago when, to be sure, the number possessing large fortunes was much smaller. To cite once more the history of my own University, with which I am best acquainted, I think it was somewhat significant that when the committee of the hierarchy sought funds for the institution in the 1880's they received only two gifts of really large size, the sum of $300,000 from Miss Mary Gwendolyn Caldwell and $100,000 from Eugene Kelly of New York. Moreover, in the sixty-six years that the University has been in existence there have not been more than about ten instances where bequests of $100,000 or more have been received from individual American Catholics of wealth, and in only one case did the amount approach the million mark when the residue of the estate of Theodore B. Basselin, who died in April 1914, brought to the University nearly $900,000 for the endowment of scholarships for students studying for the priesthood.

.   .   .   .   .

While on the subject of the laity's role in matters of this kind it is pertinent to observe that whatever assistance wealthy Catholic laymen may see fit to give to the advancement of scholarship in the Church's institutions of higher learning will, in good measure, rebound to the benefit of their fellow laymen far more than it will to the clergy. The percentage of lay teachers at every level of American Catholic education has been steadily increasing of late years, and this is especially true of the colleges and universities. For example, in the academic year 1952–1953 laymen composed 73.8 per cent of the entire faculty of the Catholic University of America, and in the same year of 753 members of the teaching staff of Marquette University 700 were drawn from the laity. This situation is entirely as it should be, for the layman and laywoman have an important part to play in the educational enterprises of the Church and, in fact, Catholic scholarship and learning, generally speaking, would be improved by giving to the laity more of a voice in the shaping of educational policy and in the active administration of the Catholic colleges and universities of the United States.

That brings us to the role played by the clerical leaders of the American Church. In anything that is said or written on the subject of either the clerical of lay leaders in the Church of the United States it should be constantly kept in mind that, *mutatis mutandis,* the vast majority of them have been men of their own generation, reflecting—apart from the dogmatic and moral views which they held as Catholics—the predominant attitudes and prevailing tendencies of their time. Thus the solemn dignity and stately bearing of Archbishop Carroll suggested the eighteenth-century gentleman of Washington's generation in a way that might even seem a trifle stuffy to a twentieth-century prelate. Again, the bold and somewhat raucous utterances of a Bishop England and an Archbishop Hughes, faced as they were by the virulent attacks on their immigrant flocks during the era of nativism and the Know-Nothings, would probably appear out of place to Bishop Russell and Cardinal Farley, their successors in the Sees of Charleston and New York forty years ago, when the Church had by that time entered upon an age of impressive strength and security. In the same sense the bishops and major superiors of the religious orders of this generation reveal, it seems to me, the characteristics of their time, for among them one will find men whose executive and administrative talents are of very high order. It is fortunate that this is so, for it is no exaggeration to say that the Catholic Church of the United States has become "big business" in the typically American meaning of that term. And, we may add, woe to Catholic interests if the bishops and the heads of the principal religious orders were not men who possessed the ability to cope with the problems that the far-flung commitments of the American Church now daily impose upon them!

Yet it is to be regretted that the pressing tasks of administration leave so little time and leisure to these spiritual superiors for a more active participation and effective encouragement to intellectual concerns. Their backgrounds do not account for the lack of it, for they are basically the same as that of the Catholic intellectuals themselves. That point was made clear by Archbishop Cushing in 1947 when he stated to the ninth annual convention of the C.I.O. meeting in his see city:

> I have said this before, but it is important to repeat it here: in all the American hierarchy, resident in the United States, there is not known to me one Bishop, Archbishop or Cardinal whose father or mother was a college graduate. Every one of our Bishops and Archbishops is the son of a working man and a working man's wife.

Many of these prelates of whom the Archbishop of Boston spoke are, of course, themselves college graduates, and a considerable number of them are the products of graduate training in fields like theology, philosophy, canon law, education, and social work. To be sure, these are not *per se* fields of vocational training, but there has been a strong tendency to make them that. On the other hand, relatively few of the higher clergy have taken graduate work in the humanities and the liberal arts. As a consequence one will find among them, I believe, a far greater emphasis on what are the professional and vocational aspects of higher education, since they serve a practical end in their diocesan chanceries, charities, and offices of the superintendents of schools, than might otherwise be the case. In this, I submit, they faithfully mirror the intense preoccupation of American leaders in all walks of life with the practical. That the practical order of things is of vital importance to the Church, no one with any understanding of its mission would attempt to deny. But by the same token the Church has a mission to the intellectual elite and this, I fear, has been allowed to suffer neglect by reason of the prevalence of the practical.

.   .   .   .   .

Part of the reason why American Catholics have not made a notable impression on the intellectual life of their country is due, I am convinced, to what might be called a betrayal of that which is peculiarly their own. The nature of that betrayal has been highlighted during the last quarter of a century by such movements as the scholastic revival in philosophy which found its most enthusiastic and hard-working friends on the campuses of the University of Chicago, the University of Virginia, Princeton University, and St. John's, Annapolis. Meanwhile the Catholic universities were engrossed in their mad pursuit of every passing fancy that crossed the American educational scene, and found relatively little time for distinguished contributions to scholastic philosophy. Woefully lacking in the endowment, training, and equipment to make them successful competitors of the secular universities in fields like engineering, business administration, nursing education, and the like, the Catholic universities, nonetheless, went on multiplying these units and spreading their budgets so thin—in an attempt to include everything—that the subjects in which they could, and should, make a unique contribution were sorely neglected.

That American educators expect Catholic institutions to be strong in the humanities and the liberal arts—to say nothing of theology and philosophy—is not surprising. Eighteen years ago (1937) Robert M. Hutchins, then President of the University of Chicago, in an address before the Middle West regional unit of the National Catholic Educational Association made that point in a very forceful way. Speaking of the Catholic Church as having what he called "the longest intellectual tradition of any institution in the contemporary world," Hutchins criticized the Catholic institutions for failing to emphasize that tradition in a way that would make it come alive in American intellectual circles. He thought the ideals of Catholic educators were satisfactory, but as far as actual practice was concerned, he said, "I find it necessary to level against you a scandalous accusation." He then went on:

> In my opinion . . . you have imitated the worst features of secular education and ignored most of the good ones. There are some good ones, relatively speaking—high academic standards, development of habits of work, and research. . . .

Hutchins listed the bad features he had in mind as athleticism, collegiatism, vocationalism, and anti-intellectualism. In regard to the first two we can claim, I think, that in recent years Catholic institutions have shown improvement, just as all other educational groups have done. As for the second two, vocationalism and anti-intellectualism, I find no striking evidence of reform in the Church's colleges and universities since 1937. Regarding the three good features of secular institutions which Hutchins named, high academic standards, development of habits of work, and the ideal of research, I would say that a better showing has been made here and there on the first, but in the development of habits of work and a cherished ideal of research, I cannot personally see much by way of a fundamental change.

A second major defect in Catholic higher education that helps to account for its paucity of scholars of distinction, is what I could call our betrayal of one another. By that I mean the development within the last two decades of numerous and competing graduate schools, none of which is adequately endowed, and few of which have the trained personnel, the equipment in libraries and laboratories, and the professional wage scales to warrant their ambitious undertakings. The result is a perpetuation of mediocrity and the draining away from each other of the strength that is necessary if really superior achievements are to be attained. I am speaking here, incidentally, only of the graduate schools, and not of the competition —amounting in certain places to internecine warfare—among the more than 200 Catholic colleges of the land. In both categories, however, the situation is serious, and if Benjamin Fine, writing in *The New York Times* of May 8, 1955, is to be believed, there is every prospect that it will become more serious. There is, and there has been for years, a desparate need for some kind of planning for Catholic higher education on a national scale. As to the likelihood of such in the immediate future, there would seem to be little room or optimism. . . .

An additional point which should find place in an investigation of this kind is the absence of a love of scholarship for its own sake among American Catholics, and that even among too large a number of Catholics who are engaged in higher education. It might be described as the absence of a sense of dedication to an intellectual apostolate. This defect, in turn, tends to deprive many of those who spend their lives in the universities of the American Church of the admirable industry and unremitting labor in research and publication which characterize a far greater proportion of their colleagues on the faculties of the secular universities. I do not pretend to know precisely what the cause of this may be, but I wonder if it is not in part due to the too literal interpretation which many churchmen and superiors of seminaries and religious houses have given to St. Paul's oft-quoted statement that "Here we have no permanent city, but we seek for the city that is to come," and their emphasis on the question of the author of the *Imitation of Christ* when he asked, "What doth it avail thee to discourse profoundly of the trinity, if thou be void of humility, and consequently displeasing to the Trinity?" Too frequently, perhaps, those training in our institutions have had the same author's famous dictum, "I had rather felt compunction than know its definition," quoted to them without a counterbalancing emphasis on the evils of intellectual sloth. Certainly no intellectual who is worthy of the name Catholic would deny the fundamental importance of humility as an indispensable virtue in the life of the follower of Christ. But the danger of intellectual pride, grave as it is, should not be allowed to obscure the lesson taught by our Lord in the parable of the talents. If that principle had been pressed too far by Albertus Magnus we might never have known the *Summa theologiae* of St. Thomas Aquinas. Many may still recall a less dignified example of this mistaken emphasis when William Jennings Bryan gave eminent satisfaction to a Baptist fundamentalist audience in New York in 1923 with his declaration: "If we have come to the stage at which we must decide between geology and Christianity, I think it is better to know the Rock of Ages than the age of rocks."

Closely connected with the question of the prevailing Catholic attitudes in education is the overemphasis which some authorities of the Church's educational system in the United States have given to the school as an agency for moral development, with an insufficient stress on the role of the school as an instrument for fostering in-

tellectual excellence. That fact has at times led to a confusion of aims and to a neglect of the school as a training ground for the intellectual virtues. No sensible person will for a moment question that the inculcation of moral virtue is one of the principal reasons for having Catholic schools in any circumstances. But that goal should never be permitted to overshadow the fact that the school, at whatever level one may consider it, must maintain a strong emphasis on the cultivation of intellectual excellence. Given superior minds, out of the striving for the intellectual virtues there will flow, with its attendant religious instruction, the formation of a type of student who will not only be able to withstand the strains which life will inevitably force upon his religious faith, but one who will have been so intellectually fortified that he will reflect distinction upon the system of which he is a product.

.   .   .   .   .

In conclusion, then, one may say that it has been a combination of all the major points made in this paper, along with others which I may have failed to consider, that has produced in American Catholics generally, as well as in the intellectuals, a pervading spirit of separatism from their fellow citizens of other religious faiths. They have suffered from the timidity that characterizes minority groups, from the effects of a ghetto they have themselves fostered, and, too, from a sense of inferiority induced by their consciousness of the inadequacy of Catholic scholarship. But who, one may rightly ask, has been responsible in the main for its inadequacy? Certainly not the Church's enemies, for if one were to reason on that basis St. Augustine would never have written the *City of God,* St. Robert Bellarmine the *Tractatus de potestate summi pontificis,* nor would Cardinal Baronius have produced the *Annales ecclesiastici.* In fact, it has been enmity and opposition that have called forth some of the greatest monuments to Catholic scholarship. The major defect, therefore, lies elsewhere than with the unfriendly attitude of some of those outside the Church. The chief blame, I firmly believe, lies with Catholics themselves. It lies in their frequently self-imposed ghetto mentality which prevents them from mingling as they should with their non-Catholic colleagues, and in their lack of industry and the habits of work, to which Hutchins alluded in 1937. It lies in their failure to have measured up to their responsibilities to the incomparable tradition of Catholic

learning of which they are the direct heirs, a failure which Peter Viereck noted, and which suggested to him the caustic question, "Is the honorable adjective 'Roman Catholic' truly merited by America's middleclass-Jansenist Catholicism, puritanized, Calvinized, and dehydrated. . . ?" When the inescapable and exacting labor of true scholarship is intelligently directed and competently expressed it will win its way on its own merits into channels of influence beyond the Catholic pale. Of that one can be certain. For example, during the last year thousands of Americans have been brought into contact with the thought and research of two Catholic scholars, Francis G. Wilson and John Courtney Murray, S.J., on vital aspects of the current crisis through the use that has been made of them by Walter Lippmann in his latest book.

Yet an effective result of this kind is only attained through unremitting labor, prolonged thought, and a sense of the exalted mission of the intellectual apostolate on the part of the Catholic scholar. It was that ideal that Newman kept before him during his famous lectures on the position of the English Catholics at the Birmingham Oratory in the summer of 1851. He challenged his hearers to be equal to the obligation they owed to their non-Catholic fellow-countrymen. As he said:

> They must be made to know us as we are; they must be made to know our religion as it is, not as they fancy it; they must be made to look at us, and they are overcome. This is the work that lies before you in your place and in your measure.

There is not a man of discernment anywhere today who is unaware that the intellectual climate of the United States is undergoing a radical change from the moribund philosophy of materialism and discredited liberalism that have ruled a good portion of the American mind for the better part of a century. Clinton Rossiter spoke of this in a thoughtful article published some months ago. He foresees a new day dawning for our country when religious and moral values will again be found in the honored place they once occupied. Concerning that ray of hope upon the horizon, he concluded: "And it will rest its own strong faith in liberty and constitutional democracy on the bedrock of these traditional, indeed eternal values: religion, justice, morality." If this prediction should prove true, and there is increasing support for the view that it will, to whom, one may ask, may the

leaders of the coming generation turn with more rightful expectancy in their search for enlightenment and guidance in the realm of religion and morality than to the American Catholic intellectuals? For it is they who are in possession of the oldest, wisest, and most sublime tradition of learning that the world has ever known. There has, indeed, been considerable improvement among American Catholics in the realm of intellectual affairs in the last half-century, but the need for far more energetic strides is urgent if the receptive attitude of contemporary thought is to be capitalized upon as it should be. It is, therefore, a unique opportunity that lies before the Catholic scholars of the United States which, if approached and executed with deep conviction of its vital importance for the future of the American Church, may inspire them to do great things and, at the end, to feel that they have in some small measure lived up to the ideal expressed by Père Sertillanges when he said of the Catholic intellectuals:

> They, more than others, must be men consecrated by their vocation. . . . The special asceticism and the heroic virtue of the intellectual worker must be their daily portion. But if they consent to this double self-offering, I tell them in the name of the God of Truth not to lose courage.

Catholic Communication with the World

GUSTAVE WEIGEL, S. J.

One of the massive facts in the actual world is the existence of a society called the Roman Catholic Church. I must insist that the massive fact is that Roman Catholicism is a society. Of course, it is also a religion; it is a world view; it is a factor in culture, politics and every phase of interhuman relations. But the basic human truth about the Catholic Church is that it is an autonomous society. It is because of this reason that the Catholic Church is so different from older religions like Judaism, which is no society though it embraces distinct societies. Hence it is also different from communism which is

"Catholic Communication with the World," from *Faith and Understanding in America,* by Gustave Weigel (New York: The Macmillan Company, 1959). Reprinted by permission of the publisher.

a world view but not a society, even though the Union of the Russian Soviet Socialist Republics is a society and to this degree is like the Catholic Church, but the communists in the non-Russian lands rarely belong to that society no matter how much they may admire it.

Now one of the basic difficulties confronting a social group is to make itself understood to those who are not of it. This difficulty need not be vexing to a loose collectivity if the members are unconcerned about an alien conception of their reality. Many a mathematician doesn't give a fig because nonmathematicians cannot understand his craft. Understood or misunderstood, most mathematicians go their merry way quite content. Such an attitude is impossible for the Catholic. While the mathematician is not obliged in logic to make all men mathematicians, the Catholic actually must desire that every human being become a Catholic.

Any society is to some degree closed so that the world can be validly divided by the logical opposition of the members and nonmembers of the given society. Unless a nonmember clearly sees advantages in entering into the narrower circle of the given organization, he will not seek admission. His field of possibilities is larger outside of the community than in it. A society dynamized by a strong proselytizing nisus is therefore necessarily anxious to show nonmembers the advantages of belonging to its fellowship. Logically, in consequence, a problem of communication is created.

Many a naive Catholic is amazed and puzzled by the fact that the majority of the world does not wish to enter into the Catholic Church. As the Catholic sees it, the Church is the supreme elevation of man into the participation of the divine nature. Hence, it seems to him unintelligible that any man should not want this great good. Yet the patent fact for everyone is that most men show either indifference, annoyance with, or even hostility to the Catholic Church. With this fact facing the Catholic, he is not only logically but existentially forced to consider the problem of communication. It is obvious that the greater part of the world does not see in Catholicism what the Catholic sees. He must therefore explain the Church in his encounter with men.

The rise of semantics in our time is the fruit of the recognition of the complexities involved in human communication. The older generations quite blithely counseled us to say what we meant, and then we would be understood. The tacit assumption was that a good dictionary and an adequate grammar would enable us to communicate. However, the studies of the Freudian psychologists, the logical positivists, the existentialists have shown us that so simplistic a belief is altogether inadequate as a starting point in the solution of the problem of communication.

For the Catholic there is an added urgency for effective communication. We are living in a pluralistic world. Our secular society, wherever it is found, is made up of members with different world views. Except in some isolated pockets, there is no homogeneity of beliefs anywhere in the world. Yet we must all live together, and we are all anxious to live in such a way that there will be peace and harmonious collaboration in our coexistence. Hence communication cannot be exclusively directed to conversion. It must more often be an apologetic task so that the great society we live in will be able to deal with us wisely and gently. Catholic communication is a task not only because it is demanded by the smaller Catholic society to which the Catholic belongs but also because it is required by the larger secular society in which he is inexorably situated. This recognition is frankly made today by Catholics. Many non-Catholics are not aware that the Catholics have made it, and they think that the Catholic is still committed to the older vision that secular society and religious society are materially identical as they were in the Western Europe of the Middle Ages.

Any particular group erects a language and a set of symbols of its own. This enterprise is usually unrecognized by the group itself because it is superficially using the same semantic instrument as the larger community in which it exists. Yet the jargon of the schoolboy is not the same language spoken by the general community. Words are used differently and the language is restricted to a small part of its possibilities. Even within a family, certain words are symbols, in a sense, not recognizable by those beyond the family circle.

This inevitable situation affects Catholicism in a special way. Perhaps the most eloquent instance is the English Bible tradition. Many believe that the Reformation broke up the medieval unity of Western Europe. Certainly Hilaire Belloc seemed to think so. However, the truth of the matter seems to be that the Reformation merely manifested an already existing division of Europe, a division it did not produce but which produced it. The Reform is as much an effect of parochial nationalism as of religious preoccupations. When

Luther and Tyndale translated the Bible they were championing the rights of the local dialects of Christendom against the ecumenical Latin which was less vital than the local tongues. The Catholic translators of Douay and Rheims bring this out unconsciously. Whereas Tyndale and Coverdale Englished the Scriptures thoroughly, the Douay translators did it in such a way that much of the ancient Latin survived. In many expressions they merely transliterated the Latin, ignoring the English word which carried the same idea. The Douay interpreters were speaking simultaneously *urbi et orbi,* to their Catholic peers and to all English-speakers at large. This double objective for the same effort necessarily produced ambiguity. But the ambiguity was not contradiction. The Catholic had to speak the Catholic language which was his for a thousand years. The non-Catholics, on the other hand, were free to use the new language of their moment.

This predicament confronts the Catholic today no less than in the days of the sixteenth century. The non-Catholics are always very much of their time, much more so than the Catholics. Non-Catholic theologians use existentialist terminology in our era, though only fifty years ago such a terminology was universally unknown. The Catholics do so likewise but clumsily and with reluctance. The new language is not natural to them, and they speak it with an alien accent. Much of existentialist terminology was actually borrowed from Scholasticism, and when the Catholic uses the word "existence," it does not make him think of phenomenology but rather of medieval metaphysics. The Catholic cannot help himself, for he is a conditioned being like all others. It will be the convert to Catholicism who will use the new language with ease and grace but he will be understood better by non-Catholics than by his fellow Catholics. This is clearly the situation in the case of Gabriel Marcel.

There are three areas of human existence which embarrass Catholics in their efforts at communication. This embarrassment may be interpreted by many as a sign of inadequacy in the Catholic answer to questions of deep concern. However, this need not be the case. In any given moment the tendency of men is to ignore one pole of a bipolar problem. When this happens, one particular answer seems simpler and obvious. Those who keep both poles in view cannot give this easy answer but their appeal of bipolarity is not successful because in the given moment, people at large myopically overlook one of the poles. With time, the existence of the second pole will be recognized but by that time the question no longer arouses any felt urgency.

The first area where communication is difficult is the field of modernity. Every generation esteems its own insights highly and feels only for its own formulation of its problems. What is modern is not only modern but by easy assumption can be assumed to be the wave of the future. By a kind of Oedipus complex the past is hated. Yet the present is much more the past than it is the future. But there is a thrill in being modern, for individual existence can be nothing else than modern; it is only now. It is society rather than the individual which has the consciousness of the past. Its very modern existence is also an affirmation of history. Hence, the Catholic Church looks simultaneously to the past and to the present. It is never a commitment simply to the present. This causes much malaise because in any given moment the past is suspect.

Yet at any time there is a paradoxical quality in the devotion to modernity. The past despised is the immediate past rather than the period of remote origins. Modernity can make peace with the archaic but not with the last generation. In fact, the archaic can take on a glow and a glory inspiring awe in moderns. The Golden Age is deep in the past which the immediate future must recapture. It was the blind willful men of the last few generations who were the spoilers. In this situation the Catholic Church is again at a disadvantage. Not only does she affirm the past but, with equal vigor, she affirms the community of the past with the present. She will not iconoclastically destroy what is at hand in favor either of the remote past or of the presumed future.

Modernity is atomistic. Catholicism is a continuum. Hence, the Church is always antimodern. This makes communication difficult in the modern moment, which, of course, is any actual moment. Modern is a word that a wise speaker will try to avoid. So many things of history were labeled in the past as modern. Yet it is ludicrous today to refer to them by the label they chose. The theological modernism of the turn of the century is hardly modern now and the *theologia moderna* of the late fifteenth century was so little modern a century later that the use of the word is sheerly nominal.

There is loss and gain in every finite event. The antimodernism of the Church gives her an advantage in history. During the last two decades of the nineteenth century and the first two decades of the twentieth, the *Syllabus of Errors* of Pio Nono was a scandal to the world. It was so antimodern. The Pope was flying into the face of the future. Non-Catholics were angered by the Syllabus and even Catholics were embarrassed. Yet, when we read the document today, we wonder what all the uproar was about. It sounds now as a pronouncement, by and large, quite acceptable to contemporary men. The reason for this change is that the optimistic and rationalistic liberalism of the nineteenth century is no longer modern. It is "old hat," a delirium of the perverse last generation. We are reminded of Will Herberg's use of Hansen's principle: What the son wishes to forget, the grandson wants to remember. The stubborn opposition of the Church to communism was embarrassing in the 'twenties and 'thirties, when it was quite the thing to be at least a fellow traveler. Today, no apology need be made for that opposition. In fact, today, the polemicist must accuse the Church of being as bad as communism, just as twenty years ago he insisted she was not as good.

However, the advantage of the Church's antimodernism is slight in comparison with its disadvantage for communication. It is a hard and awkward task to be ever forced to be uncommitted to the passing superstitions and frenzies of the moment we live in. Contemporaries see in such an aloofness a refusal to belong—and that is always an exasperating thing for the one who enthusiastically belongs. Nor is it an easy thing to hold dialogue with an exasperated man.

This difficulty is intensified by the presence of a traditional vocabulary of long standing. The Catholic language was formed gradually over the centuries, keeping the points of view of past moments of history. The completely modern man does not know this symbolic system, nor does he feel any desire to learn it. When he does hear it spoken, he is prone to misunderstand it. In consequence, the Catholic is always bilingual; he must speak his own traditional tongue, for only by it can he live his own traditional life, and he must also translate this language to the men of his day. Bilingualism is always an obstacle because no one actually speaks two languages with the same ease and fluency. One of the two languages is the individual's proper vehicle of communication while the other is a submission to a social necessity, resented rather than loved.

The antimodernism of the Catholic Church, therefore, always hampers the Catholic in his essays of communication. The second obstacle need not be so perennial, though it functions powerfully in our time. The Catholic, *qua* Catholic, is socially specified because the Church is a society. To be social puts man under authority, for anarchism simply liquidates all social bonds. Now authority is restrictive, even when the restrictions themselves are life-giving. And there are revolutionary moments in history when authority is resented and freedom extolled. We are in such a moment and the word "authoritarian" is for us a bad word.

"Authority" is a most ambiguous term. It means so many things. Perhaps the common denominator of all its uses is the notion of power. "By what authority" means, "by what power." Not all authority is arbitrary, for there is an intellectual authority with no element of voluntarism in it. When we say that in a certain field a man speaks with authority, we are saying that he knows his field. He thus becomes an authority. A witness likewise speaks with authority though his witness function is purely informative. He is a man who knows because he experienced what he relates. He gives no other proof for his testimony than the fact that he experienced what he says.

Any religious statement rests on some authority. It cannot rest on a referral to measurable public data of the empirical order because God is not of that order. Christianity has from the beginning recognized this truth. The Christian evangelists gave witness to God's good news in Jesus. Witness was the only thing they could give. The dialectic of the Greek philosophers offered no means for the authorization of their message.

Christianity today is far removed in time from the witness of the associates of Jesus. The authority of their witness can only be mediated to us. There are current three generic theories concerning this mediation. The Christians of the Reform tradition look on the Bible as their decisive mediator. The Oriental Orthodox find the medium in the spontaneously surviving and evolving traditions of a community. The Catholics believe that their society, as a living and structured organism, mediates the testimony. In Catholicism it is not a book which has the ultimate authority nor yet the floating traditions of a loosely conjoined fellowship. It is the living community itself, acting as a society with the proper hierarchical architectonic of a mystical body. Yet none of the three forms of Christianity pretends to speak without authority.

What prejudices contemporary man against the Catholic form of authority is that it is juridical. If an organized society itself is to be the decisive mediation of the Gospel, it must be jurisdictionally operative. Yet the consequence will be that belief seems to be imposed by fiat and bureaucracy. Both in the Reform churches and Eastern Orthodoxy there is fullest possibility for a personal reconstruction of the Gospel. In Catholicism this possibility is severely restricted. This restriction seems to many to be an assault on freedom. Consequently, the witness of the Church grates on the sensitivities of our time.

The non-Catholic Christian has two questions: what does the Church say, and what does God say? These questions are for him two, and the answer to the one is not necessarily the answer to the other. For the Catholic, the two questions are identical in scope, because he believes that God speaks exclusively through the Church, so that what God says and what the Church says in his name are necessarily one. He believes this because he believes that only the Church can tell us what God communicates to the world and time. But in dialogue with non-Catholic Christians this basic assumption cannot be shared by the non-Catholic. When the Catholic proves that this or that proposition is taught by the Church, the Catholic has done all he considers required. But when the non-Catholic, spontaneously and with no malice, immediately asks what God says on the same subject, the Catholic is inwardly amazed by what he deems to be an irrelevant question. He antecedently rejects the notion that one could know God's word except by the teaching of the Church. The two participants in the dialogue are at cross-purposes without even being aware of it. This explains the futility of the old-fashioned polemic between Catholic and non-Catholic, with the Bible acting as a court of appeals. The non-Catholic understood the Bible through his sincere, sometimes scholarly, but always personal reconstruction of what the Bible says. The Catholic understood the Bible as the living fellowship interpreted it. Such debate was no debate because there was no common ground to make a dialogue viable. The Bible in its material reality seemed to keep the two disputants together but the material Bible is just one more isolated fact in the universe, incapable of uniting anything. It is the formal Bible, the Bible understood, which can be the link of union between two men. When the understandings are different, there is no union. There is not even one Bible, but two. This is clear in the Protestant controversy between fundamentalists and non-fundamentalists.

The inevitable authoritarianism of Catholicism makes communication with antiauthoritarians difficult for the Catholic. The Catholic must always begin his dialogue with an exposition of the meaning of the Church. Nor will he consider this a question permitting any answer except the affirmation of the Catholic Church. That is his Christian faith. There he stands; he cannot do otherwise. The non-Catholic Christian, by the very fact of being non-Catholic, coldly or warmly bridles at the Catholic conception of Christianity, even when he understands it. When he doesn't understand it, he is simply mystified by the Catholic's position. The Protestant begins his conversasation unconsciously supposing that the Catholic comes to Christianity in the Protestant way. He can not help himself in this approach to the question, but the approach makes fruitful dialogue most problematical. It will take much reflection for the Protestant to realize that he is as authoritarian as the Catholic but in a different way. Although, like the Catholic, he follows an authority and a tradition, he will accuse the Catholic of authoritarianism and traditionalism without realizing that he too bases his beliefs on these two grounds.

The ecumenical movement in our day is a great effort to facilitate communication. However, it is a Protestant movement. The postulates of the meetings are tacitly Protestant. The free examination of the historical sources of the Christian religion is the *modus operandi*. But the question to be faced is not a historical but a religious one. Christianity is a historical phenomenon but its problems are not to be solved historiographically. Religious assent derives from the God-encounter of the individual man, conditioned by grace, his growth and environment. Two sincere men interpret historical evidence differently because all interpretation begins with principles outside the field of evidence. These initial principles are the real dynamism of inference.

The third obstacle to effective Catholic communication is the Catholic's social conception of the Gospel. He believes that the commitment of God implies a commitment to the people of God. He does not think that God can be adequately known or properly served except in the holy community, which is indestructibly holy because it is God's way to salvation, not because its members are all necessarily holy. Man's salvation is man's ultimate quest and imperative. All else is secondary and subsidiary to this primatial concern. The result is that there is a possible conflict between the authority of the secular community to which the Catholic belongs and the authority of the divine community of which he is also a member. This produces the famous problem of relation between Church and State.

The non-Catholic who knows something about Catholic ecclesiology discovers that his Catholic neighbor confronts the secular problems of the political collectivity with Catholic persuasions. This frightens him. He rarely reflects that he approaches the same problems with a Protestant or Orthodox or Jewish persuasion. This frightens the Catholic. With these two frights to confuse the issue, communication becomes ambiguous. The Witness of Jehovah refuses to bear arms in a purely secular war. The Quaker refuses to bear arms for any cause. The Methodist and the Baptist try to outlaw alcoholic drinks in the secular community. The Southern public school teaches a Protestant version of Christianity, at least by implication. Yet somehow these things do not produce great malaise in the American body politic. But the Catholic's idiosyncrasies are always more alarming.

The naturalist has a solution for all this. He demands that the individual citizen accept the authority of the political commonwealth as ultimate and final. The democratic naturalist supposes that this authority operates through a process of the showing of hands, so that the will of 51 per cent of the community is the law even for the 49. He allows every member of the collectivity to think and act as he pleases until the authority of the majority has become legally declared. Then the individual must bow not to God but to Columbia, the gem of the ocean.

As many religious non-Catholics have seen, the naturalist solution of the conflicts between the secular community and religion is not acceptable to any religious person. They have recognized that we cannot be ready to render to Caesar the things which are God's. Whenever the demand has been made, men of faith—Catholic, Protestant, Jew, Muslim, Buddhist—have refused to obey, even if their disobedience spelled death. These deaths have always been regarded by men at large as noble things, but the naturalistic statist, at least in theory, must consider them evil.

In spite of the incompatibility of the naturalist view with religious conviction, there is a tendency in this country even among religious people to accept the naturalist theory. The reason is obvious enough. The majority of the land is Protestant, even though many millions are not church-affiliated. They know in consequence that the 51 per cent of the nation will not demand something contrary to their own none-too-clear religious tenets. The only ones threatened are the Catholics, Jews and Orthodox. The rising power of any one of these groups alarms the general Protestant majority. If they are to lose their majority status, they will not enjoy the security they now have. Fear and resentment will be their attitude to the growing minority.

How can the Catholic adequately explain his position to such a majority? It is a formidable task. The Catholic talks theory and ideal democracy but the non-Catholic concentrates on practical consequences, often enough not logically entailed by the theory expounded. The Catholic must insist that he does not put the body politic above his religious community. The non-Catholic believer really makes the same profession but since he is in the majority, he does not have to insist on it. The Catholics at present are involved in the task of making their position intelligible to the total secular community. Some of the Catholics do not want any change of rhetoric in their basic doctrines, while others do want such a change. The position of the latter is most uncomfortable. They are suspected in their own fellowship; nor are they properly understood by the men beyond it. There comes for them a temptation, understandable enough, to drop the whole thing.

. . . . .

The problem of communication across the Catholic-non-Catholic barrier falls primarily on the Catholic. In a lesser way it puts some obligations on the non-Catholic.

The Catholic has no right to expect the majority of his secular community to speak and understand his distinctive language. Such an expectation is either naivete or arrogance. If I join a community where a tongue other than my own is the medium intercourse, I simply must learn the language of the place to the best of my ability. Anything less is wrong. The Catholics of our land have not reflected on this truth sufficiently. That non-Catholics do not know more of the Catholic idiom is regrettable, but that the Catholics do not know the language of their non-Catholic milieu is tragic.

Actually there is a movement on foot among the younger members of the Catholic community to learn and talk fluently the tongue of our environment. Fortunately, they are receiving encouragement from some of the elders who recognize the need and are, in their way, helping to meet it. However, there is yet a difficulty.

.   .   .   .   .

The reasons why Catholics remain aloof from some concerns common to their general environment are many. One is the defense mentality which is part of our American Catholic tradition. The Catholic in America had a tough row to hoe. His existence was under attack all through the nineteenth century. I do not refer merely to Know-Nothingism or the Ku Klux Klan. These things were symptomatic of something deeper. Through inner logic and historical circumstances, the Reform tradition was hostile to Catholicism. The first Catholics who came to this land had to face this hostility even though most of its manifestations were neither cruel nor physical. The Catholic was made to feel that he was an intruder, accepted because of the magnanimous sufferance of the masters of the house. The degree of sufferance varied in different communities, but in any community the initially small group of Catholics was greeted with less than wholehearted acceptance.

This situation produced in the Catholics a beleaguered-beachhead mentality. Long after the reaction was logical, it stayed on— even to our day. It may strike the non-Catholic reader as strange, but the average Catholic in this country expects something less than a kind reception at the hands of non-Catholics. Usually this expectation is ungrounded but every now and again it is fulfilled. Hence, the expectation does not die easily.

This situation exists even where visibly there is no real warrant for it. The old American cities like Boston, New York, and Philadelphia are today in no sense Protestant communities. In New York the Protestants are really a small minority, numbering perhaps no more than 20 per cent of the total, and of this 20 per cent, half are whites and half colored. Nor do these two halves manifest a tight solidarity. Yet, even in New York, where the Catholics represent something between 30 and 40 per cent of the population, the defense complex is still at work. It frequently manifests itself in aggressiveness, which reaction always betrays a feeling of insecurity rather than tranquil confidence.

This too will pass with time. In fact, it is just as well that the Catholics at the moment do not realize their numerical strength. They could easily be tempted to abuse it. In the interim, Catholics and non-Catholics will grow up together, neither side attacking the other. A perduring precedent of friendly living together should make future social integration easy and natural.

If the Catholic has the principal obligation of overcoming the current impasse of communication in a land culturally non-Catholic, the non-Catholic has a lesser but not less real obligation. By and large, the American non-Catholic is eager to enter into dialogue with the Catholic on a friendly basis. I do not refer to the secular social relationships where Catholic and non-Catholic have already fused. Almost everyone has Catholic and non-Catholic friends and relatives. No social aggregation in our vast society is without its representation of Catholics and non-Catholics. But these social enclaves prescind from religion. Today, the American non-Catholic also wants to encounter the American Catholic *qua* Catholic. This feeling is actually stronger on the non-Catholic than on the Catholic side. It is certainly a good movement and it should be aided by all.

However, there is a possible danger in the movement. Given the latent indifferentism in so many contemporaneous Protestants, they may receive the Catholic on an indifferentist basis. This basis is a belief that all religious groups are equally good, or putting it reversely, equally bad. No denomination, church or sect is totally bad or totally good. We can all learn from each other and must apologize to each other. Are we not all God's children, going home by different roads? Now this is an impossible approach to the Catholic. He believes, indeed, that all roads lead to God, but only because all roads lead to Rome, which certainly is not the belief of the indifferentist.

This explains a strange phenomenon in our time. In the past the stubborn antagonists of Catholicism were the Bible Christians or fundamentalists as we call them today. When the different forms of liberalism took over in the Reform denominations, this hard resistance lost much of its unyieldingness. Historically, then, the Catholic who by the structure of his faith can never be a Biblicist fundamentalist, should look more kindly on the liberals than on the fundamentalists. Yet the opposite tends to take place. The reason is simple enough. Even though the fundamentalist is traditionally opposed to the Scarlet Woman of Rome and her ways, yet he clings to certain positions which are as fundamental for him as for Catholics. He believes in the divinity of Jesus of Nazareth, the Virgin birth, the

objectively atoning death of Jesus and His physical resurrection. The
liberals vacillate ambiguously in their adherence to these dogmas. In
consequence, the Catholic feels sympathy for the fundamentalist in
spite of the latent antipathy felt by that group toward Catholicism.
The liberals are far more friendly and more cordial but the Catholic
is appalled by their radical reconstructions of Christianity. It is easier
and more pleasant to talk to a neoliberal than to a fundamentalist, but
there is a greater community of dogmas—for different reasons—in a
fundamentalist-Catholic encounter. Tradition is the main concern of
the Catholic and, surprised as the tradition-rejecting fundamentalist
may be on hearing it, he is more traditional then his neoliberal companion.

But indifferentism is not the only pitfall the Protestant must
avoid in order to help intercommunication with Catholics. A graver
and often more unconscious assumption in an interfaith dialogue can
be more deadly. The Catholic today with no little success is translat-
ing his own formulas so that they can be genuinely understood by
those outside his church. As a result, many a non-Catholic now sees
that a typical Catholic formula is not as silly as he once believed. He
may even see that he himself actually holds what the genuinely
understood Catholic proposition states. A strange reaction is now
possible. Because the non-Catholic sees the Catholic statement in a
new light, he thinks the Catholics have changed. Actually, the change
has been in the non-Catholic, but he is not sufficiently aware of it.
The non-Catholic spontaneously thinks that the Catholics are "reforming"; they are finally coming to their senses. Perhaps with a
little time they will become Protestant, not, of course, in name but in
belief. For the non-Catholic there seem to be many straws in the
wind. He is convinced that Father Leonard Feeney gave the traditional doctrine of the Catholics on the matter of the salvation of non-
Catholics and he sees therefore a welcome change in the Church's
official repudiation of this doctrine.

Yet the repudiation of Father Feeney's understanding of the
axiom: *Extra ecclesiam nulla salus,* was not based on a change of
doctrine in the Church. The Feeney doctrine was rejected because
it was not traditional. The Roman authorities were not making a
concession to Reform-adherents but judging a Catholic preacher in
the light of their inner domestic norms. The perennial Catholic

position on the saving power of God is not to be found in the Boston priest's explanation but in its opposite.

Gradual increase in mutual understanding does not mean that the two parties in the dialogue are tending to become one in belief. Crusts of misunderstanding and antipathy are being pared off a historical division, but the division itself remains. With the greatest of sympathy and comprehension on both sides, we shall still be faced by separation. Protestantism may disappear, though no one seriously thinks that such an event is near. The hypothesis of the end of Catholicism is conceivable, though not by a Catholic. But until one of the two events be realized, there will be a Catholic-Protestant separation. It is foolish to think that the two groups will fuse into some Catholic-Protestant amalgam.

The realistic acceptance of this fundamental truth is necessary for the non-Catholic in his friendly meeting with Catholics. He must not believe that the Catholic will become something else, though remaining a Catholic. The Catholic can drop his allegiance to his Church, but he cannot become a non-Catholic Catholic. If the teleology of the non-Catholic in his approach to the Catholic is to convert him to some other faith, he should not be surprised if his efforts are resented.

Nor is there any need that conversion be the objective of encounter and dialogue. It may be and probably will be the secret hope of both sides, but the hope concerns a possible consequence rather than the purpose to be achieved in coming together. A male is not a female but they can and must live together in harmony with no futile attempt to change the sex of either party. In a pluralistic society, the presence of differences is the fundamental postulate of a human situation. We are socially conjoined to each other no matter how great our lack of complete harmony, and the conjunction can be happy, fruitful and invigorating.

Christianity and the Oriental Cultures
CHRISTOPHER DAWSON

At the end of the previous chapter I distinguished between the question of oriental nationalism and that of oriental culture. The two questions are apt to be confused, naturally enough under the present circumstances, when the conflict between East and West is always seen as an international political issue. But oriental nationalism is a very recent phenomenon, and from the historical point of view the great barrier between East and West has not been due to nationalist sentiment, but to religion and culture. In the East, as in the medieval West, man's primary and fundamental allegiance was not to his nation, but to his religion, and men thought of themselves as Muslims or Hindus or Buddhists or Sikhs, rather than Egyptians or Syrians or Indians or Indonesians. The one great exception is China, and China was not a nation but a civilization—and a civilization of a unique and very exclusive character which had been identified for thousands of years with a particular tradition of thought, and distinctive ideals of moral behaviour.

Modern nationalism has brought the East nearer to the West than ever before; its success has been due to its assimilation of Western culture, and its leaders have been that part of the population which has been most deeply influenced by modern Western ideas; above all, the class of students who have studied in Western schools and universities and who use English or French as their second language. But behind this world of the new oriental intelligentsia, there is the older world of the traditional religious cultures whose roots reach back to the most remote past. Although their influence has been steadily decreasing for the last century or two, they still mould the minds and lives of their members down to the smallest details of behaviour, and even the Westernized minorities which have revolted against the tyranny of tradition and custom keep a profound bond with them which goes far deeper than any conscious loyalty, like the bond of the child with his mother's womb.

"Christianity and the Oriental Cultures," from *The Movement of World Revolution,* by Christopher Dawson (New York: Sheed & Ward, Inc., 1959). Reprinted by permission of The Society of Authors. © 1959 by Sheed & Ward, Inc., New York, N.Y.

Thus, as I said previously, when we speak of the East we are not merely speaking of a number of different nationalities but of a number of different worlds of peoples, each of which is separated from the others by thousands of years of civilization. For thousands of years the nations have travelled on different roads, and these roads have tended to diverge ever further in the course of ages. Above all, these different roads have been different approaches to reality and different ways of religious worship and doctrine. For religion in the East is not a private matter for the individual conscience, as in the modern Western world, where men of different religions and sects can share the same culture and society without any sense of strain or conflict. The religions of the East are sacred orders or liturgical cultures in which every detail of behaviour has a religious significance, so that it is possible to tell what a man's religion is by the way he eats his dinner or ties his dress.

This is most obvious in the case of Hinduism, which is an immense and intricate hierarchy of hereditary religious societies, each governed by its own religious laws and rites, and all subordinated to the highest caste of the hereditary priesthood, which preserved the monopoly of learning and ritual and legal knowledge. Thus the whole social system and the social function of the individual is of divine right and is hedged round with religious sanctions and rites. The position of the State is unimportant, since the hereditary religious societies and castes transcend the State and it is their law, not that of the State, which rules men's daily lives.

In contrast to this we have the case of China, which was the most secular in spirit of all the great civilizations and owed its unity not to a religion but to an empire, the historical origin of which is older than that of Rome, while its tradition goes back further still into the mist of prehistoric legend. Nevertheless the civilization of ancient China was also a sacred order—a liturgical civilization founded on the sacred rites—and demanded the total subordination of the individual to the sacred traditions that had been handed down from antiquity. When we consider the great ceremony that was carried out without a break by the Emperors at the Altar of Heaven and the constant emphasis of the State ritual on the dependence of the Empire on the Mandate of Heaven, it is impossible to describe ancient Chinese culture as secular. At the same time it is not religious in our sense of the word. It has a certain resemblance to the official religion of the Roman Empire in the Augustan age.

In the case of Islam, on the other hand, the religious character of the culture is much easier for us to understand, since its theological background has much in common with that of Catholicism. The Moslem theologians lay down in categorical terms that the purpose of human life is the service of God (Ibada), that Moslem society is a community expressly constituted to fulfill this purpose, and that it is the function of the State to safeguard the community in carrying out its liturgical mission both against the external enemy by the conquest of the unbelievers and against internal enemies by defending it against the perils of heresy and schism. There is no room for nationalism, since all the Moslems are brothers; and there is no room for political democracy, since Islam is a theocracy, and both the religious community and the political State exist only to assert the divine authority and to carry out the divine law.

These three worlds of culture were entirely diverse and incommensurable both in thought and in social institutions. But owing to the absence of nationalism they possessed a greater degree of internal organic unity than Western civilization. Ancient China was a single society in every sense of the word; ancient India possessed social uniformity without political unity, and Islam was a true and full spiritual community and in theory a single universal state, although it ultimately came to be divided among a number of different kingdoms which nominally recognized the universal authority of the Khalifate, somewhat as the later German and Italian principalities recognized the authority of the Holy Roman Empire.

These great unities are so impressive by their antiquity and monolithic stability that they have given rise to the idea of the "unchanging East" and of the stationary and unprogressive character of oriental culture. But in the past they were all growing organisms and enjoyed their periods of expansion and progress. The influence of Chinese culture spread all over the Far East, eastwards to Korea and Japan, westwards into Central Asia and south to Indo-China. So, too, Indian culture underwent a great movement of expansion in antiquity, and above all in the early Middle Ages, and its sphere of influence extended far to the south and east to Ceylon and Cambodia and Champa and Java, as well as northward to Tibet and Central Asia. It was this outer zone of Indian culture that provided the most favourable conditions for the expansion of Buddhism, which continued to develop there after it had failed to maintain itself in India, somewhat as Christianity continued to spread in Western Europe after it had begun to decline in Syria and the Near East. Indeed it may be argued that these outer lands of Indian culture—the Buddhist world—should be reckoned as a fourth great oriental unity which forms an intermediate civilization between those of India and China.

But the most striking example of the expansion of oriental culture is to be seen in the case of Islam, which has continued to expand from its original centre in Arabia until it has spread from the Atlantic to the Pacific and from the Volga and the Irtish to the Zambesi and the Niger. Nor can we say that this expansion is a thing of the past; Islam is still advancing in Africa and may well become the dominant power in that continent.

Thus we must recognize that down to fairly recent times it was the oriental cultures that were the main centres of world power and economic development and Christendom that was comparatively weak and poor and backward. It had been steadily pushed out of Asia and Africa by the advance of Islam, which was built on the ruins of an older Christian world. Even in Europe the situation was uncertain, since Spain and Sicily formed an integral part of the Islamic world in the early Middle Ages, Russia was incorporated in the Mongol world empire in the thirteenth century and the advance of the Ottoman Turks in southeast Europe extended the frontiers of Islam to the Danube and beyond.

Yet in spite of all this the last few centuries have seen a complete reversal of the situation: the rise of Western culture to a position of world hegemoney, and a revolutionary process of change in Asia which has destroyed the old oriental empires and changed the character of the oriental cultures.

This process of world revolution—for it is nothing less—has passed through three successive phases:

First of all there was the age of European discovery and colonization which gradually destroyed the separate worlds of the old cultures and created a global system of communication and trade under European control. Secondly, there was the breakdown of the old Asiatic empires owing to their inability to withstand the economic pressure of Western trade, the efficiency of Western technology and the influence of Western ideas.

Finally, the third phase saw the internal transformation of oriental society by the spread of Western education and the rise of the nationalist movements, which represented at the same time a revolt against the West and the acceptance by the East of Western culture and political ideology. It is unnecessary to say more of this, as I have already discussed it at length in the foregoing chapter. But I cannot help drawing attention once more to the remarkable paradox that a movement which is rallying the peoples of Asia and Africa against the West is at the same time removing the cultural barriers between them and doing all in its power to diffuse Western education, Western science and Western political ideologies.

It is obvious that these great changes must have a profound influence on the relations between Christianity and the oriental peoples. But this involves a number of very complicated issues. For the results differ according to the circumstances of each culture and each nationality. In some cases Christianity may be regarded as the spiritual aspect of colonialism and consequently resisted as a foreign and anti-national phenomenon. In other cases Christianity is itself associated with national minorities, as in the Near East, where the national conflicts of the First World War and the succeeding period led to the wholesale destruction of the Armenian and Greek communities of Asia Minor and the Nestorian and Chaldean Churches of Western Mesopotamia and northwest Persia. On the other hand, in the case of the two greatest oriental civilizations, in India and China, Christian influences played a considerable part in the rise and development of the national movements. Since nationalism was the work of the new educated classes, the fact that the introduction of Western education into Asia was largely the work of Christian missionaries made for the growth of Christian influence on culture.

Above all, the nationalist revolutions have broken down the age-old barriers of tradition and custom which in the past made it so difficult for the Christian Church to speak directly to the hundred peoples of the East. The passing of the old order means the relaxation of the social pressures which often made religious change impossible, and the secular character of the new national states usually involves the acceptance of the principle of religious toleration. Thus in the East today Christianity finds itself faced with a similar situation to that which it had to encounter in the earliest period of its history. Then also the civilized world was passing through a period of revolutionary change. The civilizations of the ancient East—Egypt, Syria and Babylonia—which were of immemorial antiquity, had been subjugated by a Western movement of colonialism and imperialism, although they still retained their cultural identity and their old religious traditions. The resistance of Egypt to the influence of alien culture was just as strong as that of China or India to the West. Yet in spite of this the Christian Church, beginning in the great cosmopolitan cities of the Mediterranean, gradually spread through the whole of the Middle East, until by the fifth century, the ancient religious culture of Egypt and Mesopotamia had been almost entirely replaced by Christianity.

Is such a change conceivable in Asia today? Certainly there is the same opportunity, since the advance of modern Western culture has broken down the barriers between the peoples in much the same way as the Roman Empire and the Hellenistic cosmopolitan culture broke down the barriers between the ancient cultures of the Near and Middle East two thousand years ago. But in the modern world the forces of religion are much weaker than they were in the ancient world and the forces making for secularization are far stronger. In the early centuries of the Christian era the world was aflame with a passionate interest in religion. It had lost its faith in the State and its interest in politics and had turned its eyes to the supernatural and to the hope of a divine saviour. To such a world the Christian Gospel came as the answer to a universally recognized need and it swept through the dry wood of the dead civilizations like a forest fire.

But today the situation is a very different one. There is the same discontent with the old order—the same thirst for something new. But the objectives are different: they are material and this-worldly: release from poverty and insecurity and admission to an equal status with the privileged classes and peoples.

Hence the appeal of Communism to the East, since Communism offers to the poor and underprivileged the hope of a kingdom of heaven on earth, while at the same time satisfying their resentment against the rich and powerful classes and nations that have exploited them.

Nevertheless, it is too early to judge. The old religions and cultures have been moulding men's lives and thoughts for thousands of years, Western influences and also Christian missionary activity have been at work for centuries—or at any rate for a century; but

Communism is something entirely new—so new that it may have changed its character by the time that it has been fully adapted to the Asiatic environment. Although the East is in a state of fermentation and change, there is still an enormous mass to be leavened, and in many countries the process of change is still confined to the educated minority, which is naturally an urban class. But the vast majority of the people of Asia still live in their villages, and their lives are more remote from those of the nationalist or Communist intelligentsia than those of the latter are from the West.

A good example of this is to be seen in the recent study of an Indian village which was carried out by a team of Indian research workers headed by Dr. S. C. Dube. The village in question was in the State of Hyderabad and consequently, no doubt, more conservative than a comparable community in what was formerly British India. Nevertheless, it is only twenty-five miles from the capital of the state, which is one of the largest cities in India, and is connected with it by a regular bus service. Yet in spite of this many of the inhabitants had never heard of Mr. Nehru or Mahatma Gandhi, little was known of the movement for Indian independence, and national consciousness was vague. The real community was the village and the sub-caste, and "to the great bulk of the people cast-mythology was their only history." Although Communism is active in the region and the Communist or rather Communist-supported candidate was successful in the first political election ever held (in 1951), its influence was very superficial and did not touch culture or religion. The religious life of the village goes on unchanged and it centres, not so much in the worship of the high gods of classical Hinduism, but in the local cult of the village goddesses—Pochamma, the goddess of smallpox, Mutyalamma, the goddess of chickenpox, Maisamman, the boundary goddess, and half-a-dozen more.

The modern world seems very remote from this little world, in which the craftsman still worships the instruments of his craft and where the Untouchables still perform religious dramas celebrating the exploits of the legendary founder of their sub-caste. But its influence is seeping in by a hundred channels and nothing can prevent its ultimate triumph.

The oriental world is being transformed before our eyes. But it is still not clear what the dominant force in the new culture will be. Will it be a drab secular materialism of the type that is so prevalent in the modern world, or a militant Communism, or some kind of reformed Hinduism such as is represented by the Arya Samaj? At first sight there seems little hope that Christianity will be the gainer or that there is any more chance of the Eastern world's becoming Christian than there was a hundred years ago. Nevertheless, though we cannot accept the cocksure historical determinism of the Marxians or the ambitious speculations of the philosophers of history, like Spengler and Toynbee, we believe as Christians that the hand of God is at work in history and that the great revolution of world culture that is taking place before our eyes is the instrument of divine purpose.

But we also have our part to play, and not the least important factor in this is the contribution that we make to the process of study and criticism and spiritual questioning upon which the peoples of the East are now engaged. They have been just as conscious as we are of the world crisis which is affecting civilization. For more than a century the impact of Western culture has made them re-examine the foundations of their civilization, so that they have been forced either to criticize or to justify their traditional way of life and the religious foundations on which it was based. In the past the influence of the Christian missions was here far from negligible. The whole history of the Indian national movement and the renaissance of Indian culture from the time of Ram Mohun Roy at the beginning of the nineteenth century to Mahatma Gandhi was penetrated through and through with specifically Christian as well as secular European influences. And the same is true of China, though in a lesser degree, since the founders of the nationalist movement were mission-educated and in some cases Christian, like Sun Yat-sen himself.

Now, the first effect of this impact was to produce reforming movements within the great religions of Asia—the Brahma Samaj and the Arya Samaj in India and the Ram Krishna Mission. On the basis of these movements and largely owing to Western influences there developed a generalized ideal of Eastern spirituality versus Western materialism: a theory that became prevalent in all the Asian civilizations and inspired the pan-Islamic ideology of Jamal ad-Din al-Afghani (1859–1897), Svami Vivekananda's vision of the world mission of Indian spirituality, and more recently in China Lian Sou-

Ming's comparison of Eastern and Western civilization and their corresponding philosophies.

These views still exercise a good deal of influence, especially among the older generation, and have contributed to form that common Asian ideology which inspires the foreign policy of India and the Bandung Asian front. The whole subject has been recently reviewed in the remarkable study of Sardar Panikkar from which we have already quoted, a book which not only takes a much more universal view than most books on oriental history, but which is almost unique in the space and attention that it devotes to the religious aspect of Western expansion of Asia and to the importance of Christian missionary action. He points out, as few non-Christian writers have done, "the unbroken religious urge of European expansion and the immense non-official and voluntary effort that it represented."

In spite of this his final conclusions are altogether negative and unfavourable. He writes: "It will hardly be denied that in spite of the immense and sustained effort made by the churches with the support of the lay public in Europe and America, the attempt to conquer Asia for Christ has definitely failed. In China, where the effort was most concentrated, the collapse has been most complete. In India, the Christian church still exists—but mission work, except in the fields of education and medical services, is insignificant. Elsewhere, in Japan, Siam and Burma, the missionaries had no serious hopes, and with the assertion of national sentiments and the revival of oriental religions the prospects have become dimmer."

Now if this view were correct it would mean that Christianity had had its chance in Asia during the last centuries and has lost it: so that the national revival of the peoples of Asia involves the vindication of the ancient religions and cultures of the East against the intrusion of Western colonial power and Christian missionary influence. This, however, is a gross simplification of a very complex problem. Western colonialism and Christian missionary action are two distinct forces, even though they are interrelated, and the former achieved its greatest success only when it had disassociated itself completely from the latter, as the Dutch and the English East India companies both did in their palmy days. It is well known that the Dutch retained their trade with Japan only by disassociating themselves entirely from Christianity, but it is even more significant that in Ceylon they took deliberate measures for the restoration of Buddhist monasteries by importing reformers from Arakan in 1684 in order to weaken the existing native Catholicism.

In the same way, in India, the East India Company, far from acting as an agent of Christian propaganda, originally prohibited any missionary from entering the country and contributed to the maintenance of Hindu temples and the celebration of religious festivals like the great Jaganath pilgrimage at Puri. It was only after the Mutiny and the transference of the dominions of the Company to the Crown that the government of India could be said to be Christian. In fact nowhere in India except in Goa and the Portuguese possessions was there any attempt to use colonial power to favour the diffusion of Christianity.

On the other hand, from 1833 onwards the English power in India did concern itself to promote Western education, and here the effects were far-reaching and continuous. For, as I have remarked again and again in the course of this study, the passing of European political power has done nothing to check the progress of Western education and consequently the influence of Western culture. The same thing is happening all over the East, among the peoples who have always retained their independence no less than among the ex-colonial states. If a common pan-Asian society is emerging, it is not due to any religious or philosophical synthesis, but to the new secular Westernized culture that is common to them all.

The idealization of Eastern spirituality against Western materialism, which was characteristic of the earlier phase of the nationalist movement, and which is still represented by elder statesmen like Sardar Panikkar, is being replaced by a spirit of historical criticism which shows no respect for the sacred traditions of the past.

This is especially the case in China, where the revolt against Confucius and the classical tradition took place long before the advent of Communism and is indeed the one common trait that unites the intellectual leaders of the Nationalists, like Hu Shih, and those of the Communists. Lu Hsun (1881–1936), the famous writer who is now treated as a classic by the Communists, was undoubtedly a most ferocious debunker of traditionalism and nationalism and every form of orthodoxy, but I doubt if he would have been any more sympathetic to the new Communist orthodoxy than to the old Confucian one. He is nearer in spirit to Swift than to Marx. He saw the history of China as four thousand years of cannibalism. The Confucian tradition said

"Benevolence and Righteousness," but reading between the lines he found nothing but a record of man-eating. Today the totalitarian state has changed the words, but has it changed anything else? The same cannibalistic process is being carried on under the new set of slogans.

When social criticism has reached this point, there is no turning back. The old civilizations have been so violently torn from their traditional roots that it is impossible to revivify them. Whatever order takes their place will be something radically new, whether it is a democratic nationalism on the Western pattern or a totalitarian state. But in either case there remains a spiritual vacuum, like that we have already experienced in the secularized civilization of the Western world. I think this is already clearly discernible in the case of Lu Hsun. His discontent is plainly spiritual, rather than political or economic; even though he is not consciously aware of a religious problem. In this Lu Hsun differs considerably from writers like Wu Chih-hui in 1923, who is a real materialist, who sees the world "as a great stage on which the two-limbed animals are actors here and now. Their chief concerns in life are eating and producing children and entertaining friends. There is neither good nor evil, and neither gods nor devils. The metaphysical spectre and the religious deity are alien invaders of humanity."

No doubt this is an extreme case. There are vast tracts of Asian and African society that are as yet unaffected by these revolutionary changes, as in the case of the Indian village I have just referred to. Moreover, the situation in the Islamic countries is different, owing to the close connection of religion and politics, the existence of a genuine pan-Islamic loyalty that often outweighs nationalist sentiments, and a general backwardness in industrial and technological change.

But wherever the new forces develop freely, and in proportion as the people of Asia and Africa take their equal share in the cosmopolitan civilization of the modern world, there will be a new religious need which will not be satisfied by the traditional answers of the old religious cultures.

As in the ancient world, there will be a free market in ideas and any apostle of any creed who is able to satisfy the spiritual needs of modern man will obtain a hearing. Not that the debate will be a philosophical and metaphysical one, as it was in the ancient world.

This is not a metaphysical age, and in the East no less than in the West men are more interested in subsistence and coexistence than in essence and existence. Yet they still seek spiritual nourishment. There is a general sense of frustration and bewilderment and a need for a common purpose and a common hope. Up to a point the new political and national movements supply this, but not permanently and not for everyone. The deeper spiritual needs of mankind must always remain, unless we can accept George Orwell's nightmare alternative of a completely dehumanized civilization.

It is easy to understand how this state of secularization has arisen as a temporary and exceptional condition, but I do not believe that it can persist indefinitely without destroying the civilization that produced it. Religion is essential to humanity and cannot be permanently banished from the modern world.

Thus the Christian Church today and in the immediate future is confronted with a tremendous opportunity. The civilization of the new world has an immense unsatisfied spiritual need. The Church has a universal spiritual mission, which she has hitherto been unable to fulfill because the nations have been separated from one another, speaking different spiritual languages, enclosed in separate worlds, each of which has been shut off from the rest by walls of custom and tradition. Now the old barriers that divided the nations have been broken down, and the sacred laws that ruled men's lives for thousands of years have lost their power.

If Christianity were just one among the other world religions, then it too would fail and fade as they are doing. But we know that it is not so, that Christ is the only answer to the world's spiritual need, and that the Church has a universal mission to bring the Gospel of Christ to all nations.

But do we Christians today possess the power and the vision to carry out this apostolate in this new world that I have described? Although the opportunity is great, the difficulties are great also, and it will need great spiritual energy to overcome them. On the one hand, there is the negative opposition of modern secularism and materialism, which has a formidable champion in Communism and which renders all Christian action in China and Central Asia most difficult. And on the other hand there is the challenge of religious nationalism, which rejects Christianity as an alien power—an instrument of foreign domination—and identifies national loyalty with loyalty to the religious traditions of the nation. This is a paradoxical attitude in that it is political rather than religious and does not necessarily involve a revival of religious faith. It does, however, lead to anti-missionary propaganda and an anti-Christian ideology which put serious obstacles in the way of missionary activity, above all in the sphere of education.

Neither of these two difficulties is insurmountable, but I do not think it has as yet been discovered how they can best be dealt with. Here there is need for much study, and possibly for new experiments and new techniques. I believe, however, that they can best be dealt with on a national rather than a cultural basis. For as I have explained, it is no longer a question of penetrating the closed worlds of the ancient civilizations—this work of penetration has already been done by the secular forces that have created the new oriental nationalism. It is now a matter of making a direct approach to each nation individually.

The approach may be made on a number of different planes. In the first place the most obvious approach seems to be to the new educated classes who are the creators and leaders of the modern Orient. They are the most accessible to us since they belong to the same world-society and are faced with the same problems as we are. Here Christianity enjoys a certain advantage, since it has a far greater experience of the religious problems of a secularized society than any other religion except perhaps Judaism. Moreover, the educated Asian tends to be educated in Western literature rather than in the classical literatures of the oriental cultures, and this provides a basis for mutual discussion and understanding. Yet on the other hand, it is on this level that the nationalist and political prejudice against Christianity and against any form of missionary activity is strongest. For the less a man practises his own religion the more he is inclined to resent the universal claims of Christianity.

On the other hand, the plane that is most remote from Western influence, that of the oriental underworld—the world of the villages and of traditional culture—is often more accessible to missionary influence, for it is here among the poor, the unprivileged and the outcasts, that the supernatural appeal of the Gospel is most evident. The ultimate test of the Christian apostolate is that which was laid down by Our Lord Himself in His message to St. John the Baptist: "The blind see, the lame walk, the lepers are made clean, the deaf hear, the dead rise again, and the poor have the gospel preached to them." And this principle has always been justified by the great representatives of the Christian apostolate from SS. Peter and Paul to St. Francis Xavier and more recently by men like Father Damien and hundreds of forgotten missionaries.

But in addition to these two widely separated worlds of the intelligentsia and the peasants, there is a third intermediate sphere which is perhaps the most important of all.

For when we read the Acts of the Apostles we find that the decisive success of the first Christian apostolate was neither with the intelligentsia nor with the peasants. St. Paul preached alike to the sophisticated Hellenist public at Athens and to the simple peasant population of Lycaonia, who hailed Paul and Barnabas as gods and brought out oxen and garlands to sacrifice to them. But the world mission of the Church was established for all time in the great urban centres of the ancient world—at Antioch and Ephesus and Corinth and Rome and among the international lower-middle-class population of the great cities—shopkeepers, artisans, merchants, slaves and freedmen of the great houses. It was in this uprooted, denationalized, cosmopolitan population that the spiritual need was greatest and that the word was most eagerly heard and accepted. And so these cities became the centres of the new Christian world, and it was from their population that the teachers and the martyrs of the new faith came forth.

Is it not possible that the same thing will happen in modern Asia: that the key points of oriental Christianity will be found in the great urban centres like Calcutta and Bombay, Tokyo, Shanghai, Canton, Singapore—that the new Churches will find their future leaders in the same urban cosmopolitan classes from which the leaders of the primitive Church were drawn? The soil must be broken—the plough and the harrow must do their work before the seed can produce a good harvest. But this is the age of the plough and the harrow, not the time of harvest.